Macquarie Monographs in Cognitive Science

Rehabilitation of spoken word production in Aphasia

Edited by
Lyndsey Nickels

Macquarie University

Psychology Press
Taylor & Francis Group

HOVE AND NEW YORK

BS

Published in 2002 by Psychology Press Ltd
27 Church Road, Hove, East Sussex, BN3 2FA
www.psypress.co.uk

Simultaneously published in the USA and Canada
by Taylor & Francis Inc.
29 West 35th Street, New York, NY 10001, USA.

Psychology Press is part of the Taylor & Francis Group
© 2002 by Psychology Press Ltd

British Library Cataloguing in Publication Data
A catalogue record for this book is available from the British Library

ISBN 1-84169-928-4 (hbk)
ISSN 0268-7038

Cover design by Ellen Seguin
Typeset in the UK by DP Photosetting, Aylesbury, UK.
Printed and bound in the UK by Hobbs the Printers, Ltd, Totton, Hampshire

11/17/03

REHABILITATION OF
SPOKEN WORD PRODUCTION
IN APHASIA

Macquarie Monographs in Cognitive Science

Series Editor: MAX COLTHEART

The Macquarie Monographs in Cognitive Science series will publish original monographs dealing with any aspect of cognitive science. Each volume in the series will cover a circumscribed topic and will provide readers with a summary of the current state-of-the-art in that field.

A primary aim of the volumes is also to advance research and knowledge in the field through discussion of new theoretical and experimental advances.

Titles in Series

Routes to Reading Success and Failure
   Nancy Ewald Jackson and Max Coltheart

Cognitive neuropsychological approaches to spoken word production
   Lyndsey Nickels (Ed.)

Rehabilitation of spoken word production in Aphasia
   Lyndsey Nickels (Ed.)

This book is the third volume in the series *Macquarie Monographs in Cognitive Science* and also forms issues 10 & 11 of Volume 16 (2002) of *Aphasiology*

Contents

APHASIOLOGY, 2002, *16* (10/11), 935–979

Therapy for naming disorders: Revisiting, revising, and reviewing

Lyndsey Nickels

Macquarie University, Sydney, Australia

Background: Impairments of word retrieval and production are a common and distressing feature of aphasia, and much clinical time is devoted to attempts at their remediation. There are now many research papers devoted to case studies examining treatments for word-retrieval impairments using a wide range of tasks with individuals who have varying levels of impairment.

Aims: This paper aims to continue the selective review of this literature carried out by Nickels and Best (1996a). It summarises in table form those published papers since 1980 which present single case studies of treatment for word-retrieval impairments and which satisfy minimal methodological criteria.

Main Contribution: Several main themes are derived from the literature and discussed in more detail, these include strategic approaches and facilitative or repair approaches to remediation, the contrast between semantic and phonological tasks in therapy, generalisation in therapy tasks and the relationship between impairment, therapy task, and outcome. Further discussion relates to the relationship between impairment level treatments, and measures of disability and handicap, and between therapy research and therapy practice.

Conclusions: There are now many research papers devoted to impairments of word retrieval, and there can be no doubt that therapy for word-retrieval impairments can be highly successful, resulting in long-term improvements which can be of great communicative significance for the individual with aphasia. However, predicting the precise result of a specific treatment task with a specific individual with certainty is still not possible. For clinicians the recommendation is to use analyses of functional impairments to guide the choice of task, but to ensure that efficacy is tested and not assumed. Furthermore, structured multi-modal and multicomponent tasks (e.g., "semantic" or "phonological" cueing hierarchies) may hold the most promise for many individuals. For researchers, there remains a need to further dissect tasks, impairments, and their interactions across series of single cases.

Address correspondence to: Dr Lyndsey Nickels, Macquarie Centre for Cognitive Science (MACCS), Macquarie University, Sydney, NSW 2109, Australia. Email: lyndsey@maccs.mq.edu.au

Thanks to all the contributing authors who have worked so hard to comply with my demands, and also to the reviewers of their papers. Thanks to Chris Code for inviting me to compile and edit the volume, and to Deborah Maloney and the production team at Psychology Press for their patience. Wendy Best, Britta Biedermann, Ruth Fink, Julie Hickin, David Howard, and Stacie Raymer made helpful comments on an earlier version of this paper. Thanks too to Britta Biedermann who gave invaluable assistance in gathering together the references, and translating those not in English. This paper was prepared while the author was supported by an Australian Research Council QEII fellowship.

DOI:10.1080/02687030244000563

Of the symptoms associated with aphasia, none are more pervasive than *anomia*, a difficulty in finding high information words, both in fluent discourse and when called upon to identify an object of action by name.

(Goodglass & Wingfield, 1997, p. 3)

The majority of people with aphasia have some degree of difficulty in retrieving and producing the words they need to communicate, and this can be reported as one of the most frustrating and distressing aspects of their problems. Clearly then, remediation of impairments of spoken word production is of the utmost importance for the person with aphasia and for those communicating with them.

In 1996, Wendy Best and I reviewed (selectively) the literature on the remediation of spoken word production in aphasia (Nickels & Best, 1996a). Our paper focused on research addressing the remediation of spoken word retrieval impairments, published after 1980 and that satisfied minimum methodological requirements. This paper will continue that review.[1] The papers excluded from this review are those that either present only group data, or where pre- and post-testing do not allow clear conclusions to be drawn (i.e., it is not possible to distinguish effects of treatment from non-specific treatment effects or spontaneous recovery). Although some papers have been included that do not have statistical analysis of results, this has only been the case where the patterns from visual inspection seem reasonably clear, and adequate baseline testing has occurred.

Inevitably, there have been more papers published in the last 7 years that fulfil the criteria than there were in the previous 15![2] Hence, discussion of each paper individually is not possible, rather this paper will discuss general issues pertaining to remediation of word production in aphasia,[3] with illustrative examples being drawn from the literature. The scope of this review will also be somewhat broader, including not only the remediation of spoken word retrieval, but also written word retrieval, and disorders of phonological encoding and semantics (in so far as semantic impairments impact on word retrieval). Nevertheless this review remains restricted—it focuses on impairment-level treatments of spoken word production in aphasia that aim to improve word production itself. I will not address treatments that aim to use alternative (non-linguistic) means of communication to overcome a word-retrieval/production impairment (e.g., drawing,

---

[1] Although I have attempted to track down as many relevant papers as possible, it is probable that some studies that meet the criteria for this review have been omitted. The authors of these papers should accept my apologies and I hope will understand that this is no reflection on their work or any bias on my part, but rather the limitations of keyword searching of electronic databases (which don't always make life easy when, for example, "anomia" is frequently transcribed as "anemia"!).

[2] Although there are now many published reports of remediation for word retrieval in aphasia, and some are of the highest quality, it is of note that many remain methodologically or analytically weak. Although most reports incorporate baseline testing, all too often authors claim evidence for treatment effects on the basis of visual inspection of data (rather than statistical analysis), data sets are small, treatment underspecified, and the functional impairments of participants poorly described. We can only hope that the increase in quantity of reports will swiftly be followed by an increase in quality.

[3] The review also excludes treatments of aphasia as a result of progressive brain diseases (e.g., Alzheimer's disease, cortico-basal degeneration). Although a number of studies have now shown positive effects of treatment with individuals with these pathologies using similar approaches to the treatment of non-progressive aphasia (e.g., Abrahams & Cramp, 1993), they are excluded here due to the different methodological considerations in interpretation of the data.

Hunt, 1999; Sacchet, Byng, Marshall, & Pound, 1999), neither will I address treatments that focus on impairments at an articulatory level (e.g., those treatments focusing on apraxia of speech, for review see Ballard, Granier, & Robin, 2000, and Wambaugh & Doyle, 1994), nor treatments "beyond the single word" (e.g., sentence processing—see Mitchum, Greenwald, & Berndt, 2000, for a review of the issues in this field). In addition, this review will not address rehabilitation primarily focused at reducing levels of handicap/disability where the rehabilitation is not impairment-based (e.g., Lesser & Algar, 1995).[4] Finally, this review will restrict itself to papers published in peer-reviewed journals and books (hence excluding unpublished conference papers, oral paper presentations, and theses).

APPROACHES TO THE REMEDIATION OF WORD-RETRIEVAL IMPAIRMENTS IN APHASIA

Howard and Hatfield (1987) gave a historical review of approaches to the treatment of aphasia—these included surgical, pharmacological (e.g., crocodile grease), and behavioural treatments. However, the vast majority of treatments over the past 100 years have been behaviourally based. It is only more recently that pharmacological approaches to the treatment of aphasia have been demonstrated to show some promise, using, for example, amphetamine or piracetam (e.g., Enderby, Broeackx, Hospers, Schildermans, & Deberdt, 1994; Walker-Batson et al., 2001). However, there remains a general consensus that these treatments are helpful primarily when paired with effective behavioural language therapy (see Shisler, Baylis, & Frank, 2000, for a review). Hence, it is not the case that there is little point in devoting research effort to evaluating behavioural approaches to the remediation of aphasia because of the promise of pharmacological approaches; there is little doubt that there will be a role for behavioural approaches for many years to come.

Behavioural approaches take many forms, and in particular can be divided into those that aim to rehabilitate the impaired process(es) and those that attempt to provide an alternative mechanism to achieve a goal (such as successful word production) using processes not normally implicated. I shall discuss these latter approaches first.

Strategic, re-organisational, or compensatory approaches

One approach to treatment of word-production/retrieval impairment aims to facilitate naming by reorganising the processes utilised, such that intact processes are used to compensate for or support the impaired processes (Howard & Patterson; 1989). Table 1 summarises the studies that have set out with the aim of taking this approach (as we will see aims and results do not always converge).

Common to most of these approaches is the use of knowledge of the written form of a word to help retrieve the spoken form. Clearly this approach will be of most benefit to

---

[4] This is not meant to suggest that impairment-based approaches do not have an impact on levels of disability/handicap, far from it, underlying every clinician's impairment-based treatment is the belief that it will have an impact on the levels of disability and/or handicap of the individual treated. The evidence for the truth of this statement will be discussed later.

TABLE 1

Summary of papers taking a "reorganisation" approach to treatment

Paper	Aphasic individual	Impairment	Intact skills	Treatment	Outcome (treated)	Generalisation (to untreated)	Comments	Problems with interpretation
Bachy-Langedock & De Partz (1989)	SP	Phonological encoding; grapheme–phoneme conversion	Written naming (marginally better cf spoken naming)	Reading aloud: Letter–sound correspondences, blending	N/A	✓		Spontaneous recovery possible; a second therapy (silent phonology tasks & spelling) was carried out in parallel
Bastiaanse et al. (1996)	GD	Access to POL; grapheme–phoneme conversion	Initial letter knowledge; phonemically cueable	Letter–sound correspondences, resulting in self-generated phonemic cues	✓	✓	Unable to learn to blend	
Best et al. (1997a,b); Best & Nickels (2000); Howard (1994)	JOW (aka JWO)	Word-retrieval (good semantics), failure to activate lemma representations	Phonemically cueable (but poor initial letter knowledge)	Cueing aid (point to letter, phoneme generated)	✓	✓	?Improved letter knowledge, and the automatic use of this knowledge in word retrieval?	Multi-component task
Best & Nickels (2000); Howard (1994)	RD	Word-retrieval (good semantics)	Written naming (cf spoken naming); phonemically cueable		✓ (and benefit from using the cueing aid)	×		
Best & Nickels (2000)	MF	Word-retrieval (good semantics)	Initial letter knowledge, (NOT phonemically cueable)		✓	×	?Post-lexical locus of treatment effects?	
Best & Nickels (2000)	PG	Word-retrieval (good semantics)	Not cueable; no initial letter knowledge		✓	✓	Improved letter knowledge, and the automatic use of this knowledge in word retrieval?	
Howard (1994)	JG	Word-retrieval	Initial letter knowledge, (NOT phonemically cueable)		✓	✓		
	JGR	Word-retrieval	Phonemically cueable (but poor initial letter knowledge)		✓	✓		
	LM	Word-retrieval	Initial letter knowledge, phonemically cueable		✓	✓		

Study	Subject	Impairment	Initial letter knowledge	Cueing aid (point to letter, phoneme generated)			Comments	Individual statistics not given for effects of treatment on treated and untreated items without the aid
Bruce & Howard (1987)	PAB	"Broca's aphasia"; word-finding impairment	Initial letter knowledge, phonemically cueable	Cueing aid (point to letter, phoneme generated)	✓	✓	Learned to generate his own phonemic cues—hence no benefit from using the aid, post-treatment. Dramatic improvements in naming success	Individual statistics not given for effects of treatment on treated and untreated items without the aid
	LIN	"Broca's aphasia"; word-finding impairment	Initial letter knowledge, phonemically cueable		✓ (significant benefit from using cueing aid)	✓ (significant benefit from using cueing aid)		
	MAA	"Broca's aphasia"; word-finding impairment	Initial letter knowledge, phonemically cueable		✓ (significant benefit from using cueing aid)	✓ (significant benefit from using cueing aid)		
	OLI	"Broca's aphasia"; word-finding impairment	Initial letter knowledge, phonemically cueable		✓ (significant benefit from using cueing aid)	✗		
	DAV	"Broca's aphasia"; word-finding impairment	Initial letter knowledge, phonemically cueable		✓ (significant benefit from using cueing aid)	✗		
Hillis & Caramazza (1994)	HW	Word-retrieval (good semantics)	Written naming (cf. spoken naming)	Letter–sound correspondences, blending	✗	✗	Poor learning of letter–sound correspondences, unable to learn to blend, not helped by initial phoneme cue	
Howard & Harding (1998)[1]	SD	Access to POL; grapheme–phoneme conversion; letter naming; unable to form letters (write)	Initial letter identification (by pointing)	Pointing to initial letters on an alphabet board	N/A	✓	Thought to be effective by a lexically mediated cascade of activation from input orthography to output phonology	

(Continued overleaf)

TABLE 1
(Continued)

Paper	Aphasic individual	Impairment	Intact skills	Treatment	Outcome (treated)	Generalisation (to untreated)	Comments	Problems with interpretation
Holland (1998)	RR	Access to POL; grapheme–phoneme conversion	Written naming	Letter–sound correspondences, resulting in self-generated phonemic cues	N/A	✓	Specific additional treatment successfully focused on carry-over into spontaneous language use outside the clinic	No statistics
Nickels (1992)	TC	Access to POL; grapheme–phoneme conversion	Written naming (cf. spoken naming); phonemically cueable	Letter–sound correspondences, resulting in self-generated phonemic cues	N/A	✓	Rapid acquisition & spontaneously used technique in conversation; unable to learn to blend	
White-Thomson (1999)	BC	Semantics & Access to POL	Written naming (cf. spoken naming)	Encouraging use of written form in naming; letter–sound correspondences; reading aloud	✓	× (or marginal)	Strategy use WAS apparent in conversation	Multi-component task, likely to have also facilitated word retrieval directly

Phon.: Phonological; POL.: Phonological Output Lexicon

[1] Although this study is not strictly speaking a treatment study, the effects of the technique are so marked that it is felt useful to include it.

Note: Kiran, Thompson, and Hashimoto (2001) is not included as although the title of this paper suggests it trains grapheme–phoneme conversion, in fact it does not!

those individuals who have better written naming when compared to spoken naming; for those individuals who are equally impaired in both modalities it is unlikely to be as helpful.[5] Bachy-Langedock and De Partz (1989) used this technique with SP, a man who on 18% of occasions could correctly write a name that he could not produce. As SP was also severely impaired at reading he was unable to subsequently read the word aloud. Bachy-Langedock and De Partz reasoned that if SP could read aloud the words he was able to write but not say, then his communication would be improved (see also Nickels, 1992, and later). Thus, they retaught SP letter–sound correspondences and how to blend these sounds to read words (and nonwords) aloud, with a resulting improvement in both reading and naming.

One of the most widely used methods for utilising orthographic knowledge rests on the fact that some individuals who have word-retrieval impairments benefit from phonemic cues. In other words, if, when unable to retrieve a target, they hear the initial phoneme of that item, they are often then able to produce the word successfully. It follows, then, that if an individual could generate their own phonemic cue when unable to retrieve a word, their word-finding would be improved. Unfortunately this is not as easy as it sounds! Bruce and Howard (1988) argued that in order to be able to cue themselves, individuals with aphasia need to have three skills: access to the initial letter of the word they are unable to retrieve,[6] an ability to convert letters to sounds, and to benefit from the provision of phonemic cues. It is rare for an individual to have this combination of skills.[7] Nevertheless, self-generation of phonemic cues has been successfully used as a rehabilitation strategy by a number of different authors, using slightly different methods. All the studies have in common that the individuals were able to identify the first letter for words that they were unable to name, and were phonemically cueable. However, the individuals were unable to convert letters to sounds—it is in the approach to bridging this "intermediate" stage that the studies differ.

Bruce and Howard (1987) used a computer to generate the phonemes from the initial letter (see also Best & Nickels, 2000; Best, Howard, Bruce, & Gatehouse, 1997a,b; Howard, 1994). Individuals were presented with a picture, they selected the initial letter of the picture name, then pressed the corresponding key on the "cueing aid" which then produced the phoneme associated with that letter. After treatment, Bruce and Howard's five aphasic individuals were significantly better at naming treated words with the aid than without.[8]

---

[5] It is likely that some individuals automatically use the written form to help their spoken word production, but that for the most part we are unaware of this fact, occasionally, however, it becomes clear. For example, MK (Howard & Franklin, 1988) when attempting to name a picture of a comb, produced /kɒmb/ (as opposed to the target /kəʊm/). How does this arise? Unable to access the phonological form, MK visualises the spelling and reads it aloud, however, as he is unable to read irregular words he uses grapheme–phoneme correspondences—which for this irregular word result in the regularisation error /kɒmb/.

[6] It is the individual's knowledge of the initial letter that is important, rather than the initial sound—it is likely that if they already "knew" the initial sound of the word then they would not be assisted by provision of the initial sound as a cue.

[7] Alternatively, of course, if an individual has these skills perhaps they use their initial letter knowledge to implicitly/automatically cue spoken word retrieval. In this case, there would no longer be an advantage for initial letter knowledge over and above spoken naming. Thus, perhaps it would be more accurate to say that it is rare to find individuals with this combination of skills precisely because the majority of those that do will mask the effect by self-cueing!

[8] With the exception of one individual whose naming after treatment was at ceiling even without the aid.

In contrast, rather than using a computer to generate the cues, Nickels (1992) retaught letter–sound correspondences to a man with anomia, TC, which enabled him to generate his own cues.[9] Critically, TC had considerably more accurate written than spoken naming.[10] TC learned the correspondences with relative ease. He had no difficulty in using a strategy of visualising the initial letter, identifying and producing the corresponding sound, to provide a phonemic cue for word finding. This resulted in significantly improved spoken picture naming and spontaneous use of the strategy in communicative contexts.

The description earlier suggests the story is simple—unfortunately as is so often the case in aphasia therapy research, this is deceptive. Best et al. (1997b) report 13 individuals treated using the cueing aid, some had both the skills required to benefit from using the aid (knowledge of initial letters for words they could not name and ability to benefit from phonemic cues), while others lacked one or both skills and were hence predicted not to benefit. However, at least 12 of the 13 individuals treated showed significant improvement—despite the fact that only two individuals had both skills required in order to be predicted to benefit. The answer to this paradoxical finding, is that the same treatment can work in different ways for different individuals. This treatment was multicomponent—involving orthography, phonology, and semantics (via presentation of the picture) and hence the opportunities for facilitating the language system are many. Howard (1994), when discussing the results of this treatment, notes that for those individuals who are not assisted by the cueing aid, the treatment essentially comprises naming with a phonemic cue or repetition in the presence of a picture. As we will see later, these tasks are identical to those included under the mantle of "phonological therapy", however, in this case much greater generalisation was observed than is usually found in "phonological therapy". Best et al. (1997b) argue that for one of their participants (JOW), the treatment had allowed him to use partial orthographic knowledge to aid word finding. Even though this was available to JOW prior to therapy, it is suggested that the treatment drew attention to the relationship between orthography and phonology and altered automatic (not strategic) processes in his word retrieval. Best and Nickels (2000; Best et al., 1997 a,b) use a microanalysis of impairments and retained skills to further dissect the complex effects of this treatment for other individuals.

Howard and Harding (1998) also report a case where initial letter knowledge is used to cue word retrieval, but not via phonological cues. SD had relatively poor spoken picture naming, argued to be due to impaired access to the phonological output lexicon in the context of good semantics. When given an alphabet board, SP's naming improved; she was able to correctly name 50% of those pictures she failed previously. However, it was unlikely that SD was using self-generated phonemic cues, as she was unable to convert letters to sounds. Moreover, a letter board also helped her produce words where the initial letter does not predict the phoneme (e.g., KNEE or AERIAL). Instead, Howard and Harding argue that identifying the letter on the alphabet board activates the representations of words corresponding to that letter in the orthographic input lexicon. This activation cascades through the language system, and combines with the activation produced from looking at the picture to increase the chances of retrieval from the phonological output lexicon. It is important to note that SD was unable to form letters (in the absence of a motor impairment), hence it was only when given the opportunity to select a letter that she had access to the form of the letters. As Howard and Harding note,

---

[9] The original aim of treatment was, in fact, to reinstate the sublexical reading route. However, it became apparent that whereas TC seemed to find it impossible to reacquire one of the necessary skills (blending) for nonword reading, once generated, the initial phoneme was a successful cue.

[10] In fact all that is required is (written) initial letter accuracy to be superior to spoken naming.

it is possible that for those individuals who can and do write or visualise letters, this orthographic cueing is already occurring.

In summary, the use of orthographic information to assist spoken naming can be a very effective strategy and one that may be utilised in different ways. Of course, spoken naming can also be used to facilitate written naming (see for example, Hillis & Caramazza, 1994, SJD), but somehow this is less surprising. Indeed it is rare to find an individual who does not automatically verbalise when having difficulty in writing.

However, as was alluded to earlier, it is important to note that even a treatment that is explicitly aiming to take a reorganisational (and/or prosthetic) approach, may in fact result in improved naming by amelioration of the underlying functional impairment (rather than by circumvention of the impairment).

Facilitation, repair, and reteaching approaches

Although, as we have seen, alternative strategies can be a highly effective way to assist word retrieval, there are relatively few individuals who have retained the skills necessary to be able to utilise these techniques. Hence, the ultimate goal remains to find techniques that will improve the impairment(s) that underlie poor word retrieval and/or production for an individual.

A number of different tasks have now been shown to be effective in the remediation of word-retrieval/production impairments (e.g., Hillis & Caramazza, 1994; Howard, Patterson, Franklin, Orchard-Lisle, & Morton, 1985b): they can produce durable effects (e.g., Pring, White-Thomson, Pound, Marshall, & Davis, 1990), which can carry over into connected speech and conversation (e.g., Hickin, Herbert, Best, Howard, & Osborne, 2002b), can be administered by clinican and/or computer (e.g., Fink, Brecher, Schwartz, & Robey, 2002) and can be obtained on verbs as well as the more commonly treated nouns (e.g., Murray & Karcher, 2000; Raymer & Ellsworth, 2002 (see Appendix for a summary review). However, the fact remains that treatment tasks are not invariably effective. For example, Howard et al. (1985b) note that when they studied the effects of the same treatment task for twelve aphasic individuals, only eight showed improvement. Of course this is unsurprising: impaired word production is a symptom and can have as its cause a number of different types of impairment. Just as we would not expect antibiotics to cure any cough (only those that were the result of bacterial infection), we have no reason to believe that any one treatment task will be equally effective with every type of word-production impairment. A widely accepted current hypothesis is that each different level of breakdown in word production will be best remediated by a different type of treatment (e.g. Hillis & Caramazza, 1994; Nettleton & Lesser, 1991). For example, a word-finding difficulty that has as its cause impaired word meaning (semantics) will require a treatment focusing on meaning (e.g., matching a word to one of a choice of pictures), whereas a problem retrieving the sounds of a word (phonology) will require a treatment focusing on word sounds (e.g., repeating a spoken word) (e.g., Miceli, Amitrano, Capasso, & Caramazza, 1996; Nettleton & Lesser, 1991). This leads us to a point that urgently needs clarification—there is much talk about the contrast between ''semantic'' therapy and ''phonological'' therapy, but what precisely do we mean by these terms?

Task type and impairment type

Howard et al. (1985a,b) compared two different types of tasks—those focusing on semantic processing (e.g., word–picture matching) and those focusing on phonological processing (e.g., repetition, phonological cueing). It is clear in these papers that the classification ''semantic'' or ''phonological'' therapy refers to the type of task rather than the nature of the impairment that the task is targeting. However, the two factors task type and impairment type are often mistakenly assumed to be the same.

Therapy for semantic impairments or semantic tasks as therapy? Many if not all tasks will involve semantic processing even those, such as repetition, that intend to focus on phonology (in the unimpaired speaker it is virtually impossible to repeat a word and not understand it). However, some tasks clearly focus on semantic processing to a greater extent, for example, selecting the "odd one out" of a set of pictures from the same semantic category, or matching a spoken or written word to one of a set of semantically related pictures. In both of these tasks, difficulty is graded by the "semantic similarity" of the distractors to the target (whether the distractors are unrelated to the target, or from within the same semantic category as the target). These tasks are widely used in the remediation of word-retrieval impairments; however, their use is not restricted to those individuals with semantic impairments.

Thus we can divide the reports using semantic tasks into those where the aim is to remediate impaired semantic processing, and those where the aim is to improve word retrieval in the absence of (severe) semantic impairments.

First, therapy for semantic impairments. In my experience, because of the centrality of semantics to all language tasks, much of an aphasia specialist's time is spent attempting to improve semantic processing: Improve semantic processing and there will be "knock on" effects to every aspect of language behaviour. Yet there is a remarkable lack of published single case studies reporting therapy for semantic impairments (Table 2 summarises these studies; also see Nickels, 2000, for a review). If one restricts these reports to those where effects of semantic remediation are demonstrated on and/or aimed at word retrieval, the list becomes shorter still.

One technique that characterises the general philosophy behind many treatments for semantic impairments in aphasia is semantic feature analysis (SFA). In this technique, the aphasic individual is provided with a picture, asked to name it, and then encouraged to describe the semantic features of a target, prompted by "is a..." "has a..." "is used for..." etc to generate features relating to group, properties, use, action, location, and association (Boyle & Coelho, 1995; Coelho, McHugh, & Boyle, 2000). Hillis (1991, 1998) used a similar technique to remediate the semantic impairment and improve (written) naming for HG. HG was asked to attempt to name a picture, if this attempt failed and a semantic error was produced, a drawing of her error was made. This drawing was compared to the target picture and semantic distinctions between the two were discussed. Both treatments are argued to be successful. In the case of HG, there is a clear demonstration that there is improvement not only in written naming, which was treated, but also in spoken naming and word comprehension (as would be predicted for a treatment targeting semantic processing).

How might these semantic treatments be having their effects? Hillis is explicit that HG's improvement was "improvement at the semantic level itself—perhaps through increased specificity of semantic representations of trained items" (Hillis, 1998, p. 654). Coelho et al. (2000) do not appear to advocate a relearning of semantic distinctions, but instead focus on the facilitative effects of SFA "by activating the semantic network surrounding the target word, that word may be activated above its threshold, thereby facilitating retrieval" (p. 135). Indeed they are explicit in suggesting that SFA is a strategy for word retrieval, noting that the aphasic individual treated by Boyle and Coelho (1995) was "less able to internalise the SFA strategy to facilitate word retrieval" (Coelho et al., 2000, p. 140). Nickels and Best (1996b) discuss a similar account for a man with a

TABLE 2
Summary of papers focusing on remediation of semantic impairments

Semantic tasks focused on the remediation of semantic comprehension impairments

Paper	Aphasic individual	Impairment	Treatment	Outcome (treated)	Generalisation	Comments	Problems with interpretation
Behrmann & Lieberthal (1989)	CH	Semantic	Teaching superordinate features, then specific details	✓ (and carry-over to other tasks using the same stimuli)	Partial: ✓ untreated items in treated categories ✗ untreated categories		Effects not consistent across all categories: one untreated category improved; only one treated category showed marked generalisation
Byng (1988); Byng & Coltheart (1986)	BRB	Semantic (abstract words)	word-picture match (abstract words) with feedback	✓ (but restricted to that task)	None	Possibly just paired-associate learning of word–picture correspondences	
			Dictionary therapy—generate synonyms for abstract words using the dictionary	✓ (and carry-over to other tasks using the same stimuli)	None		
Grayson et al. (1997)	LR	Semantic	Word–picture match; categorisation, associate matching	n.t.	Comprehension	Naming not tested	Spontaneous recovery
Hough (1993)	RC	"Wernicke's aphasia with jargon": semantic & probable additional input and output requirements	Written word–picture matching & word–word matching: (e.g., synonyms, associates, categorisation); Sentence comprehension: sentence–picture matching, following questions, answering questions	✓ (Data only provided for sentence comprehension)	BDAE: word–picture matching, confrontation naming, Boston naming test	Change from neologistic to semantic jargon	Single baseline, for sentence comprehension therapy tasks; no testing of treated items for word comprehension; no statistics

(Continued overleaf)

TABLE 2
(Continued)

Studies focusing on semantic tasks in individuals with semantic impairments

Paper	Aphasic individual	Impairment	Treatment	Outcome (treated)	Generalisation	Comments	Problems with interpretation
Boyle & Coelho (1995)	HW	Eroca's aphasia, "anomic"	Semantic Feature Analysis: Picture Naming & discussing semantic features;	✓	Control items (tested weekly)	No generalisation to connected speech	Impairment unspecified. Small numbers of items, no statistics
Coelho et al. (2000)	TH	Anomic (semantic and phonclogical errors)	(Repetition of target if unable to name)	✓	? (++ variable)		Small numbers of items, no statistics
Hillis (1991, 1998)	HG	Semantic, POL (surface dyslexia)	Picture naming: emphasising/reteaching semantic distinctions using drawing when semantic errors produced	✓	Within semantic category and to comprehension	Treatment for WRITTEN naming	
Kiran & Thompson (2001)	P1	Semantics and/or access to POL	TYPICAL exemplars of a single semantic category:	✓	×	Short report, limited detail	No statistics, small number of items (n = 8 per subset)
	P3		Naming, category sorting, identifying semantic attributes, y/n questions regarding semantic features	✓	×		
	P2		ATYPICAL exemplars of a single semantic category:	✓	✓ (to untreated typical exemplars within the category)		
	P4		Naming, category sorting, identifying semantic attributes, y/n questions regarding semantic features	✓	✓ (to untreated typical exemplars within the category)		
Nickels & Best (1996b)	AER	Semantic	Function judgements "Do you (VERB) an (OBJECT)?"	×	Only for nouns having homophonic verb forms (e.g. iron, hammer)	No change on measures of comprehension (but ceiling effects)	
			Relatedness judgements (judging associative and categorical relationships)	✓	✓ (Only when feedback was given on the task)	Relatively error prone on this task	Provision of feedback is confounded with order of treatment
			Written word–picture matching	✓	× (Significant generalisation at 1 week post therapy, but no lasting effects at 1 month)	Relatively accurate at this task	

Study	Case		Task				
Visch-Brink et al. (1997)	Patient A	Visual and lexical-semantic	'BOX' Lexical semantic therapy: e.g. semantic categories, word semantic association	n.t.	× (no change in naming but gains in word (but not picture) comprehension)	This paper is part of an *Aphasiology* "clinical forum"; see commentaries for further discussion	Single baseline, no testing of treated items
	Patient B	Visual and lexical-semantic	'BOX' Lexical semantic therapy: e.g. semantic categories, word semantic association, semantic gradation	n.t.	× (no change in naming but gains in word and picture comprehension)		
Studies manipulating presence of word form information in semantic tasks							
Drew & Thompson (1999)	1	Severe semantic	Semantic tasks with no provision of phonological or orthographic form: Sorting pictures by category, by features; semantic feature judgements; definition to picture matching	×	×		No statistics, relatively small numbers of items (n = 15)
	2	Semantic		✓ (inconsistent across categories)	Inconsistent	Increased semantic errors in naming. After treatment	
	3	Semantic		✓ (inconsistent across categories)	Inconsistent	Increased semantic errors on naming. After treatment	
	4	Semantic		×	×		
	1	Severe semantic	Semantic tasks providing phonological and orthographic form: semantic judgements; word-picture matching; naming to definition	✓	×		
	4	Semantic		✓	×		
Le Dorze et al. (1994)	RB	Access to phonological form?	Formal-semantic: word-picture matching	✓	×	*Strictly speaking a facilitation rather than therapy study	Controls were at ceiling at baseline
			Semantic: definition–picture matching	×	×		

Phon.: Phonological; POL: Phonological Output Lexicon.

semantic impairment, AER, following "relatedness" judgements (and following "function" judgements). They suggest that naming improvement showed generalisation by "the use of a strategy (which may be unconscious) of exploring the semantics of an item (when naming fails) which facilitates retrieval of that item (perhaps by increasing the semantic information addressing the output lexicon to a 'critical' level where retrieval can occur)" (p. 119). Hence, techniques promoting reflection on semantic properties may be better viewed as teaching a strategy rather than remediating semantic processing, at least for some of the individuals targeted.

Second, addressing semantic tasks as therapy. As discussed earlier, semantic tasks are not restricted in their use to those individuals who have semantic impairments. Indeed there is some evidence that semantic tasks can improve word production even for those individuals with good semantic processing and even when the tasks are performed accurately (e.g., Nickels & Best, 1996b). There is now a large body of research that demonstrates that these tasks (usually word–picture matching) are widely effective and can have long-lasting effects (e.g., Marshall, Pound, White-Thomson, & Pring, 1990; Nickels & Best, 1996b; Pring et al., 1990). However, in general, lasting benefits from treatment are item-specific (see later for further discussion of apparent generalisation). One issue that has received some attention is, to what extent is semantic processing the source of the benefit from so-called semantic tasks? The majority of studies have used semantic tasks where the word-form is also provided, usually as a (written or spoken) stimulus for matching to a picture, although the participant is not always required to explicitly produce the word-form (Nickels & Best, 1996b, discuss the role of explicit production in task efficacy).

Few studies have explicitly attempted to examine the effects of semantic treatments where no word form is provided. Drew and Thompson (1999) demonstrate that for two of their participants with semantic impairments, there was no benefit from semantic tasks unless the word form was also provided. However, although Drew and Thompson argue that their other two participants did benefit from the "pure" semantic task, the data are unclear, with inconsistent results for these participants across the two categories treated. Le Dorze, Boulay, Gaudreau and Brassard (1994) used a facilitation task with one aphasic individual to investigate whether provision of the word form in a semantic task affected the efficacy of that task in improving naming. Whereas "Show me the octopus" improved naming, "Show me the mollusc with long legs" did not. Hence it appears that the provision of the word form may be important in at least some cases, although clearly more research is needed to establish the generality of these findings.

Therapy for phonological impairments or phonological tasks as therapy?   So-called "phonological tasks" are possibly an even more mixed bag than semantic tasks. They range from repetition of the target, phonological (and orthographic) cueing of picture naming, tasks involving phonological judgements such as rhyme judgements, syllable and phoneme counting, and phoneme segmentation to tasks combining orthography and phonology using reading, anagrams, and scrabble tiles. In much the same way as with semantic tasks, many of these have been used to facilitate word retrieval and not exclusively in individuals with phonological impairments.

First, therapy for phonological impairments. The first point to be made here is what do we mean by a phonological impairment? The easiest definition of a phonological impairment is symptomatic—the individual makes phonological errors in all tasks requiring speech output and these are more common on words with more phonemes. What is more controversial is what the underlying impairment might be. Most authors agree that a post-lexical impairment is one possible cause; an impairment in activating phonemes or inserting those phonemes into their syllable positions, or maintaining those phonemes in a buffer. However, authors disagree as to whether an impairment at the level of retrieval of a phonological representation from the lexicon will result in phonological errors (compare, for example, Nickels, 1997; Kohn 1989; and Dell, Schwartz, Martin, Saffran, & Gagnon, 1997; Nickels, 2001b). Current theories of word production appear to restrict phonological errors primarily to post-lexical impairments (see Nickels, 2001a; Nickels & Howard, 2000, for reviews).

Surprisingly, there are relatively few papers that address the remediation of phonological encoding/assembly impairments (characterised by phonological errors in output; see Table 3), indeed in 1986 Marshall noted that there were "no specific testable proposals for the remediation of fluent paraphasic ... speech" (p. 16). However, there seem to be two main approaches taken clinically to treatment—improvement of the phonological assembly processes themselves, and improvement of monitoring and correction of errors. Franklin, Buerk, and Howard (2002) aimed to use the latter approach. MB produced long sequences of phonologically related responses in all speech-production tasks, however these rarely resulted in a correct response. Franklin et al. describe therapy that used an approach and tasks commonly used clinically when attempting to remediate self-monitoring (including phoneme discrimination tasks, judgements of accuracy of target attempts).[11] However, they argue that the treatment (which showed generalised improvement across items and modalities) was not effective by improving self-monitoring, indeed they suggest (with hindsight) that MB had good monitoring. Rather, they propose that treatment improved the phoneme selection impairment itself (but admit they do not know how or why). Hence, as is so often the case, the aim of treatment (influencing the choice of treatment task) and the means by which improvement is actually effected are at odds!

Second, addressing phonological tasks as therapy. Phonological tasks have been widely argued to be the most appropriate for impairments in retrieval of (or damage to) the phonological form from the phonological output lexicon (e.g., Miceli et al., 1996; Nettleton & Lesser, 1991). Miceli et al. (1996) argue that as these tasks focus at the level of activation of individual entries in the phonological output lexicon, their effects should be item-specific—a result of "priming" retrieval of the phonological form. Indeed, that is what has been found in several studies (e.g., Miceli et al., 1996; Hillis & Caramazza, 1994, HW; Nettleton & Lesser, 1991, DF). However, there are several reports where generalisation to untreated items is argued to have been observed. For example, Robson, Marshall, Pring, and Chiat (1998) treated GF (a woman with jargon aphasia who was argued to have an impairment in retrieval of the phonological form) using a range of phonological tasks including syllable counting, pointing to the letter corresponding to the initial phoneme, phonological cueing, and repetition. Following therapy, GF showed significant improvement on both treated and untreated items, in clear contradiction to the predictions of Miceli et al. (1996). Why might this be? One possibility is that the therapy was similar to that used with JOW (Best et al., 1997a, b; Best & Nickels, 2000; Howard, 1994) as discussed earlier. JOW also showed generalisation, and Best et al. argued that the use of orthography and phonology may have drawn links between the two and led to automatic use of orthography to facilitate access to phonological lexical representations. Hence, tasks that involve both orthography and phonology (and perhaps specifically

---

[11] It should be noted that while termed "monitoring tasks", it is clear that they were very similar to tasks labelled in other studies as "phonological" tasks in that they involved comparing a phonological form to a target and provided phonological information regarding the target (as occurs in phonological cueing).

TABLE 3
Studies focusing on remediation of post-lexical phonological impairments

Paper	Aphasic individual	Impairment	Treatment	Outcome (treated)	Generalisation (to untreated items in naming)	Comments	Problems with interpretation
Cubelli et al. (1988)	FC, PB, IS	'Conduction aphasia' — phonological encoding	Word–picture matching with visual distractors, reading, repetition, sentence–picture matching; anagrams (syllables, letters)	n.t.	✓ (and reading, repetition, written naming & connected speech)		Spontaneous recovery, multicomponent task
Franklin et al. (2002)	MB	Phonological encoding	Phoneme discrimination & monitoring	✓	✓ (and to connected speech)	Argued that therapy had improved phoneme selection (NOT monitoring)	

Kohn, Smith, and Arsenault (1990) is excluded from this table as the authors are explicit that their aim is to improve fluency rather than increase the accuracy of CM's word production.

letters and sounds) may produce their effects in a different way from those that only involve phonology (or whole word orthographic forms). A second possibility is that while GF did have impaired lexical retrieval, perhaps he also had post-lexical impairments in phonological encoding. If this is the case, the tasks used may have produced similar effects to those found by Franklin et al. (2002) for MB—improvement of the phonological encoding impairment, and hence generalisation to all word production tasks.[12] A final possibility for why some studies may find generalisation is related to the repeated exposure to "control" stimuli during treatment in daily naming probes. This will be discussed further later.

It is also important to note that while phonological tasks are argued to be most appropriate for phonological retrieval impairments, they have also been successful in improving naming for individuals with semantic impairments (e.g., Nickels & Best, 1996b, PA; Raymer, Thompson, Jacobs, & Le Grand, 1993). However, it is worth reflecting on the results of a semantic impairment on activation at the lexical level— underspecified semantic representations or weak activation at the semantic level will result in weak activation at the lexical level, hence any task that increases activation at the lexical level (as is argued for phonological tasks) will increase the chance of retrieval of the phonological form. This is true whether the reason for the weak lexical activation is a phonological impairment or a semantic impairment. Hence phonological tasks might improve naming for individuals with semantic impairments but this would not be because they remediate the semantic impairment itself.

Semantic and phonological tasks and word retrieval

Traditionally, so-called "semantic" and "phonological" tasks were argued to have very different effects on word retrieval (see e.g., Mitchum & Berndt, 1995; Nickels & Best, 1996a,b). This view originated from the literature on facilitation of aphasic naming (e.g., Howard et al., 1985a; Patterson, Purell, & Morton, 1983). Facilitation is similar to priming—it examines the effect of performing a task *once* on naming. For example, is someone more likely to be able to name a picture accurately having been asked to repeat the name of the picture, than if they simply had a second attempt at naming. The results of the facilitation tasks were clear: "phonological" tasks only improved naming for a very short time (six items later, with no effects at 10–15 minutes; Howard et al., 1985a); whereas "semantic" tasks improved naming for up to 24 hours (Howard et al., 1985a).

However, when used as treatment tasks the distinctions are no longer so clear.[13] Howard et al. (1985b) found equivalent effects of both tasks when used as treatment, and other studies have now also demonstrated long-lasting effects of "phonological" treatments on word retrieval (e.g., Davis & Pring, 1991; Hickin, Herbert, Best, Howard, & Osborne, 2002a; Raymer, Thompson, Jacobs, & Le Grand, 1993; Rose, Douglas & Matyas, 2002). Howard (2000) suggests that the difference between semantic and phonological tasks may well be overstated. In the majority of the studies with semantic treatments, the form of the word is provided (as a spoken or written word), and as we have already noted, in "phonological" tasks, the picture is usually present (evoking

---

[12] Only one piece of data would seem to counter this argument—GF showed no change in nonword repetition following treatment—however, it is possible that an additional impairment to the procedures required for successful nonword repetition may have caused this result.

[13] In fact more recent facilitation studies have also suggested that phonological cues can produce durable effects (Best, Herbert, Hickin, Osborne, & Howard, 2002).

semantic processing) and/or a word provided for repetition, which will also access word meaning. Hence in both tasks there is semantic and phonological information available. Howard (2000) argues that the difference between these tasks is indeed more apparent than real and that both tasks are indeed having their effects in exactly the same way—by strengthening mappings between semantics and phonological form when both are simultaneously active. This predicts equivalent effects for semantic and phonological tasks for most individuals. Unfortunately, there are few studies that examine this issue. Howard (2000), in a reanalysis of Howard et al. (1985b), found a very high correlation between the rate of improvement during the two types of therapy, and naming accuracy on items treated by the two methods. Moreover, a homogeneity test on the difference between the effects of the two treatments confirmed that there was no evidence that any patient benefited more from one treatment than the other. Nevertheless, one of the cases studied by Nickels and Best (1996b), PA, does seem to counter Howard's prediction— she benefited from tasks providing the word form (in her case the written word) but failed to benefit from semantic tasks (including the word form). Clearly, once again, further investigation is warranted.[14]

Other tasks and word retrieval

I have focused on treatments involving phonological, orthographic, and semantic tasks, yet these have been fairly narrowly defined. Semantic tasks have generally involved matching words or definitions to pictures, or categorising the pictures themselves. Yet other tasks may also be tapping these same processes: For example, Rose et al. (2002) investigate the efficacy of gesture using both iconic gesture (which can be thought of as another semantic task) and cued articulation (which systematically maps onto phonology in a similar way to letter–sound correspondences). Similarly, drawing can be perceived as a semantic task and has been used as part of some of the treatments described earlier (e.g., Hillis, 1991, 1998). Even the use of hypnosis (Thompson, Hall, & Sison, 1986) has incorporated description of semantic attributes. In essence, every task that has been used to facilitate word retrieval in the past, or is likely to be used in the future, will most probably impact on semantic and/or phonological processing to some degree.

Generalisation in the treatment of word retrieval

There is a sense in which the most successful treatment is one that effects improvement not only for the items used in therapy but also for any other item. In other words, a treatment for naming that improves naming of all items (and in all contexts). Of course, strategic approaches by their very nature often result in generalisation, but this is less often true for treatments aiming to remediate impaired retrieval and production processes themselves. While many treatments produce clear long-lasting effects on the treated items, generalisation to untreated items is less common, and when obtained, often less robust (e.g., Nickels & Best, 1996b). In fact, Howard (2000) has recently argued that for many treatment studies, so-called "generalisation" may in fact be treatment effects. Howard et al. (1985b) included a set of "naming controls" in their treatment design.

---

[14] It is also probable that the choice of stimuli has an influence on the success of treatment. Martin, Laine, and colleagues (Laine & Martin, 1996; Martin, Fink, Laine & Ayala, 2001; Martin & Laine, 1997, 2000) have recently observed that some individuals benefit from facilitation using sets of either phonologically or semantically related items, whereas others are impaired by these contexts.

These items were not given treatment but were presented for naming along with the treated items at every treatment session. These "naming controls" were found to have improved significantly at the end of the treatment period (although less than the treated items). Although these gains have been widely interpreted as generalisation, Howard (2000) suggests that they are more probably a result of the repeated attempts at naming. Nickels (2002) directly examined this issue, and found that for one aphasic man, JAW, repeated attempts at naming did indeed increase his naming success. Both Nickels (2002) and Howard (2000) argue for the same mechanism: many aphasic individuals are inconsistent in their naming ability—some names will be successfully retrieved on one occasion but not on another. When, by chance, an individual produces a picture name successfully, both the semantic representation and the phonological representation for that item are simultaneously active. This will then strengthen the mapping for that item, making it more likely that the word will be produced correctly on a subsequent occasion (which will again strengthen the mapping). It is likely that some perceived generalisation in other studies can also be the result of the same process—either stimuli are deliberately introduced during therapy (e.g., as naming controls, daily pre- or post-therapy probes, or distractor items) or appear accidentally (e.g., in stimuli where multiple distractors are used). Hence, it would appear that greater caution needs to be used before improvement in control stimuli is attributed to "generalisation" of treatment effects.

Relationship between task, impairment, and efficacy

The ideal for the clinician would be the ability to unambiguously pair a particular functional impairment with a treatment task that has guaranteed success for that impairment. However, over and over again we find authors noting that we cannot yet predict which therapy task will be effective for which impairment (e.g., Best & Nickels, 2000; Hillis, 1993, 1994; Howard, 2000; Pring, Davis & Marshall, 1993; Nickels & Best, 1996a,b). Best and Nickels (2000) argued that this expectation is naïve—we cannot hope to obtain a 1:1 relationship between impairment and treatment task; at the very least one has to consider an individual's preserved language skills (and impairments in other language domains) but there will also be interactions with non-linguistic factors such as memory (and impairments thereof), learning style, and psychological state (see also the discussion later regarding "theory of therapy"). Howard (2000) recommends that what is required is a series of single case studies which can examine how different individuals with different impairments (and retained skills) respond to a treatment—comparing one *identical* treatment across subjects (e.g., Hickin et al., 2002a). In addition, examining the effect of different treatments within the same individual will also inform us as to which aspects of a task effect change for that individual (e.g. Nickels, 2002; Rose et al., 2002). Moreover, if we are truly to understand how a task has its effect and the interactions between task and impairment, then we need first to examine the most simple tasks with the fewest components. As Byng (1995) explicitly states, "most therapies described do not represent a single therapeutic process, even if they involve a single task. A single task might require a number of complex processes, but it may not be clear which of these processes was the most important for effecting change" (p. 10).

Having said this, are there any generalisations that can be drawn from the recent literature? I think the answer to this question is "yes"—there are certain types of tasks that seem to "generally" be effective for certain types of problems *but* for all of these there have been demonstrated exceptions to the rule. Why these exceptions occur we still don't fully understand. As Howard (2000) notes, it may be that the individuals fail to respond to a treatment task for reasons that are not related directly to the task itself; they might, for example, not practise as much with one treatment task (see e.g., Best et al., 1997a), or the treatment might occur over a period when, for some reason the patient was less likely to benefit (e.g., illness, depression). However, once again, the more cases we can study using the same treatment tasks, the more we should be able to draw sensible generalisations.

What tentative generalisations can we draw to date? First, the majority of individuals with impaired retrieval of phonological forms (anomia) seem to benefit from tasks that combine semantic and phonological activation. These tasks can be those that have been traditionally labelled "semantic" (e.g., word–picture matching) or "phonological" (e.g., repetition, phonemic cueing, reading aloud in the presence of the picture), and usually have long-lasting item-specific benefits for treated items. The individuals who benefit can have impairments at a semantic level or in retrieval of the phonological form (in the absence of a semantic impairment).

Second, individuals with semantic impairments seem to benefit from semantic tasks where there is explicit feedback and discussion regarding semantic features of the target (e.g., Hillis, 1991, 1998). However, the number of studies examining this issue is still extremely limited.

Any other conclusions drawn must be even more tentative, nevertheless, it would appear that tasks that combine phonology and orthography in the form of letter and sound cueing and identification, and semantics in the form of the picture, are very often successful in improving word retrieval: They can produce generalisation for some individuals, and for many others they produce item-specific effects (e.g., Best et al., 1997a,b; Hickin et al., 2002a; Robson et al., 1998).

THEORY AND THERAPY

No method of treatment is better than the principles on which it is based, and the search for principles should concern us no less than the immediate clinical situation.

(Zangwill, 1947, p. 7; cited in Howard & Hatfield, 1987, p. 6)

Can cognitive neuropsychological theory inform therapy?

The relationship between cognitive neuropsychology and remediation has been much debated in the last 10 years (see for example, Basso & Marangolo, 2000; Caramazza, 1989; Hillis, 1993; Howard, 2000; Mitchum & Berndt, 1995; Shallice, 2000; Wilshire & Coslett, 2000; Wilson & Patterson, 1990). Some authors doubt that cognitive neuropsychology has advanced the theoretical basis of our therapy (e.g., Basso & Marangolo, 2000). Moreover, there is a general consensus that while cognitive neuropsychology can inform our assessment, it does not tell us what should be done in treatment nor how it should be done, nor does it provide a "theory of therapy" (see later). Nonetheless, cognitive neuropsychological theory can benefit treatment, as eloquently stated by Basso and Marangolo (2000, p. 228):

The most important contribution of cognitive neuropsychology to aphasia therapy lies in the massive reduction of the theoretically-motivated choices left open to the therapist. Clearly articulated and detailed hypotheses about representations and processing of cognitive functions allow rejection of all those strategies for treatment that are not theoretically justified. The more detailed the cognitive model, the narrower the spectrum of rationally motivated treatments; whereas the less fine-grained the cognitive model, the greater the number of theoretically justifiable therapeutic interventions.

Moreover, as discussed earlier, if one is ever to achieve (or even attempt) prediction in treatment, between task and impairment, a clearly articulated theory of the levels of processing that can be impaired is essential. Indeed, one of the limitations remains that while theories of language processing are becoming increasingly specified (e.g., Levelt, Roelofs & Meyer, 1999), how these models will function once damaged is not at all clear (but see Dell et al., 1997, for a computationally implemented theory that has investigated the effects of "lesioning").

Can therapy inform theory?

Cognitive neuropsychology plays a clear role in the development of theories of cognitive processing (see Rapp, 2001, for a review). However, to date, much of the focus of therapy research has been to demonstrate that therapy can be effective and to develop theories of how the therapy may have been having its effects. Yet therapy can also play a role in testing the adequacy of theories of language processing. For example, Biedermann, Blanken, and Nickels (2002) present a preliminary study which demonstrates how evidence from the patterns of generalisation in therapy might be used to argue for theories incorporating a single phonological representation for homophones. Best et al. (2002) examined phonological and orthographic cueing techniques in a facilitation paradigm (the therapeutic task is only performed once followed by subsequent reassessment). The pattern of results across a case series was used to inform theoretical accounts of how phonemic and orthographic cues might have their effects in language processing. Hence, while using therapy as evidence for theory is relatively under-utilised, it is a role that has great potential and should not be overlooked.

Theory of therapy

As Howard and Hatfield (1987) note, and as was alluded to earlier, a theory of language processing and a hypothesis regarding the individual's level of impairment within such a theory are necessary to specify treatment, but they are not sufficient—a "theory of therapy" is also required. Hillis (1993) discusses some of the mimimal requirements for such a theory of rehabilitation. These requirements include analysis of the pre- and post-therapy (damaged) states of the language system, a specification of how the change between these occurred, and a determination of which characteristics of the individual and their profile of impairments are relevant to the treatment outcome. Clearly we are still some way from having a comprehensive theory of therapy, but progress has been made—even if only to clarify the limits of our understanding! The greatest focus has been on the last of Hillis's requirements, but increasingly there is also discussion of "how" the therapy might be having its effects.

We have described, earlier, the problems with identifying the components of task and impairment that are relevant to outcome, and advocated the need for "microanalysis". However even this may not be sufficient. Byng (1995) notes that one of the assumptions that underlie approaches to aphasia therapy, is that therapy is synonymous with the task. However as Basso and Marangolo (2000) discuss, this is far from true: "Therapy takes place at the interaction between the aphasic patient and the speech pathologist. The patient is not a passive recipient of therapy and the therapist is not a machine. They must continually adapt their behaviour to what the partner does and says" (p. 228). This process of interaction between therapist and the individual with aphasia during treatment is rarely made explicit, and to do so is far from easy, as is made clear by Horton and Byng (2000). As they note, although they have developed a system for documenting the discourse of therapy, there is still a long way to go before we can answer the question of whether the way in which a task is enacted has a significant impact on the outcome (see also Ferguson, 1999). This is particularly true when we go beyond the "gross" differences such as presence or absence of feedback, but instead examine, for example, the nature and timing of that feedback (see for example, Simmons-Mackie, Damico, & Damico, 1999). Nevertheless, this is yet another emerging strand in our (slow and painful) development of a "theory of therapy".

Function, activities, and participation

This section refers to the World Health Organisation 2001 International Classification of Functioning, Disability and Health (ICF). The distinction is made between "impairment" (problems in body function or structure such as a significant deviation or loss), "activity limitations" (difficulties an individual may have in executing a task or action), "participation restrictions" (problems an individual may experience in involvement in life situations), plus additional consideration of environmental factors.

Every clinician has as his or her aim to reduce the limitation in communication activities and restrictions to participation experienced by the person with aphasia. However, there is considerable debate as to whether impairment-based approaches such as those described here are the most appropriate way to achieve this, or even whether they achieve any functionally useful outcomes at all. We will not debate whether impairment-based treatments (for word-retrieval/production impairments in particular) are an appropriate goal for therapy. It is my strong belief that they are, and that different approaches to therapy are complementary rather than mutually exclusive: impairment-based therapy at many levels of description (impaired word retrieval, sentence processing, discourse, conversation) can and should be combined with "functional" therapies and those derived from social models (e.g., Kagan & Gailey, 1993; Pound, Parr, Lindsay, & Woolf, 2000; Simmons-Mackie, 2001).

Can, and do, impairment-based treatments for word-retrieval and production disorders impact on functional skills and increase activity and participation? Many studies do not address this issue, although the "traditional" response might be that as word retrieval/production underlies every attempt at verbal communication, improving word-retrieval impairments is of course functionally relevant. Unfortunately, this argument is simplistic at best and fundamentally misguided at worst. If indeed treatments are successful in remediating word-retrieval impairments themselves, then indeed verbal communication should be improved across all contexts. However, few studies can claim to have done more than improve retrieval of a small set of treated items as measured in one context (picture naming). Nevertheless, as many authors have noted, the importance of an increased ability to name treated items following therapy should not be underestimated. Indeed, in her treatment of word production with HG, Hillis (1998) notes that while treatment effects were restricted to treated items, and hence there was only a moderate change in impairment, there was a large reduction in disability. Following treatment, HG (without training) used treated words in appropriate functional contexts (e.g., while shopping or out at dinner). HG also started generating lists of words she wished to be able to produce (e.g., "Bacardi and Coke"), and learned a vocabulary that would help her obtain and carry out a job. Hence, even item-specific gains and a small change in level of impairment can result in significant gains in activity and participation, but only with the use of functionally relevant items.

Hickin et al. (2002b) were unusual in measuring generalisation of improvement from treatment of word-retrieval disorders into connected speech and conversation for two individuals. Although both of the two individuals treated, MH and HP, improved on naming treated items, only one, MH, showed generalisation to untreated items (although for treated items the gains from therapy were smaller than for HP). When conversational measures were examined, MH showed improvements that were evident even before the phase of therapy that specifically targeted using words in conversation. In contrast HP showed no evidence of change.

Reorganisation approaches to word retrieval can often result in clear changes in functional language use. For example, Nickels (1992) notes that TC spontaneously and effectively used the taught self-cueing strategy in conversation.

Hence, in summary, there remain few studies that have formally evaluated the effects on disability of impairment-based remediation. However, it is clear that functional gains can be achieved although they are by no means guaranteed. It seems particularly important given the prevalence of item-specific effects that remediation should include personally relevant stimuli.

Rehabilitation research and rehabilitation practice

In many ways, there is no conflict between the requirements of the researcher and the needs of the clinician—both aim to remediate the impairment (and impact on the disability) and both need to know whether or not their therapy has been effective. Moreover, should therapy prove ineffective, both need to understand why it may have failed in order that they might "get it right next time". However, when it comes down to the choice of task, the two can diverge: the clinician is most concerned with choosing a therapy that has the best chance of succeeding (and understanding why it might have succeeded is a luxury), whereas the researcher needs not only to prove that a therapy has succeeded but also to understand why. Hence, for the clinician a task that has successfully improved naming for a wide variety of people with differing types of spoken word production impairments is often the most sensible choice. As we have seen, these are often multicomponent approaches such as cueing hierarchies or multimodality/multi-task therapies (e.g., Hickin et al., 2002a). However, as discussed earlier, if we are ever to reach the goal of being able to predict which treatment task is effective for which impairment and under which conditions, research must take a different approach. Hence researchers need to use the most simple task they can (comprising as few elements as possible) and undertake to investigate the efficacy of that task with different individuals (with a range of clearly defined functional impairments and retained skills). In addition, they need to use different tasks (but varying minimally, e.g., contrasting reading aloud with and without the picture present) with each individual to establish the "active" ingredient of the task for that individual.

This is all very well, but clinicians need to be able to match individuals to effective therapy tasks now—not when research has finally enabled us to write a "prescription guide" (if that is ever going to be possible). Is there any way to decide which task to use? One possibility is to use the approach demonstrated by Best et al. (1997a; see also Nickels & Best, 1996b, PA) where pilot studies are carried out using different tasks for short periods (e.g., 1 week) to establish which tasks seem effective and which do not prior to continuing with the most effective therapies over a longer period. A more "extreme" version of this method is to use one application of the task in a single session ("facilitation") to attempt to predict which tasks will be effective (e.g., Rose et al.,

2002). Hickin et al. (2002a) found that all of the individuals who benefited from cues when provided in a facilitation design (Best et al., 2002) also benefited from the use of cues as therapy.

However, possibly the most important recommendation for both clinicians and researchers is to ensure that it is possible to establish whether or not a particular therapy is effective by using a sound methodology. Although the researcher often has the luxury of more time to establish baselines, develop stimuli, and statistically analyse results, some minimal methodological controls can and should be used by clinicians too. We have a duty to be able to demonstrate that a therapy is effective to the individuals with aphasia, their families/friends/carers, those funding the treatment, and not least to ourselves. Unfortunately, clinicians cannot always be guided by published research papers in their search for guidance on a methodology for demonstrating efficacy of treatment—many studies have methodological flaws. The following list notes some of the key points that should be considered when embarking on therapy, in order to have an optimum chance of being able to evaluate the efficacy of the therapy.[15]

(1) The same assessments should be repeated before and after therapy.

Even if it appears obvious that the individual has improved, and the task used before therapy is likely to be performed with ease and accuracy, it still needs to be demonstrated.

(2) These assessments should contain at least one measure of the skill that has been treated and this measure should contain enough items to allow change to be demonstrated.

For example, in the case of word retrieval, measured by picture naming, the use of the Boston Diagnostic Aphasia Examination (BDAE, Goodglass & Kaplan, 1983) would not be recommended as a pre- and post-therapy measure. As the BDAE only incorporates five line drawings for confrontation naming, even the largest benefit from therapy could not be demonstrated. It would be far better to use a specific assessment of picture naming, and possibly this more general assessment in addition. The specific assessment may, and often should, comprise the set of "to-be treated" stimuli.

(3) Ideally perform more than one pre-therapy baseline (i.e., do the assessment on more than one occasion) to establish degree of spontaneous recovery and/or variability.

If the baseline assessments show no difference in performance but there is change following treatment, then there is a strong argument that the treatment caused the change. However without stable baselines, if treatment generalises perfectly across items (with untreated items improving as much as treated items), it is often difficult to argue that the effect is due to the treatment, rather than due to spontaneous recovery or non-specific effects (e.g., increased motivation, reduced depression).

(4) Divide the assessed and "to-be-treated" stimuli into two sets of equal difficulty based on pre-treatment performance, treat one set first, reassess and then treat the second set and reassess (a "cross-over" design).

---

[15] Although some of these points may seem trivial, or possibly patronising, they are included on the basis of my observation of real behaviours by clinicians and researchers.

This design allows the degree of generalisation to be observed. If treated items improve more than untreated items, then it can be argued that the treatment has had an effect, even if spontaneous recovery is a factor (that possibly resulted in all or part of the improvement of the untreated items).

(5) Select a control task that you would not expect to be affected by the treatment and assess before and after therapy. For example, auditory lexical decision could be used as a control task when word retrieval is being treated. Any change in the control task will suggest spontaneous recovery or non-specific treatment effects

(6) Evaluate your results objectively. Ideally, statistical comparisons such as McNemar's Test should be used to identify whether any change in performance is greater than might be expected by chance. At the very least, clinicians should be aware that a change from 4/10 to 7/10, although in percentage terms a change from 40% correct to 70% correct, could still not represent true improvement. Instead it might represent the same level of performance with the difference in scores being the result of chance (due to natural variability in performance). In contrast, a change from 12/30 to 21/30 (still 40% to 70%) is unlikely to be the result of chance variations in performance (hence the importance of using reasonable numbers of stimuli).

Some studies have used daily post-tests (and/or pretests) of treated stimuli to observe the effects of treatment during the treatment period (see for example, Fink et al., 2002; Raymer & Ellsworth, 2002; Rose et al., 2002). This can be useful, in that it allows tracking of the effects of treatment, and termination if no effect is being observed or if ceiling has been reached. However, this method cannot be used easily with home programmes, and for some participants may be too onerous (particularly when sufficient items are used to enable accurate assessment of treatment efficacy).

Figures 1 to 3 present idealised hypothetical treatment results to illustrate different designs and patterns of results and their interpretation.[16] In sum, for both the clinician and the researcher it is important to ensure that efficacy is tested and not assumed; visual inspection alone is not adequate (see Rose et al., 2002 for further discussion). For further discussion of single case study design and statistical analysis refer, for example, to: Coltheart, 1983; Franklin, 1997; Howard, 1986; Howard and Hatfield, 1987; Pring, 1986; Wertz, 1995; Willmes, 1990, 1995; Wilson, 1987, 1993.

CONCLUSION

It has now been clearly demonstrated that therapy for word-retrieval and production disorders can be effective. However, we still cannot predict which therapy will work for which impairment—this is a conclusion that has been drawn several times in the past (e.g., Hillis, 1993; Nickels & Best, 1996b), and is likely to remain for several years to come. Nevertheless, there are clear pointers for future research and for clinical practice, which should lead to continued benefits for impairment-based remediation for the person with aphasia.

---

[16] Although statistical analysis is not presented for these figures, it should be emphasised once again that only with statistical analysis can the results be interpreted with confidence.

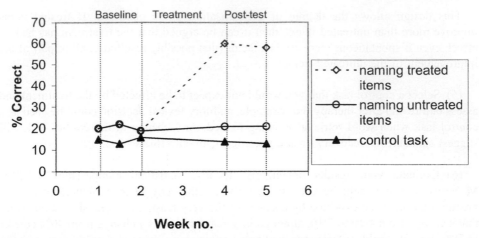

Figure 1a. An example of a multiple baseline study with item-specific improvement. Baselines are stable (no consistent improvement in naming performance over three pre-therapy baselines). Following treatment of one set of items, they improve in naming. However, there is no change in untreated items in picture naming, indicating item-specific effects of treatment. Similarly there is no change in a control task chosen to be unaffected by the treatment process (e.g., auditory lexical decision). Hence we can conclude (assuming statistical significance) that the treatment is effective, and there is no generalisation to untreated items or tasks, nor is there spontaneous recovery or non-specific effects of treatment.

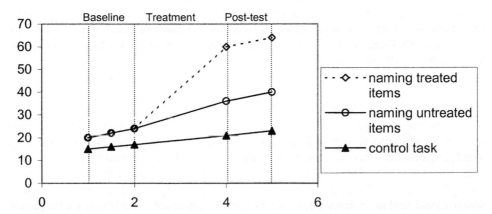

Figure 1b. An example of a multiple baseline study, with item-specific improvement and spontaneous recovery. Baselines are rising, indicating spontaneous recovery. However, following treatment of one set of items, they improve in naming at a faster rate than during the baseline period. However, there is no change in the rate of improvement for untreated items in picture naming. Similarly there is no change in rate of improvement for a control task. Hence we can conclude (assuming statistical significance) that the treatment is effective and there is no generalisation to untreated items or tasks, although there is also spontaneous recovery (or non-specific effects of treatment).

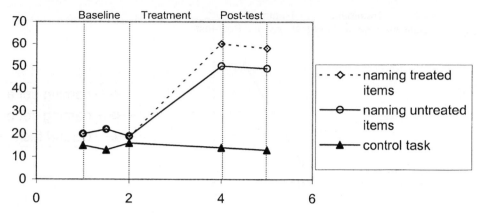

Figure 2a. An example of a multiple baseline study with generalisation to untreated items in the same task. Baselines are stable (no consistent improvement in naming performance over three pre-therapy baselines). Following treatment of one set of items, they improve in naming. However, there is also improvement for untreated items in picture naming, indicating generalisation of treatment effects across items. There is no change in a control task. Hence we can conclude (assuming statistical significance) that the treatment is effective, and there is generalisation to untreated items but not to an untreated (and unrelated) task, nor is there spontaneous recovery or non-specific effects of treatment.

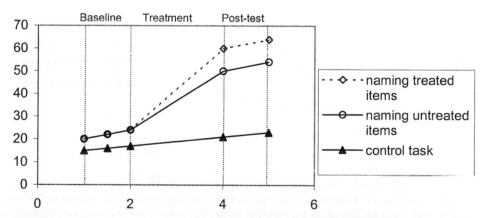

Figure 2b. An example of a multiple baseline study with generalisation to untreated items in the same task, and spontaneous recovery. Baselines are rising, indicating spontaneous recovery. However, following treatment of one set of items, they improve in naming at a faster rate than during the baseline period. There is also an increase in the rate of change of improvement for untreated items in picture naming, indicating generalisation of treatment effects across items. There is no difference in the rate of change for the control task. Hence we can conclude (assuming statistical significance) that the treatment is effective, there is generalisation to untreated items but not to an untreated (and unrelated) task, and there is spontaneous recovery.

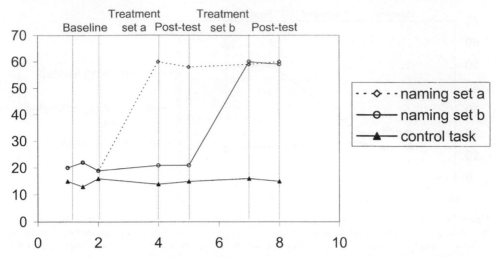

Figure 3a   An example of a multiple baseline study with item specific improvement, and a cross-over design. Baselines are stable (no consistent improvement in naming performance over three pre-therapy baselines). Following treatment of set a, naming improves on that set. However, there is no change in untreated items (set b) in picture naming, indicating item specific effects of treatment. Similarly there is no change in a control task. When in the second phase of treatment, set b are treated, they now show improvement. Hence we can conclude (assuming statistical significance) that the treatment is effective, there is no generalisation to untreated items or tasks, nor is there spontaneous recovery or non-specific effects of treatment.

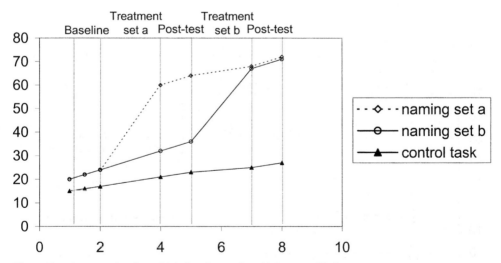

Figure 3b.   An example of a multiple baseline study, with item-specific improvement, spontaneous recovery, and a cross-over design. Baselines are rising, indicating spontaneous recovery. However, following treatment of set a, naming improves at a faster rate than during the baseline period. However, there is no change in the rate of improvement for untreated items (set b) in picture naming. Similarly there is no change in rate of improvement for a control task. When the previously untreated items (set b) are treated, they now show an increase in the rate of change of improvement. Hence we can conclude (assuming statistical significance) that the treatment is effective and there is no generalisation to untreated items or tasks, although there is also spontaneous recovery (or non-specific effects of treatment).

REFERENCES

Abrahams, J.P., & Camp, C.J. (1993). Maintenance and generalization of object naming training in anomia associated with degenerative dementia. *Clinical Gerontologist, 12*, 57–71.

Aftonomos, L.B., Steele, R.D., & Wertz, R.T. (1997). Promoting recovery in chronic aphasia with an interactive technology. *Archives of Physical Medicine Rehabilitation, 78*, 841–846.

Annoni, J.M., Khater, A., Custodi, M.C., Debeauvais,V., Michel, C.M., & Landis, T. (1998). Advantage of semantic language therapy in chronic aphasia: A study of three cases. *Aphasiology, 12*, 1093–1105.

Bachy-Langedock, N., & de Partz, M-P. (1989). Coordination of two reorganization therapies in a deep dyslexic patient with an oral naming disorder.In X. Seron and G. Deloche (Eds.) *Cognitive approaches in neuropsychological rehabilitation.* Hillsdale, NJ: Lawrence Erlbaum.

Ballard, K.J., Granier, J.P. & Robin,D.A. (2000). Understanding the nature of apraxia of speech: Theory, analysis and treatment. *Aphasiology, 14*, 969–995.

Basso, A. & Marangolo, P. (2000) Cognitive neuropsychological rehabilitation: The emperor's new clothes? *Neuropsychological Rehabilitation, 10*, 219–230.

Basso, A., Marangolo, P., Piras, F., & Galluzzi, C. (2001). Acquisition of new "words" in normal subjects: A suggestion for treatment of anomia. *Brain and Language, 77*, 45–59.

Bastiaanse, R., Bosje, M. & Franssen, M. (1996). Deficit-oriented treatment of word-finding problems: Another replication. *Aphasiology, 10*, 363–383.

Beeson, P. (1999). Treating acquired writing impairment: Strengthening graphemic representations. *Aphasiology, 13*, 767–785.

Behrmann, M., & Lieberthal, T. (1989). Category-specific treatment of a lexical-semantic deficit: A single case study of global aphasia. *British Journal of Disorders of Communication, 24*, 281–299.

Best, W.M., Herbert, R., Hickin, J., Osborne, F., & Howard, D. (2002). Phonological and orthographic facilitation of word-retrieval in aphasia: Immediate and delayed effects *Aphasiology, 16*, 151–168.

Best, W.M., Howard, D., Bruce, C., & Gatehouse, C.E.P. (1997a). Cueing the words: A single case study of treatments for anomia. *Neuropsychological Rehabilitation, 7*, 105–141.

Best, W.M., Howard, D., Bruce, C., & Gatehouse, C.E.P. (1997b). A treatment for anomia combining semantics, phonology and orthography. In S. Chiat, J. Law, & J. Marshall (Eds.), *Language disorders in children and adults: Psycholinguistic approaches to therapy.* London: Whurr.

Best, W.M., & Nickels, L.A. (2000). From theory to therapy in aphasia: Where are we now and where to next? *Neuropsychological Rehabilitation, 10*, 231–247.

Biedermann, B., Blanken, G., & Nickels, L.A. (2002). The representation of homophones: Evidence from remediation. *Aphasiology, 16*, 1115–1136.

Boyle, M., & Coelho, C.A. (1995). Application of semantic feature analysis as a treatment for aphasic dysnomia. *American Journal of Speech-Language Pathology, 4*, 94–98.

Bruce, C., & Howard, D. (1987) Computer-generated phonemic cues: An effective aid for naming in aphasia. *British Journal of Disorders of Communication, 22*, 191–201.

Bruce, C., & Howard, D. (1988). Why don't Broca's aphasics cue themselves? An investigation of phonemic cueing and tip-of-the-tongue information. *Neuropsychologia, 26*, 253–264.

Byng, S. (1988). Sentence processing deficits: Theory and therapy. *Cognitive Neuropsychology, 5*, 629–676.

Byng, S., & Coltheart, M. (1986). Aphasia therapy research: Methodology requirements and illustrative results. In E. Hjelmquist & L.-G. Nilsson (Eds.), *Communication and handicap: Aspects of psychological compensation and technical aids.* New York: Elsevier Science.

Byng, S. (1995). What is aphasia therapy? In C. Code & D. Müller (Eds.), *The treatment of aphasia from theory to practice.* London: Whurr.

Caramazza, A. (1989). Cognitive neuropsychology and rehabilitation: An unfulfilled promise? In X. Seron & G. Deloche (Eds.), *Cognitive approaches in neuropsychological rehabilitation.* Hillsdale, NJ: Lawrence Erlbaum Associates Inc.

Carlomagno, S., Pandolfi, M., Labruna, I., Colombo, A., & Razzano, C. (2001). Recovery from moderate aphasia in the first year post-stroke: Effect of type of therapy. *Archives of Physical Medicine Rehabilitation, 82*, 1073–1080.

Coelho, C.A., McHugh, R.E., & Boyle, M. (2000). Semantic feature analysis as a treatment for aphasic dysnomia: A replication. *Aphasiology, 14*, 133–142.

Coltheart, M. (1983) Aphasia therapy research: A single case study approach. In C. Code, & D.C. Muller (Eds.), *Aphasia therapy.* London: Edward Arnold.

Cubelli, R., Foresti, A., & Consolini, T. (1988). Reeducation strategies in conduction aphasia. *Journal of Communication Disorders, 21*, 239–249.

Davis, A., & Pring, T. (1991). Therapy for word finding deficits: More on the effects of semantic and phonological approaches to treatment with dysphasic patients. *Neuropsychological Rehabilitation, 1*, 135–145.

Dell, G.S., Schwartz, M.F., Martin, N., Saffran, E.M., & Gagnon, D.A. (1997). Lexical access in normal and aphasic speech. *Psychological Review, 104*, 801–838.

Deloche, G., Dordain, M., & Kremin, H. (1993). Rehabilitation of confrontation naming in aphasia: Relations between oral and written modalities. *Aphasiology, 7*, 201–216.

Deloche, G., Hannequin, D., Dordain, M., Metz-Lutz, M-N., Kremin. H., Tessier, C., Vendrell, J., Cardebat, D., Perrier, D., Quint, S., & Pichard, B. (1997). Diversity of patterns of improvement inconfrontation naming: Some tentative hypotheses. *Journal of Communication Disorders, 30*, 11–22.

Drew, R.L., & Thompson, C.K. (1999). Model based semantic treatment for naming deficits in aphasia. *Journal of Speech, Language, and Hearing Research, 42*, 972–989.

Eales, C., & Pring, T. (1998). Using individual and group therapy to remediate word finding difficulties. *Aphasiology, 12*, 913–918.

Enderby, P., Broeckx, J., Hospers, W., Schildermans, F., & Deberdt, W. (1994). Effect of Pireacetam on recovery and rehabilitation after stroke: A double-blind, placebo-controlled study. *Clinical Neuropharmacology, 17*, 320–331.

Ferguson, A. (1999). Learning in aphasia therapy: Its not so much what you do, but how you do it! *Aphasiology, 13*, 125–140.

Fink, R., Brecher, A., Schwartz, M., & Robey, R. (2002). A computer implemented protocol for the treatment of naming disorders: Evaluation of clinician-guided and partially self-guided instruction. *Aphasiology, 16*, 1061–1086.

Francis, D.R., Clark, N., & Humphreys, G.W. (2002). Circumlocution-induced naming: A treatment for effecting generalisation in anomia? *Aphasiology, 16*, 243–259.

Franklin, S.E. (1997). Designing single case treatment studies for aphasic patients. *Neuropsychological Rehabilitation, 7*, 401–418.

Franklin, S.E., Buerk, F., & Howard, D. (2002). Generalised improvement in speech production for a subject with reproduction conduction aphasia. *Aphasiology, 16*, 1087–1114.

Goodglass, H., & Kaplan, E. (1983). *The assessment of aphasia and related disorders, Second Edition.* Philadelphia: Lea & Febiger.

Goodglass, H., & Wingfield, A. (1997). *Anomia: Neuroanatomical & cognitive correlates.* San Diego: Academic Press.

Grayson, E., Hilton, R., & Franklin, S. (1997). Early intervention in a case of jargon aphasia: Efficacy of language comprehension therapy. *European Journal of Disorders of Communication, 32*, 257–276.

Greenwald, M.L., Raymer, A.M., Richardson, M.E., & Rothi, L.J.G. (1995). Contrasting treatments for severe impairments of picture naming. *Neuropsychological rehabilitation, 5*, 17–49.

Hickin, J., Herbert, R., Best, W., Howard, D., & Osborne, F. (2002a). Phonological therapy for word finding difficulties: A re-evaluation. *Aphasiology, 16*, 981–999.

Hickin, J., Herbert, R., Best, W., Howard, D., & Osborne, F. (2002b). Efficacy of treatment: Effects on word retrieval and conversation. In S. Byng, C. Pound, & J. Marshall (Eds.), *The aphasia therapy file 2.* Hove, UK: Psychology Press.

Hillis, A.E. (1989). Efficacy and generalisation of treatment for aphasic naming errors. *Archives of Physical Medicine Rehabilitation, 70*, 632–636.

Hillis, A.E. (1991). Effects of separate treatments for distinct impairments within the naming process. In T. Prescott (Ed.), *Clinical aphasiology Volume 19.* Austin, TX: Pro-Ed.

Hillis, A.E. (1992). Facilitating written production. *Journal of Clinical Communication Disorders, 2*, 19 33.

Hillis, A.E. (1993). The role of models of language processing in rehabilitation of language impairments. *Aphasiology, 7*, 5–26.

Hillis, A.E. (1994). Contributions from cognitive analyses. In R. Chapey (Ed.), *Language intervention strategies in adult aphasia (3rd Edn.).* Baltimore: Williams & Wilkens.

Hillis, A.E. (1998). Treatment of naming disorders: New issues regarding old therapies. *Journal of the International Neuropsychological Society, 4*, 648–660.

Hillis, A., & Caramazza, A. (1994). Theories of lexical processing and rehabilitation of lexical deficits. In M.J. Riddoch & G.W. Humphreys (Eds.), *Cognitive neuropsychology and cognitive rehabilitation.* Hove, UK: Lawrence Erlbaum Associates Ltd.

Holland, A.L. (1998). A strategy for improving oral naming in an individual with a phonological access impairment. In N. Helm-Estabrooks & A.L. Holland (Eds.), *Approaches to the treatment of aphasia.* San Diego: Singular Publishing Group.

Horton, S., & Byng, S. (2000). Examining interaction in language therapy. *International Journal of Language and Communication Disorders, 35*, 355–375.

Hough, M.S. (1993). Treatment of Wernicke's aphasia with Jargon: A case study. *Journal of Communication Disorders*, 26, 101–111.

Howard, D. (1986). Beyond randomised controlled trials: The case for effective case studies of the effects of treatment in aphasia. *British Journal of Disorders of Communication*, 21, 89–102.

Howard, D. (1994). The treatment of acquired aphasia. *Philosophical Transactions of the Royal Society London*, B, 346, 113–120.

Howard, D. (2000). Cognitive neuropsychology and aphasia therapy: The case of word retrieval. In I. Papathanasiou (Ed.), *Acquired neurogenic communication disorders: A clinical perspective*. London: Whurr.

Howard, D., & Franklin, S. (1988). *Missing the meaning?* Cambridge, MA: MIT Press.

Howard D., & Harding D. (1998). Self-cueing of word retrieval by a woman with aphasia: Why a letter board works. *Aphasiology*, 12, 399–420.

Howard, D., & Hatfield, F.M. (1987). *Aphasia therapy; historical and contemporary issues*. Hove, UK: Lawrence Erlbaum Associates Ltd.

Howard, D., & Patterson, K.E. (1989). Models for therapy. In X. Seron & G. Deloche (Eds.), *Cognitive approaches in neuropsychological rehabilitation*. Hillsdale, NJ: Lawrence Erlbaum Associates Inc.

Howard, D., Patterson, K.E., Franklin, S., Orchard-Lisle, V., & Morton, J. (1985a). The facilitation of picture naming in aphasia. *Cognitive Neuropsychology*, 2, 49–80.

Howard, D., Patterson, K.E., Franklin, S., Orchard-Lisle, V., & Morton, J. (1985b). The treatment of word retrieval deficits in aphasia: A comparison of two therapy methods. *Brain*, 108, 817–829.

Hunt, J. (1999). Drawing on the semantic system: The use of drawing as a therapy medium. In S. Byng, K. Swinburn, & C. Pound (Eds.), *The aphasia therapy file*. Hove, UK: Psychology Press.

Jokel, R., & Rochon, E. (1996). Treatment for an aphasic naming impairment: When phonology met orthography. *Brain & Cognition*, 32, 299–301.

Kagan, A., & Gailey, G.F. (1993). Functional is not enough: Training conversation partners for aphasic adults. In A.L. Holland & M.M. Forbes (Eds.), *Aphasia treatment: World perspectives*. San Diego: Singular Publishing Group.

Kiran, S., & Thompson, C.K. (2001). Typicality of category exemplars in aphasia: Evidence from reaction time and treatment data. *Brain and Language*, 79, 27–31.

Kiran, S., Thompson, C.K., & Hashimoto, N. (2001). Training grapheme–phoneme conversion in patients with oral reading and naming deficits: A model-based approach. *Aphasiology*, 15, 855–876.

Kohn, S.E. (1989). The nature of the phonemic string deficit in conduction aphasia. *Aphasiology*, 3, 209–239.

Kohn, S.E., Smith, K.L., & Arsenault, J.K. (1990). The remediation of conduction aphasia via sentence repetition: A case study. *British Journal of Disorders of Communication*, 25, 45–60.

Laine, M., & Martin, N. (1996). Lexical retrieval deficit in picture naming: Implications for word production models. *Brain and Language*, 53, 283–314.

La Dorze, G. (1991). Étude des effects de l'intervention auprès d'un cas d'aphasie de conduction avec trouble d'accès au lexique. *Journal of Speech Language Pathology and Audiology*, 17, 5–14.

Le Dorze, G., Boulay, N., Gaudreau, J., & Brassard, C. (1994). The contrasting effects of semantic versus a formal-semantic technique for the facilitation of naming in a case of anomia. *Aphasiology*, 8, 127–141.

Le Dorze, G., & Pitts, C. (1995). A case study evaluation of the effects of different techniques for the treatment of anomia. *Neuropsychological Rehabilitation*, 5, 51–65.

Lesser, R., & Algar, L. (1995). Towards combining the cognitive neuropsychological and pragmatic in aphasia therapy. *Neuropsychological Rehabilitation*, 5, 1–16.

Levelt, W.J.M., Roelofs, A., & Meyer, A.S. (1999). A theory of lexical access in speech production. *Behavioural and Brain Sciences*, 22, 1–38.

Li, E.C., Kitselman, K., Dusatko, D., & Spinelli, C. (1988). The efficacy of PACE in the remediation of naming deficits. *Journal of Communication Disorders*, 21, 491–503.

Lowell, S., Beeson, P. & Holland, A. (1995). The efficacy of a semantic cueing procedure on naming performance of adults with aphasia. *American Journal of Speech-Language Pathology*, 4, 109–114.

Marshall, J.C. (1986). The description and interpretation of aphasic language disorder. *Neuropsychologia*, 24, 5–26.

Marshall, J., Pound, C., White-Thomson, M., & Pring, T. (1990). The use of picture/word matching tasks to assist word retrieval in aphasic patients. *Aphasiology*, 4, 167–184.

Marshall, J., Robson, J., Pring, T., & Chiat, S. (1998). Why does monitoring fail in jargon aphasia? Comprehension, judgement and therapy evidence. *Brain and Language*, 63, 79–107.

Martin, N., Fink, R., Laine, M., & Ayala, J. (2001). Differential effects of contextual priming on word retrieval impairments in aphasia. *Brain & Language*, 79, 138–141.

Martin, N., & Laine, M. (1997). Contextual priming of lexical retrieval in two severely anomic patients. *Brain & Language*, 60, 20–23.

Martin, N., & Laine, M. (2000). Effects of contextual priming on impaired word retrieval. *Aphasiology*, *14*(1), 53–70.

Massaro, M. & Tompkins, C.A. (1994). Feature analysis for treatment of communication disorders in traumatically brain-injured patients: An efficacy study. *Clinical Aphasiology*, *22*, 245–256.

McNeil, M.R., Doyle, P.J., Spencer, K., Goda, A.J., Flores, D., & Small, S. (1997). A double-blind, placebo controlled, pharmacological and behavioural treatment of lexical-semantic deficits in aphasia. *Aphasiology*, *11*, 385–400.

McNeil, M.R., Doyle, P.J., Spencer, K., Goda, A.J., Flores, D., & Small, S. (1998). Effects of training multiple form classes on acquisition, generalisation and maintenance of word retrieval in a single subject. *Aphasiology*, *12*, 575–585.

Miceli, G., Amitrano, A., Capasso, R., & Caramazza, A. (1996). The remediation of anomia resulting from output lexical damage: Analysis of two cases. *Brain and Language*, *52*, 150–174.

Mitchum, C.C., & Berndt, R.S. (1995). The cognitive neuropsychological approach to treatment of language disorders. *Neuropsychological Rehabilitation*, *5*, 1–16.

Mitchum, C.C., Greenwald, M.L., & Berndt, R.S. (2000). Cognitive treatments of sentence processing disorders: What have we learned? *Neuropsychological Rehabilitation*, *10*, 311–336.

Murray, L.L., & Karcher, L. (2000). A treatment for written verb retrieval and sentence construction skills. *Aphasiology*, *14*, 585–602.

Nettleton, J., & Lesser, R. (1991). Therapy for naming difficulties in aphasia: Application of a cognitive neuropsychological model. *Journal of Neurolinguistics*, *6*, 139–157.

Nickels, L.A. (1992). The autocue? Self-generated phonemic cues in the treatment of a disorder of reading and naming. *Cognitive Neuropsychology*, *9*, 155–182.

Nickels, L.A. (1997). *Spoken word production and its breakdown in aphasia*. Hove, UK: Psychology Press.

Nickels, L.A. (2000). Semantics and therapy in aphasia. In W. Best, K. Bryan & J. Maxim (Eds.), *Semantic processing in theory and practice*. London: Whurr.

Nickels, L.A. (2001a). Producing spoken words. In B. Rapp (Ed.), *A handbook of cognitive neuropsychology*. New York: Psychology Press.

Nickels, L.A. (2001b). Words fail me: Symptoms and causes of naming breakdown in aphasia. In R. Berndt (Ed.), *Handbook of neuropsychology* (2nd Edn.). Amsterdam: Elsevier Science.

Nickels, L.A. (2002). Improving word-finding: Practice makes (closer to) perfect? *Aphasiology*, *16*, 1047–1060.

Nickels, L.A., & Best, W. (1996a). Therapy for naming deficits (part I): Principles, puzzles and progress. *Aphasiology*, *10*, 21–47.

Nickels, L.A., & Best, W. (1996b). Therapy for naming deficits (part II): Specifics, surprises and suggestions. *Aphasiology*, *10*, 109–136.

Nickels, L.A., & Howard, D. (2000). When the words won't come: Relating impairments and models of spoken word production. In L. Wheeldon (Ed.), *Aspects of language production*. Hove, UK: Psychology Press.

Pashek, G. (1997). A case study of gesturally cued naming in aphasia: dominant versus nondominant hand training. *Journal of Communication Disorders*, *30*, 349–366.

Pashek, G. (1998). Gestural facilitation of noun and verb retrieval in aphasia: A case study. *Brain and Language*, *65*, 177–180.

Patterson, K.E., Purell, C., & Morton, J. (1983). Facilitation of word retrieval in aphasia. In C. Code & D.J. Muller (Eds.), *Aphasia therapy*. London: Edward Arnold.

Pedersen, P.M., Vinter, K., & Olsen, T.S. (2001) Improvement of oral naming by unsupervised computerised rehabilitation. *Aphasiology*, *15*, 151–169.

Pound, C., Parr, S., Lindsay, J., & Woolf, C. (2000). *Beyond aphasia: Therapies for living with communication disability*. Bicester, UK: Speechmark.

Pring, T. (1986). Evaluating the effects of speech therapy in aphasia: Developing the single-case methodology. *British Journal of Disorders of Communication*, *21*, 103–115.

Pring, T., Davis, A., & Marshall, J. (1993). Therapy for word finding deficits: Can experimental findings inform clinical work? In F.J. Stachowiach (Ed.), *Developments in the assessment and rehabilitation of brain-damaged patients*. Tubingen, Germany: Gunter Narr Verlag.

Pring, T., White-Thomson, M., Pound, C., Marshall, J., & Davis, A. (1990). Picture/word matching tasks and word retrieval; some follow-up data and second thoughts. *Aphasiology*, *4*, 479–483.

Rapp, B. (Ed.) (2001). *A handbook of cognitive neuropsychology*. New York: Psychology Press.

Raymer, A.M., & Ellsworth, T. (2002). Response to contrasting verb retrieval treatments: A case study. *Aphasiology*, *16*, 1031–1045.

Raymer, A.M., Thompson, C.K., Jacobs, B., & Le Grand, H.R. (1993). Phonological treatment of naming deficits in aphasia: Model-based generalisation analysis. *Aphasiology*, *7*, 27–53.

Robson, J., Marshall, J., Pring, T., & Chiat, S. (1998). Phonological naming therapy in jargon aphasia: Positive but paradoxical effects. *Journal of the International Neuropsychological Society, 4*, 675–686.

Rose, M., & Douglas, J. (2001). The differential facilitatory effects of gesture and visualisation processes on object naming in aphasia. *Aphasiology, 15*, 977–990.

Rose, M., Douglas, J., & Matyas, T. (2002). The comparative effectiveness of gesture and verbal treatments for a specific phonologic naming impairment. *Aphasiology, 16*, 1001–1030.

Sacchet, C., Byng, S., Marshall, J., & Pound, C. (1999). Drawing together: Evaluation of a therapy programme for severe aphasia. *International Journal of Language and Communication Disorders, 34*, 265–289.

Sbisa, S., D'Andrea, J., Semenza, C., & Tabossi, P. (2001). Rehabilitating anomia: A case study. *Brain & Language, 79*, 46–47.

Shallice, T. (2000). Cognitive neuropsychology and rehabilitation: Is pessimism justified? *Neuropsychological Rehabilitation, 10*, 209–218.

Shisler, R.J., Baylis, G.C., & Frank, E.M. (2000). Pharmacological approaches to the treatment and prevention of aphasia. *Aphasiology, 14*, 1163–1186.

Simmons-Mackie, N. (2001). Social approaches to aphasia intervention. In R. Chapey (Ed.), *Language intervention strategies in aphasia and related neurogenic communication disorders (4th Edn.)*. Baltimore: Lippincott, Williams & Wilkins.

Simmons-Mackie, N., Damico, J.S., & Damico, H.L. (1999). A qualitative study of feedback in aphasia treatment. *American Journal of Speech-Language Pathology, 8*, 218–230.

Spencer, K.A., Doyle, P.J., McNeil, M.R., Wambaugh, J.L., Park, G., & Carroll, B. (2000). Examining the facilitative effects of rhyme in a patient with output lexicon damage. *Aphasiology, 14*, 567–584.

Sugishita, M., Seki, K., Kabe, S., & Yunoki, K. (1993). A material-control single-case study of the efficacy of treatment for written and oral naming difficulties. *Neuropsychologia, 31*, 559–569.

Thompson, C.K., Hall, H.R., & Sison, C.E. (1986). Effects of hypnosis and imagery training on naming behaviour in aphasia. *Brain and Language, 28*, 141–153.

Thompson, C.K., Raymer, A. & Le Grand, H. (1991). Effects of phonologically based treatment on aphasic naming deficits: A model-driven approach. In T. Prescott (Ed.) Clinical Aphasiology, Vol 20, 239–261.

Visch-Brink, E.G., Bajema, I.M., & Van De Sandt-Koenderman, M.E. (1997) Lexical semantic therapy. BOX. *Aphasiology, 11*, 1057–1115.

Walker-Batson, D., Curtis, S., Natarajan, R., Ford, J., Dronkers, N., Salmeron, E., Lai, J., & Unwin, D.H. (2001). A double-blind, placebo-controlled study of the use of amphetamine in the treatment of aphasia. *Stroke, 32*, 2093–2098.

Wambaugh, J.L., & Doyle, P.J. (1994). Treatment for acquired apraxia of speech: A review of efficacy reports. *Clinical Aphasiology, 22*, 231–243.

Wertz, R.T. (1995). Efficacy. In C. Code & D. Muller (Eds.), *Treatment of aphasia: From theory to practice*. London: Whurr.

White-Thomson, M. (1999). Naming therapy for an aphasic person with fluent empty speech. In S. Byng, K. Swinburn, & C. Pound (Eds.), *The aphasia therapy file*. Hove, UK: Psychology Press.

Willmes, K. (1990). Statistical methods for a single-case study approach to aphasia therapy research. *Aphasiology, 4*, 415–436.

Willmes, K. (1995). Aphasia therapy research: Some psychometric considerations and statistical methods of the single-case study approach. In C. Code & D. Muller (Eds.), *Treatment of aphasia: From theory to practice*. London: Whurr.

Wilshire, C.E., & Coslett, H.B. (2000). Disorders of word retrieval in aphasia: Theories and potential applications. In S.E. Nadeau, L.J. Gonzalez-Rothi, & B. Crosson (Eds.), *Aphasia and language: Theory to practice*. New York: Guilford Press.

Wilson, B. (1987). Single case experimental designs in neuropsychological rehabilitation. *Journal of Clinical and Experimental Neuropsychology, 9*, 527–544.

Wilson, B. (1993). Editorial: How do we know that rehabilitation works? *Neuropsychological Rehabilitation, 3*, 1–4.

Wilson, B., & Patterson, K. (1990). Rehabilitation for cognitive impairment: Does cognitive psychology apply? *Applied Cognitive Psychology, 4*, 247–260.

World Health Organisation (2001). *International Classification of Functioning, Disability and Health*. Geneva, Switzerland: WHO.

Zangwill, O.L. (1947). Psychology, speech therapy and rehabilitation. *Speech, 11*, 4–8.

APPENDIX

Summary of papers reporting treatment for impaired word retrieval

(Massaro & Tompkins, 1994, is excluded here despite using a feature analysis similar to that of Lowell et al., 1995, as no clear measure of word retrieval is included; instead, the measure is number of features retrieved.)

Paper	Aphasic individual	Impairment	Treatment	Outcome (treated)	Generalisation (to untreated items in naming)	Comments	Problems with interpretation
Primarily Semantic tasks							
Lowell et al. (1995)	BB	Conduction aphasia (good comprehension)	Semantic feature analysis: subjects generated 4 written semantic cues for each item—used on each	✓	✓?	Generalisation was most likely largely an effect of repeated attempts at naming in the treatment session	Small numbers of items per set (n = 6/7), no statistics
	BG	Anomic aphasia (good comprehension)		✓	✓?		
	SB	Conduction aphasia (good comprehension)	subsequent naming attempt (and reading aloud if incorrect)	✗	✗		
Marshall et al. (1990)	RS	Access to POL	Written word–picture matching with reading aloud	✓	✗		
	IS	Semantic		✓	✗	Comprehension improved	
	FW	Semantic		✓	✓		lack of control tasks
Marshall et al. (1998)	CM	Access to POL	Associate picture with semantically related word (from pairs of words) then written word–picture matching	✗	✗	Better monitoring of accuracy of responses to treated items, following treatment	
McNeil et al. (1997)	BO	Anomic aphasia	L-SAIT (Lexical-Semantic Activation Inhibition Therapy) generating antonyms/synonyms with cueing hierarchy—form classes trained sequentially	✓	✗		Small numbers of items per set (n = 10), variable baselines, no statistics
McNeil et al. (1998)			L-SAIT—different form classes trained concurrently	✓	✗		
Nettleton & Lesser (1991)	PD	Semantic	sem. (various)	✓	n.t.	spontaneous recovery	
	FF	Semantic		✗	n.t.		
	MH	Phon. Encoding		✗	n.t.	Therapy designed to be "impairment inappropriate"	Would impairment-appropriate treatment be effective?
	NC	Phon. Encoding		✗	n.t.		

Study	Case	Process	Task				Comments
Nickels & Best (1996b)	AER	Semantic	Function judgements "Do you (VERB) an (OBJECT)?"	×	Only for nouns having homophonic verb forms (e.g. iron, hammer)	No change on measures of comprehension (but ceiling effects)	Provision of feedback is confounded with order of treatment
			Relatedness judgements (judging associative and categorical relationships)	✓	✓ (Only when feedback was given on the task)	Relatively error prone on this task	
			Written word–picture matching	✓	× (Significant generalisation at 1 week post therapy, but no lasting effects at 1 month)	Relatively accurate at this task	
	TRC	Semantic and access to POL	Written word–picture matching/verification	✓ (in both written and spoken naming)	× (Significant generalisation at 1 week post therapy, but no lasting effects at 1 month)	Relatively accurate performance	
			Spoken word–picture matching/verification	×	×	Relatively accurate performance	Crossover design not used—treated set was the same as in written word–picture matching

Both semantic & phonological tasks

Study	Case	Process	Task				Comments
Aftonomos et al. (1997)	VAMC patients 1, 2, 3	?	Linigraphic® software—interactive icons within semantic categories or in	n.t.	✓ (PICA %ile scores improved)	Unclear what tasks involved, and to what extent they differed for different subjects	Only aphasia classification provided, no functional localisation. Unclear what tasks involved, and to what extent they differed for different subjects. No statistics for individual subjects
	Patients 1, 2, 9, 11, 18, 20	?	syntactic sequences; written word & auditory form provided	n.t.	✓ (Boston naming test scores improve)	Unclear how many items in BNT were included in treatment. Single pretest only	
	Patients 4, 8, 16, 17	?		n.t.	× or ?		
Annoni et al. (1998)	JNH	Semantic & phonological	A: semantic tasks (multiple & including provision of phonological form). B: phonological tasks (multiple, including pictures)	n.t.	✓ (only for semantic treatment)		Order effects? Statistics may not include both baselines
	GE	Semantic	phonological tasks (multiple, including pictures)	n.t.	✓ (only for semantic treatment)		Very small effect size—unlikely to be significant difference between treatments
	EG	?(phonological input)	A: phonological tasks (multiple, including pictures). B: semantic tasks (multiple & including provision of phonological form)	n.t.	×		Ceiling effects in naming? Single baseline (but chronic aphasic)

Phon.: Phonological; PGL: Phonological Output Lexicon

APPENDIX

(Continued)

Paper	Aphasic individual	Impairment	Treatment	Outcome (treated)	Generalisation (to untreated items in naming)	Comments	Problems with interpretation
Best et al. (1997a,b); Best & Nickels (2000); Howard (1994)	JOW (aka JWO)	Word-retrieval: failure to activate lemma representations	Cueing hierarchy: Cueing aid (point to initial letter, hear phoneme, repeat word)		✓	?Improved letter knowledge, and the automatic use of this knowledge in word retrieval?	
Best et al. (1997a)			Lexical therapy (written naming & delayed copying)	×	×		
			Semantic therapy (word–picture matching & delayed copying)		✓	Effects no longer significant 1 month later	
Deloche et al. (1993)	RB	Surface dysgraphia (written naming relied on phonological retrieval)	**Written naming treatment:** Computer assisted Orthographic & Semantic: Anagrams; Written sentence completion	✓	✓ (to untreated) ✓ (to treated & untreated items in spoken naming)	Generalisation to spoken naming for both treated and untreated items	NB Even untreated items were written in every treatment session. No control tasks
	GC	"Morpholexical" & word-retrieval	**Written naming treatment:** Computer assisted Orthographic Anagrams; Written syllable cues	✓	✓ (to untreated) ✓ (only to treated items in spoken naming)	WRITTEN naming treated. Generalisation to spoken naming but only for treated items	
Deloche et al. (1997)	B	Word finding:	**Written naming treatment:** Computerised Orthographic & syntactic/semantic: 2 of anagrams, written syllable cues, written letter cues, gender cues, semantic sentence completion	✓ (treated items in written naming)	✓ (to untreated) ✓ (treated & untreated items in spoken naming)	B, written naming reliant on spoken naming	Single baseline, no control for spontaneous recovery, nonspecific effects of treatment. Participants received different combinations of cues
	L			✓ (treated items in written naming)	✓ (to untreated) ✓ (treated items in spoken naming) × (to untreated in spoken naming)	L, spoken naming relies on written naming	
	A, D, J, Q, C, K			✓ (treated items in written naming)	× (to untreated written & spoken) ✓ (only to treated items in spoken naming)	A, D, J, Q, written naming reliant on spoken; C, spoken naming relies on written naming	

Study	Case	Word finding:	Written naming treatment:	✓ (treated items in written naming)	✓ (to untreated written) × (to spoken naming)		
Deloche et al. (1997) cont.	I, O		Computerised Orthographic & syntactic/semantic: 2 of anagrams, written syllable cues, written letter cues, gender cues, semantic sentence completion	✓ (treated items in written naming)	✓ (to untreated written) × (to spoken naming)	I, O written naming reliant on spoken naming	
	H, G, P, M, R			✓ (treated items in written naming)	× (to untreated written or to spoken naming)	H spoken naming relies on written naming	
	N			×	× (to untreated written & spoken) ✓ (only to treated items in spoken naming)	N spoken naming relies on written naming	
	E			×	× (to untreated written & treated spoken) ✓ (only to UNtreated items in spoken naming)		
	F			×	×		
Eales & Pring (1998)	MB	Semantic	Reading; repetition; naming with semantic and/or phonological cues; word–picture matching	✓	×	After individual therapy, group 'conversational' therapy focused on the stimuli (topic based on 'shopping' or 'holidays')	
	NO	?POL		✓	✓		Spontaneous recovery, single baseline only
	PU	Semantic	picture matching	✓	×		
	SK	?POL		✓	✓		Spontaneous recovery, single baseline only
Greenwald et al. (1995)	SS	Semantic & access to POL	Naming to auditory definition, with a phonological cueing hierarchy (C, CV cue, repetition)	✓	?	Generalisation from naming to definition, to picture naming, but not reading	Small no. items pers condition (n = 10). Daily probes of naming to definition, picture naming, semantic associate picture matching and reading aloud
			Visual-semantic cueing hierarchy (attempt naming at each stage): elicit category, elicit visual feature, elicit more visual features, elicit size, repetition	✓	×		
			Repetition (with picture present)	×	×		

Phon.: Phonological; POL: Phonological Output Lexicon

Paper	Aphasic individual	Impairment	Treatment	Outcome (treated)	Generalisation (to untreated items in naming)	Comments	Problems with interpretation
Greenwald et al. (1995) cont.	MR	Semantic and access to POL	Semantic & phonological: Naming to auditory definition, with a phonological cueing hierarchy (C, CV cue, repetition)	✓	×	Generalisation from naming to definition, to picture naming, but not reading	Small no. items per condition (n = 10). Daily probes of naming to definition, picture naming, semantic associate picture matching and reading aloud
			Visual-semantic cueing hierarchy: As above	✓	×		
			Repetition (with picture present)	×	×		
Hillis (1989)	Patient 1 (KE)	Semantic	Orthographic Cueing Hierarchy written naming, anagrams (with & without distractors), letter cue, writing to dictation, delayed copying	✓	Within semantic category & to spoken naming	Written naming treated	No statistics, small number of items per set (n = 10)
	Patient 2 (HW)	Access to POL (and graphemic output buffer impairment)		✓	× (nor to treated items in spoken naming)		
			Verbal Cueing Hierarchy: naming, writing & reading, questions about function, function provided, reading aloud, verbal sentence completion, initial phoneme	✓	× (nor to treated items in written naming)		
Hillis (1991, 1992, 1998)	HG	Semantic, POL (surface dyslexia)	Semantic (emphasising semantic distinctions)	✓	Within semantic category & to spoken naming & comprehension	Treatment for WRITTEN naming	
			Phonological (reading)	✓	×	Reteaching lexical forms for irregularly pronounced words	No statistics
Hillis (1998)			Orthographic cueing hierarchy (see Hillis, 1989)	✓ (only with 5 day/ week treatment)	×	Treatment for WRITTEN naming	No statistics
			Verbal cueing hierarchy (see Hillis, 1989)	✓ (only with 5 day/ week treatment)	×		No statistics

Study	Patient	Impairment	Task			Notes
Hillis & Caramazza (1994)	JJ	Semantic	sem. (w–p matching)	✓	✓	Unclear whether read targets aloud
	HW	Access to POL	phon. (read)	×		
			sem. (w–p matching)	×		Unclear whether read targets aloud
			phon. (read)	✓	n.t.	
			sem./phon. cueing hierarchy for naming: sentence completion, phonemic cues, repetition	✓	×	
	KE	Semantic	sem./phon. cueing hierarchy for naming: sentence completion, phonemic cues, repetition	✓	✓	
Le Dorze (1991)	LR	Access to POL	Semantic & orthographic: word–picture matching, definition; letter cueing and reading	✓	✓	Summary from Le Dorze & Pitts (1995), original in French
Le Dorze & Pitts (1995)	RT	Semantic & access to POL	Semantic & Phonological/ Orthographic: Word–picture matching with reading aloud (semantically related distractors) & naming; reading aloud/letter cue naming	✓	×	Only five items per condition
			Semantic & Phonological/ Orthographic: Word–picture matching with reading aloud (unrelated distractors) & naming; reading aloud/letter cue naming	?	×	
			Semantic: Word–picture matching with reading aloud (semantically related distractors) and naming	?	×	
			Semantic: Word–picture matching with reading aloud (unrelated distractors) & naming	×	×	

Phon.: Phonological; POL: Phonological Output Lexicon

APPENDIX

(Continued)

Paper	Aphasic individual	Impairment	Treatment	Outcome (treated)	Generalisation (to untreated items in naming)	Comments	Problems with interpretation
Li et al. (1988)	–	Conduction aphasia & impaired comprehension	"Stimulation therapy": carrier phrases, sentence completion, associated word cues, phonemic cueing, reading aloud	×		Scoring of naming includes as 'correct' gestural, circumlocution, drawing responses that would be encouraged in PACE. Hence, word retrieval itself may not have improved, but instead there was increased strategic use of alternative means of communication when word-finding fails	Results do not discriminate between treated and untreated stimuli. No statistics
			PACE therapy: "natural interaction sequences … communicating the identity of a picture on a card" using object and action pictures	✓			
Nickels & Best (1996b)	PA	Semantic & access to POL	Semantic (word–picture verification): Study 1	×	×		
			Orthographic (letter cues & reading aloud)	✓	×		
			Phonological (reading aloud)	✓	×		
Pedersen et al. (2001)	KB	POL	Unsupervised computerised	✓	×	Very small treatment effects	Single baseline, spontaneous recovery cannot be excluded
	JI	Semantic lexicon	rehabilitation—Semantic: simultaneous auditory & written word–picture matching (and picture–word matching); Phonological: word–picture matching with phonological distractors; Initial letter/sound completion. Orthographic: copying; anagrams; written naming	✓	×		
	RI	POL		✓	✓		

974

Raymer & Ellsworth (2002)	WR	Semantic	Phonological (initial phoneme and rhyme judgements) & repetition	✓	✗	Treatment of VERB retrieval; generalisation from naming to sentence production	
			Semantic (verb similarity judgements; noun relatedness judgements) & repetition	✓	✗		
			Repetition (in the presence of the picture)	✓	✗		
Sbisa et al. (2001)	ML	Access to POL?	Phonological: naming & repetition	✓	? (controls improve significantly)	Short report, statistics provided but no raw data	Controls were named before and after every treatment session. No statistical demonstration that controls improve less than treated items
			Semantic: word-picture matching	✓	? (controls improve significantly)		
Spencer et al. (2000); Doyle et al. (1998)	NR	Access to POL	Semantic category rhyme therapy (cueing hierarchy): ask for a target within a superordinate category that rhymes (e.g. clothing that rhymes with boat); phonemic cue; letter cue; repetition & reading & writing of target	✓ (spoken and written naming)	? (Improvement on output tasks not used in treatment)	Control items from a different semantic category named in daily probes but never treated show improvement = generalisation or effects of repeated naming?	Small numbers of stimuli per condition, particularly for untreated items in a category (n = 5); Nonword repetition improves (not predicted or explained)
Thompson & Kearns (1981)	Subject with anomia	Access to POL? (impaired naming with relatively preserved auditory comp & repetition)	Sentence completion (SC) cueing hierarchy: SC cue (giving semantic information), SC plus phonemic cue, SC plus target for repetition	✓	✗ (not even to semantically related stimuli)	Control stimuli were semantically related	Small numbers of stimuli per condition (n = 10), no statistics
Primarily phonological/orthographic tasks							
Basso et al. (2001)	RF	Anomia (omissions in naming)	Orthographic: Letter cue	✓	✗	Treatment on items with no response in naming & accurate comprehension. Orthographic (letter) cue had greater immediate effects which maintained compared to other tasks	Single baseline, but little change for control stimuli
			Repetition	✗	✗		
			Reading aloud	✓ (not maintained 1 week later)	✗		
	MR	Word-retrieval	Letter cue	✓	✗		
			Repetition	✓ (not maintained 1 week later)	✗		
			Reading aloud	✓ (not maintained 1 week later)	✗		

Phon.: Phonological; POL: Phonological Output Lexicon

Paper	Aphasic individual	Impairment	Treatment	Outcome (treated)	Generalisation (to untreated items in naming)	Comments	Problems with interpretation
Beeson (1999)	ST	Loss of Orthographic representations, graphemic output buffer impairment	Orthographic cueing hierarchy: written naming, anagrams, delayed copying	✓	×	Treatment of WRITTEN naming. Improvements continued with home programme	Small numbers of items per set (n = 6, but probably necessary due to severity of impairment and hypothesised 'relearning' required); no statistics
Carlomagno et al. (2001)	Patients 1–8		'Lexical' therapy—Written naming with 'visuo-lexical cues': number of letters, initial letter, anagrams (cues faded out during treatment)	n.t.	✓ P1, 2, 4, 7, 8; × P3, 5, 6	Treatment of WRITTEN NAMING (in Italian). Reduced disability observed on the CADL read/write subtest. Spoken naming also improved for P2 & P4—self cued spoken naming using initial letter	Separate scores on reading and writing of words, nonwords not provided, nor functional localisation of impairment
			'Non-lexical' therapy: repetition, phoneme segmentation, letter-sound matching, writing syllables or nonwords	n.t.	✓ P3, 5, 6, 7, 8; × P1, 2, 4		
Fink et al. (2002)	GM	Phonological encoding	Clinician guided cueing	✓	✓		
	AS	Semantics & Access to POL	hierarchy: phonemic cues, letter cues, sentence	✓	✓		
	BM	Semantics & Access to POL	completion (spoken/written), reading aloud repetition	✓	×		
	EL	Access to POL & phonological encoding	Partially self-guided computer implemented	✓	×		
	EG	Phonological encoding	Cueing Hierarchy: phonemic cues, letter cues, sentence	✓	×		
	RH	Access to POL	completion (spoken/written)	✓	×		

Study		Deficit	Treatment tasks		? (no sig. difference between treated and untreated; untreated approaching significance compared to baseline)	No significant difference between orthographic and phonological treatments for any subject	
Hickin et al. (2002a)	HM	Access to POL & phonological encoding	Orthographic: letter choice; syllable choice, or word choice (unrelated distractors), repetition. Phonological: choice of phonemes; choice of syllables, repetition	✓		No significant difference between orthographic and phonological treatments for any subject	
	PH	Access to POL		✓	×		
	SC	Semantic & phonological encoding		×	×		
	DC	Access to POL & phonological encoding		✓	✓ (but treated sig. better)		
	OL	Access to POL		✓	×		
	IK	Semantic and phonological encoding		✓	×		
	NK	Access to POL		✓	×		
	KR	Semantic		✓	×		
Hickin et al. (2002b)	MH	Lexical semantic, Access to POL, & phonological encoding	Orthographic: letter choice syllable choice, or word choice (unrelated distractors), repetition. Phonological: choice of phonemes; choice of syllables, repetition	✓	✓ (and to measures of connected speech)	No significant difference between orthographic and phonological for either subject. Second phase of treatment, on using stimuli in everyday speech—effective for MH	
	HP	Access to POL	Phonological: choice of phonemes; choice of syllables, repetition	✓	×		
Jokel & Rochon (1996)	PD	Access to POL	Repetition	×	n.t.		Short report, full data not available, unclear why repetition and reading differ
			Reading	✓	n.t.		
			Sentence completion	×	n.t.		
Kiran et al. (2001)	RN, RD	Phonological (probably phonological encoding—diagnosis of "conduction aphasia")	Orthographic (reading, spelling, letter identification) & phonological (reading, repetition)	✓	✓ (partial—not to irregular items, seen less often)	Grapheme-phoneme conversion is NOT explicitly trained	Small n: 10 in each set (treated, untreated, irregular). No statistical analysis. Irregular items were seen less often than 'untreated'. Hence, generalisation could be effects of repeated presentation
Miceli et al. (1996)	RBO	POL	Phonological (read & repeat)	✓	×		Delayed change in untreated items
	GMA	POL	Phonological (read, name with phonological cues)	✓	×		

Phon.: Phonological; POL: Phonological Output Lexicon

APPENDIX

(Continued)

Paper	Aphasic individual	Impairment	Treatment	Outcome (treated)	Generalisation (to untreated items in naming)	Comments	Problems with interpretation
Murray & Karcher (2000)	HR	?semantic +	Orthographic cueing hierarchy: anagrams (with & without distractor letters), letter cues, copying	✓	×	Treatment of WRITTEN Verb retrieval (& sentence construction)	No statistics, small number of items per set (n = 10)
Nettleton & Lesser (1991)	DF	POL	Phon. (various)	✓	×		Lack of control tasks
	MF	POL	Phon. (various)	✓	✓		
Raymer et al. (1993); Thompson et al. (1991)	S1: CG	"POL" (encoding?)	Hierarchy of cues: rhyme cue, initial phoneme cue, repetition	✓	× (possibly to untreated but related items—rhyming & semantically related words)	Reading aloud and written naming performed in the same session	No stats, inconsistent baseline performance, small numbers of items (n = 10 per set). Unclear whether untreated rhyming words were used in therapy
	S2: RJ	Lexical-semantic		✓	✓ (only to untreated but related items—rhyming & semantically related words)		
Raymer et al. (1993)	S3: MR	Lexical-semantic		?	?		
	S4: RE	Lexical-semantic		✓	×		
Robson et al. (1998)	GF	Access to POL	Phonological (syllable judgements, initial phoneme judgements—pointing; +/– naming)	✓	✓	Similar to Best et al. (1997)—cueing aid study	Only 1 pre-therapy baseline (but 2yrs post onset)
Sugishita et al. (1993)	HK, MH, SK	Not specified	Naming, repetition, writing, copying	✓ (written & spoken naming)	×	Only treatment 1 reported here	
	MK, BY, ST, MT, TI, YA, YK			✓ (written naming alone)	×		
	AI, TD			✓ (written naming alone)	✓ (written naming alone)		No control for spontaneous recovery—NOTE authors do not claim therapy to have been effective
	YH			✓ (written & spoken naming)	✓ (written & spoken naming)		
	TZ, TE			×	×		

Study	Subject	Impairment	Task			Comment	Notes
Pashek (1997)	KR	Apraxia of speech, (& word retrieval?)—repetition accurate for 1 & 2 syll words) (good comprehension)	gesture plus speech: (naming/repetition)	✓	×	Gesture plus speech seemed more effective. Effects maintained for at least 6 months	No statistics
			Verbal only: repetition	✓	×		
Pashek (1998)	WT	"noun & verb retrieval"	Verbal (phonological): repetition	✓	×	No difference between tasks for nouns; verbal + gestural more effective for verbs. Nouns generalised to connected speech, but not verbs	Short report no detail of impairment. No statistics
			Verbal + gestural: repetition & pantomime	✓	×		
Rose et al. (2002)	AB	Access to POL and phonological encoding	Verbal (Phonological/orthographic): syllable counting, identify first phoneme of erroneous sylls, written syll anagrams, identify stressed syll, repetition	✓	×	See Rose & Douglas (2001) for facilitation with AB using these tasks and more	Improvement observed in untreated language tasks/items—but only a single baseline & AB only 6 months post-onset
			Gestural: Iconic gesture, cued articulation of first and last phoneme, repetition	✓	×		
			Gestural & Verbal combined	✓	×		
Other Tasks							
Francis et al. (2002)	MB	Phonological access	Encouraging to circumlocute until word retrieved (Circumlocution induced naming—CIN)	n.t.	✓		Spontaneous recovery
Thompson et al. (1986)	S1	Word retrieval	Hypnosis & guided imagery: look at picture, notice the size, shape & texture of the object; then with subject's eyes closed, examiner	?	×		No statistics, small numbers of items per set (n = 5). Twice daily naming of treated and untreated stimuli
	S2		described the physical attributes and function of object. NO Verbal label provided	✓	✓	Cannot exclude the results being due to the repeated naming attempts rather than treatment per se	
	S3			×	×	When verbal label added, some improvement in treated stimuli	

Phon.: Phonological; POL: Phonological Output Lexicon

APHASIOLOGY, 2002, *16* (10/11), 981–999

Phonological therapy for word-finding difficulties: A re-evaluation

Julie Hickin

De Montfort University, Leicester, UK

Wendy Best and Ruth Herbert

University College, London, UK

David Howard

University of Newcastle-upon-Tyne, UK

Felicity Osborne

Birkbeck College, University of London, UK

Background: Treatments for word-finding difficulties in aphasia using semantic techniques have been shown to be effective (e.g., Marshall, Pound, White-Thomson, & Pring, 1990). The evidence with regard to phonological treatment is more equivocal, however, with some studies reporting only short-term improvement in word retrieval (e.g., Howard, Patterson, Franklin, Orchard-Lisle, & Morton, 1985a) and other studies reporting lasting effects (e.g., Miceli, Amitrano, Capasso, & Caramazza, 1996). There is also little in the literature on the use of orthographic cues in treatment (Howard & Harding, 1998). Additionally, whereas several studies have reported the results of using cues in facilitation of word-finding difficulties (e.g., Patterson, Purrell, & Morton, 1983), none so far has attempted to relate response to facilitation and response to treatment using similar techniques in the same individuals.

Aims: This study set out to investigate whether the use of phonological and orthographic cues in the treatment of word-finding difficulties could produce lasting improvements in word retrieval. The response of the participants to phonological and orthographic cues in a facilitation study was also related to their response to treatment using similar cues.

Methods & Procedures: The study used a case series design. The participants were eight people with acquired aphasia who were all at least 1 year post-onset, had a single left CVA, and had word-finding difficulties as a significant aspect of their aphasia. Detailed assessment of each participant was carried out to identify the nature of their word-finding difficulties and this was related to response to treatment.

Outcomes & Results: Results are given for the eight participants, seven of whom benefited overall from treatment. Both phonological and orthographic cues were effective in improving word retrieval. For the group as a whole there was a significant correlation between the overall outcome of facilitation and response to treatment.

Address correspondence to: Julie Hickin, Division of Psychology and Speech and Language Therapy, De Montfort University, Scraptoft Campus, Leicester LE7 9SU, UK. Email: JHickin@dmu.ac.uk

This research was supported by a grant from the Tavistock Trust for Aphasia. Further funding was given by the Psychology Department, Birkbeck College and by the Department of Human Communication Science, University College London. Thanks are also due to Kevin Baker and Tim Grant for their helpful comments. Finally, we wish to record our gratitude to the people with aphasia who participated in the research.

---

http://www.tandf.co.uk/journals/pp/02687038.html   DOI:10.1080/02687030244000509

Conclusions: The theoretical and clinical implications of the relationship between the individual's level of language impairment and their response to therapy are discussed. It is also suggested that the results from facilitation appear to have potential in predicting the outcome of phonological/orthographic therapy with aphasic participants. Finally, it is concluded that phonological and orthographic treatments for word-finding difficulties can be highly effective and that they represent an under-utilised and under-researched tool in the clinician's armoury.

Word-finding difficulties are probably the commonest symptom of aphasia. There is anecdotal evidence (see Parr, Byng, Gilpin, & Ireland, 1997) and evidence from the field of conversational analysis (e.g., Lesser & Algar, 1995) of the significant impact that problems with word finding have on everyday communication. It seems imperative therefore that we develop effective means of treatment.

Treatments for word-finding difficulties using semantic techniques have been shown to be effective (e.g., Howard et al., 1985a,b; Marshall et al., 1990). The evidence with regard to phonological treatment is more equivocal. In 1985 Howard et al. published two seminal papers comparing the effectiveness of semantic and phonological techniques in both facilitation and treatment of word-finding difficulties. (*Facilitation* studies investigate the effectiveness of using a cue on *one* occasion on later word finding, usually a few minutes or days later. *Treatment* refers to the *repeated* use of a therapy task, e.g., a cue, in an attempt to improve word finding in the long term, ideally permanently.) Early reports had suggested that phonological facilitation was less effective than semantic (Patterson et al., 1983) and this seemed to be confirmed by Howard et al.'s 1985 study. The latter concluded that phonological facilitation techniques (e.g., phonemic cues, word repetition) resulted in only short-term improvement in word retrieval, whereas semantic facilitation techniques (e.g., word-to-picture matching, semantic judgements) resulted in relatively long-lasting improvement. When they went on to compare these two tasks in a treatment study, the differences in the effects of the two types of task were minimal (Howard, 2000; Howard et al., 1985b). However, their facilitation findings had a powerful influence on the type of research and therapy carried out for word-finding difficulties, with the emphasis being placed on semantic techniques (e.g., Horton & Byng, 2000).

More recently a number of studies have shown that phonological approaches to both facilitation and treatment of word-finding difficulties *can* be effective. Best, Hickin, Herbert, Howard, and Osborne (2000) report the results of a phonological facilitation study related to the treatment study described here (see also Best, Herbert, Hickin, Osborne, & Howard, 2002). This showed improvement in word-retrieval more than 10 minutes after the use of a phonological cue. These results contradict those of both Patterson et al. (1983) and Howard et al. (1985a, Experiment 4). Regarding treatment studies, there are a number of papers reporting the effective use of phonological techniques. These include Davis and Pring (1991), Raymer, Thompson, Jacobs, and Le Grand (1993), and Miceli et al. (1996). It has indeed been suggested that phonological approaches should be the treatment of choice for those whose word-finding difficulties lie at the post-semantic/lexical level (e.g., Nettleton & Lesser, 1991).

The differing outcomes from semantic and phonological techniques raise a number of questions. First, why is it that semantic tasks may produce longer-lasting changes in word retrieval than phonological tasks? One difference between the two is the element of choice. In semantic tasks the aphasic client is generally expected to make a choice (for example choosing one picture from a set to match a word), whereas in phonological tasks information about the word-form is generally presented without the need to make a choice (e.g., the initial phoneme of a word is presented as a cue in a straightforward manner). Byng and Jones (1993) postulated that the extent to which an individual is required to actively manipulate information/problem solve may be important in determining the effectiveness of therapy. Thus, it could be that the act of making a choice encourages deeper processing of the therapy task, thereby producing long-term changes in word retrieval. This may also relate to the claim by Robertson and Murre (1999) that active attention to the stimuli is necessary for effective rehabilitation. In this study we provide a choice of phonological or orthographic cues as part of therapy.

Second, given that the effects of phonological cues in *facilitation* may be long-lasting (Best et al., 2000), would it be possible to use phonological cues successfully in *treatment*, thus adding weight to those more recent studies showing positive outcomes from such treatment (e.g., Davis & Pring, 1991)? It has indeed been proposed that effective facilitation techniques would also be effective in treatment (e.g., Howard et al., 1985a) but without supporting evidence. In this study, we were able to test this by examining whether two of the cueing techniques used in the facilitation study (word-initial CV spoken and written letter cues) would be effective in treatment.

Third, we were interested to see if there was a relationship between a participant's response to cues in facilitation and in treatment—a relationship that has never been explored. In particular, would an individual's response to facilitation (which could be given as part of background assessment) enable us to predict response to treatment using the same cues? Investigating this link pertains to the issue of developing a theory of therapy. Crucial to the latter is the ability to predict response to treatment for an individual from the results of background assessment (Byng & Black, 1995; Caramazza & Hillis, 1993; Howard & Hatfield, 1987). This is investigated further in our study by considering how the person's handling of phonological and orthographic information in lexical and sublexical tasks in assessment relates to their response to treatment using phonological and orthographic cues.

The inclusion of orthographic cues in the study warrants discussion. There are only a few studies of the use of written cues to improve word finding, e.g., Nickels (1992), Howard and Harding (1998) and Basso, Marangolo, Piras, and Galluzzi (2001). This may partly reflect the findings from a study by Bruce and Howard in 1988. They investigated 20 people with Broca's aphasia and found that none of the people studied had all three of the abilities deemed necessary to generate their own phonemic cues from written letters (i.e., that they showed ability to indicate the initial letter of a word they were unable to say, to convert letters to sounds, and to benefit from phonemic cues). However, Bruce and Howard (1987) successfully treated five people with word-finding difficulties by using a cueing aid which provided the missing link of converting letters to sounds. This was replicated by Best, Howard, Bruce, and Gatehouse (1997) in a single case study. They found that it was only necessary to show *some* ability to benefit from phonemic cues and *some* awareness of orthography in order to benefit from treatment using the cueing aid. In the latter study treatment took place once a week for 5 weeks and resulted in improved word finding for treated words. This improvement also generalised to untreated words beginning with the treated letter/sound, and to words beginning with other sounds. Improvement was not dependent on the presence of the aid. Best et al. suggest that treatment enabled their client to make use of his existing knowledge of orthography and link this with phonology but not as a conscious strategy. Rather, "It appears that the treatment affected a fundamental change in (his) word-finding, altering automatic and not strategic processes in his linguistic system" (p. 134). Thus the use of orthographic cues in the treatment of word-finding difficulties merits further investigation.

Finally, we will consider the issue of generalisation of treatment for word-finding difficulties. Ideally, treatment of a limited set of items would result not only in improved ability to retrieve that set, but also improved ability to retrieve words in general (although this is not to underestimate the benefits of improved ability to retrieve a functionally useful set of items only—e.g., Hickin, 1997, who worked on a small vocabulary of colour and flower names with an aphasic woman who was a keen gardener and artist). One might predict that semantic treatment—which often involves thinking about the relationships between words—would result in generalisation of treatment at least to untreated items that are semantically related to the treatment set. This may be mediated by activation of shared semantic features in a connectionist model such as that proposed by Dell (1986). There is some evidence that this can occur, e.g., FW in Marshall et al.'s 1990 study, and AER and TRC in Nickels and Best (1996). Phonological treatments that focus on the output form of the individual word might, on the other hand, be predicted to result in item-specific improvement (e.g., both participants in Miceli et al.'s study and DF in Nettleton & Lesser, 1991). However, there are contradictory examples of clients given semantic therapy showing improvement only on treated items (e.g., RS, Marshall et al., 1990) and of people treated using phonological techniques showing generalisation (e.g., MF, Nettleton & Lesser, 1991). It has been suggested that a factor influencing whether generalisation occurs or not is the nature of the deficit, i.e., that clients with post-semantic deficits may show item-specific improvement whereas those with semantic deficits may show generalisation. For example, Miceli et al. (1996) argue that if output representations are selectively impaired and are addressed by fully intact semantics then what is required by treatment is the precise restoration of these damaged/inaccessible lexical entries, and that on this basis generalisation would not be expected. Nickels and Best (1996) discuss the possibility that the lexical therapy they carried out with PA (which resulted in item-specific improvement) may be working by strengthening the links between the semantic system and the phonological output lexicon. It also seems possible that the distinction may be between treatment that involves simply producing the item (e.g., by repetition/reading aloud) relatively automatically and others where deeper processing is required. In this latter case generalisation may occur if the processing involves making a new link or developing a new strategy that may be applied across items (see Best et al., 1997).

METHOD

Design

In considering the effectiveness of aphasia therapy, there has been much debate over recent years concerning the appropriate research methodology (e.g., Howard, 1986; Robey, 1998; Robey, Schulz, Crawford, & Skinner, 1999). Nickels and Best (1996) advocate the use of a case series design. This "allows the results of therapy to be related to individual deficits and strengths" (p. 110) which informs us as to how therapy might be working, while at the same time demonstrating the efficacy of therapy with a number of different individuals. Thus, we have used a case series design in our study and will present both the group results and also comment on the response of individual participants within the group where this informs us as to the mechanisms by which therapy may be working.

The overall study consists of three phases each lasting approximately 8 weeks. First, there is an assessment phase—including a facilitation trial—which is reported in the related special issue (Best et al., 2002). Next, there is a treatment phase which focuses on improving word finding by using cues in a picture-naming task. The results of this phase will be reported here. Finally, there is a second phase of treatment which aims to enable the use of treated words in real-life conversation. This phase is reported by Herbert et al. (2002). Progress is monitored via five assessments, one at the beginning and end of each phase of the study. This is summarised below. Only the results of baseline assessments (i.e., Assessments 1 and 2) and Assessment 3 are reported in this paper.

Assessment 1
Assessment and facilitation study
Assessment 2
Phase 1 of treatment
Assessment 3
Phase 2 of treatment
Assessment 4
No intervention
Assessment 5 (follow-up)
The assessments are composed of the following on each occasion:

1. A quantified measure of word finding in real-life conversation.
2. A measure of word finding in connected speech using Cinderella (Bird & Franklin, 1996).
3. Naming of 200 items.
4. A questionnaire pertaining to feelings about communication skills.
5. A set of control tasks: written sentence comprehension; reading aloud words (n – 52); reading aloud nonwords (n = 26), short-term memory (STM) (picture pointing).

Participants

The participants in the study were eight people with aphasia (see Table 1). For ease of comparison, participants are listed in the same order as in Best et al., 2002). All were at least 1 year post-onset and had suffered a single left hemisphere CVA. They all presented with word-finding difficulties as a significant aspect of their aphasia, but also presented with a range of severity and types of aphasia ascertained via a battery of comprehensive assessment (see Table 2 and following section). None had severe comprehension problems, hearing loss, oral or verbal dyspraxia.

Procedure

Assessment. Participants were first asked if they wished to be involved in the research via an aphasia-friendly consent form specifically designed for the study. This used simple text and pictures combined with a spoken explanation to try to ensure that truly informed consent was given by the aphasic participants despite their communication difficulties (see Osborne, Hickin, Best, & Howard, 1998).

During the first phase of the study detailed assessment was carried out to identify the nature of the individual word-finding difficulties. Tasks were drawn from a range of assessments and looked at several different stages of language processing. These are summarised in Table 2.

TABLE 1
Background information

Participant	Years post-onset	Age	Aphasia type
HM	6	45	Broca's
PH	3	77	Anomic
SC	5	65	Mixed/Wernicke's
DC	5	70	Anomic
OL	2	65	Anomic
NK	3	52	Anomic
IK	3	68	Broca's
KR	8	38	Broca's

Initials for participants, years post-onset, age at the start of their involvement in the study, and aphasia type as assessed by the Comprehensive Aphasia Test (Swinburn et al., 2002).

Naming was assessed using a set of 200 pictures. These were black and white line drawings taken from a number of naming tests (including Nickels, 1992; European Naming Test, unpublished; our own materials). Naming was tested at the beginning and end of the assessment phase (Assessments 1 and 2) to establish baseline naming performance. Written naming was assessed using a subset of 40 items taken from this set. Comprehension was assessed using a variety of tasks (see Table 2). These included the Pyramids and Palm Trees Test (Howard & Franklin, 1992) and tests of spoken and written word–picture matching from the Comprehensive Aphasia Test (Swinburn, Baker, and Howard, 2002) in order to identify difficulties at the semantic stage of lexical retrieval. The tests of auditory discrimination and STM (using picture pointing, and phoneme, digit, and letter spans) were included as the skills tapped by these tests may have an important influence on retention of cues during treatment. Reading and repetition were assessed using both real words and non-words. This was to allow us to examine whether the ability to respond to cues depended on the ability to convert between input and output lexically or sub-lexically.

Facilitation.   Participants' response to the single application of a cue was assessed using a set of pictureable CVC items. Participants were presented with a picture to name and if unable to do so within 5 seconds they were given one of three types of help: (i) they were given extra time (5 seconds) to name the picture (the *control* condition); (ii) they were given a single cue (the *single cue* condition); or (iii) they were given a choice of two cues—the target and a distractor—(the *choice* condition). Four types of cue were investigated in each condition: CV spoken, CV written, rime, and repetition. Only one type of cue was investigated during each facilitation assessment. To give an example of the procedure for the CV written cue, when a participant was unable to name a picture (e.g., cage) it would go into one of the three conditions: if the picture entered the *control condition* the participant would be given 5 extra seconds to name it, in the *single cue condition* they would be shown the letters CA and told "It begins with this", and in the *choice condition* they would be shown the letters RO (distractor) and CA (target) and told "It begins with either this or this". (The distractor cue was always derived from a semantically and phonologically unrelated word, here "rock"). The immediate effect of the cue on naming was then recorded (*immediate naming*). Testing continued until the

TABLE 2
Scores on background assessments

Test	n	HM	PH	SC	DC	OL	IK	NK	KR	mean	s.d.
Picture naming tests 1 and 2: mean	200	0.45	0.36	0.32	0.67	0.52	0.24	0.56	0.40	0.39	0.16
Semantic tests:											
CAT Spoken word to picture matching test	30	1.00	0.93	0.87	1.00	0.97	0.93	0.93	0.93	0.92	0.06
CAT Written word to picture matching test	30	0.87	0.97	0.77	0.97	0.93	0.80	0.97	0.90	0.86	0.17
Pyramids and Palm Trees Test three-picture version	52	0.94	0.90	0.88	0.92	0.96	0.92	0.87	0.77	0.85	0.15
Picture naming: Semantic errors as a proportion of total errors		0.52	0.25	0.28	0.50	0.16	0.18	0.33	0.16	0.29	0.14
Phonological tests:											
ADA Auditory discrimination test	40	0.82	0.68	0.95	0.85	0.70	0.65	0.90	0.65	0.72	0.18
Short-term memory test: phoneme span		1.40	2.50	2.30	2.30	2.90	1.70	2.70	1.70	2.10	0.60
Repetition of words	152	0.73	0.97	0.57	0.95	0.99	0.52	0.99	0.90	0.80	0.23
Repetition of non-words	26	0.31	0.58	0.27	0.50	0.92	0.23	0.81	0.69	0.54	0.29
Repetition of non words: Initial phoneme correct	26	0.54	0.88	0.50	0.85	1.00	0.38	0.96	0.81	0.78	0.22
Picture naming: Phonological errors as a proportion of total errors		0.20	0.05	0.02	0.11	0.00	0.22	0.00	0.02	0.09	0.10
Reading real words	152	0.70	0.97	0.15	0.97	0.91	0.31	0.92	0.64	0.65	0.32
Reading non-words	26	0.00	0.35	0.00	0.15	0.23	0.00	0.08	0.00	0.11	0.15
Reading non-words: Initial phoneme correct	26	0.38	0.85	0.00	0.92	0.81	0.23	0.92	0.00	0.52	0.34

Participants' performance on the following: CAT—Comprehensive Aphasia Test (Swinburn et al., 2002); Pyramids and Palm Trees (Howard & Patterson, 1992); ADA Auditory Discrimination from Action for Dysphasic Adults Comprehension Battery (Franklin et al., 1992). The remaining assessments are unpublished.

participant had failed to name 36 pictures providing 12 for each of the three conditions. Entry of items into the control, single cue, or choice of cue conditions, was counterbalanced.

After a delay of at least 10 minutes during which therapist and participant had a drink and conversation (i.e., no further language testing occurred) naming of the 36 cued items was retested (*delayed naming*). This whole procedure was then repeated for the remaining cue types (CV spoken, rime, and repetition) each on a different occasion, generally 1 week apart. (Full details of the facilitation study are reported by Best et al., 2002.)

Therapy. During Phase 1, 100 words were treated that were drawn from the set of 200 items named at Assessments 1 and 2. The 200 items were divided into two sets of 100 matched for baseline naming accuracy. These two sets were randomly assigned as treatment and control sets. The treated set was divided into two sets of items matched for baseline naming accuracy: 50 were treated using phonological cues and 50 using orthographic cues. In addition to the 100 treated items, each participant chose 20 words of their own. These were words that they felt would have a useful impact on their everyday lives if treatment resulted in improved ability to retrieve them. These 20 words were assessed at Assessment 2 (i.e., before treatment) and Assessment 3 (i.e., after treatment) only, and were treated following the same procedure used for the 50 orthographic items.

Treatment took place once a week for 8 weeks. All treated items were seen once in each session and each session lasted about one to one and a half hours. Items were presented for naming and, if unsuccessful, participants were presented with a choice of cues. In the phonological condition, the first phoneme (plus schwa) of the target and an unrelated distractor were presented. If still not named successfully, the amount of information given in the cues was increased (i.e., the first syllable was given) and, if still not named, the whole of the target word and the distractor was presented for the participant to choose between. Where the participant still could not name the picture the word form was provided for repetition. So, for example, if someone couldn't name a picture of a penguin they were told "It begins with either /pɛ/ or /kɛ/". If still unable to name the picture they were told "It begins with /pEŋ/ or /koŋ/", then "It's penguin or concrete". Finally, the target word would be modelled for repetition where necessary. Exactly the same procedure was followed in the orthographic condition except that the cues given were written letters.

The number of distractors was increased gradually across the treatment sessions. Thus in the first two sessions one distractor was used, the next two sessions had two distractors, and in the final four sessions, three distractors were used. The order in which the target cue and the distractor cues were presented was randomised for each picture. The order in which the set of items to be treated using phonological cues and the set treated using orthographic cues was also varied (i.e., sometimes the 50 items to be treated using phonological cues were presented first in the session and sometimes second). The order of items within the sets was also randomised across the sessions.

RESULTS

Effects of treatment

As a result of treatment, seven of the eight participants showed a significant improvement in naming the 200 tested items (see Table 3). A statistical comparison of the amount of improvement on the treated and untreated sets shows that five of the seven participants (PH, DC, OL, IK, and NK) who showed overall improvement improved significantly more on the treated items than the untreated items. Only one of these participants showed significant improvement on the untreated items: DC ($z = 1.83$, $p = .033$), indicating for her partial generalisation. The remaining four participants show treatment effects that are item-specific—confined to the treated items.

HM shows no significant difference in the change on the treated and untreated sets. His improvement on the untreated set approached significance ($z = 1.55$, $p = .068$) suggesting that, in his case, there may be generalisation of improvement to the untreated items.

TABLE 3
Improvement in naming the 200 items

Participant	Assessment 1 Pre-therapy	Assessment 2 Pre-therapy	Assessment 3 Post-therapy	z score
HM	0.450	0.420	0.550	3.12***
PH	0.325	0.375	0.485	3.57***
DC	0.720	0.735	0.885	4.95***
SC	0.335	0.370	0.370	0.61
OL	0.520	0.505	0.605	2.54***
IK	0.240	0.220	0.335	3.16***
NK	0.555	0.590	0.710	3.96***
KR	0.400	0.370	0.460	2.29***

Figures given are the proportion of items named successfully within 5 seconds, (n = 200).
Treatment took place after Assessment 2. The z score is from a Wilcoxon test comparing naming accuracy in the two pre-therapy assessments with accuracy after therapy (*$p < .05$ **$p < .01$ ***$p < .001$, one-tailed).

There is also no significant difference between improvement on the treated and untreated sets for KR. Her improvement was the smallest of those who showed significant improvement (7.5%). Improvement on the untreated items (3%) was not significant, but also not significantly less than the 12% improvement on the treated items. Her performance therefore provides no strong evidence for the generalisation of improvement to untreated items.

None of the participants showed significant change on the control tasks—i.e., written sentence comprehension; read aloud words (n = 52); read aloud nonwords (n = 26); short-term memory (STM: picture pointing).) There was also no significant change between the two baseline assessments for any of the participants. Taken together with the item-specific treatment effects, these findings show that improvement during therapy cannot be attributed to spontaneous recovery or non-specific effects of intervention.

Table 4 reports improvement in naming for the phonologically treated, orthographically treated, and control sets individually. When improvement from the phonological treatment and orthographic treatment is compared (Table 4), there are no significant differences for any participant. KR shows a trend towards greater benefit from phonological than orthographic therapy.

Progress during treatment

Figure 1 shows how naming progressed over the treatment sessions for the group as a whole. This figure shows the mean number of items named spontaneously (i.e., without cueing) during each treatment session (mean of phonologically treated and orthographically treated sets n = 100).[1] It is interesting to note that the effect of treatment appears to be cumulative. In other words, there is not a dramatic immediate improvement in naming as a result of treatment. This was a general pattern shown by all seven of the eight participants who benefited overall from treatment. Finally, in looking at the data from the individuals, it is clear that the starting place for treatment has a strong bearing on

[1] For DC who had seven sessions of treatment the score for session 8 is projected from average performance in sessions 6 and 7.

TABLE 4
Improvement in treated and untreated sets

Participant		Assessment 1 Pre-therapy	Assessment 2 Pre-therapy	Assessment 3 Post-therapy	Improvement in treated vs untreated	Improvement in p treated vs o treated
HM	Phonological	.46	.40	.56	0.94	−0.20
	Orthographic	.42	.44	.60		
	Untreated	.46	.42	.52		
PH	Phonological	.32	.36	.60	4.26***	−0.93
	Orthographic	.32	.38	.68		
	Untreated	.33	.38	.33		
DC	Phonological	.70	.72	.94	3.01***	−0.24
	Orthographic	.72	.74	.98		
	Untreated	.73	.74	.81		
SC	Phonological	.32	.36	.36	0.39	0.19
	Orthographic	.34	.38	.38		
	Untreated	.34	.37	.37		
OL	Phonological	.52	.50	.70	1.94*	0.72
	Orthographic	.52	.50	.62		
	Untreated	.52	.51	.55		
IK	Phonological	.24	.22	.44	1.86*	0.86
	Orthographic	.24	.20	.36		
	Untreated	.24	.23	.27		
NK	Phonological	.56	.58	.86	4.36***	0.36
	Orthographic	.54	.58	.82		
	Untreated	.56	.60	.58		
KR	Phonological	.40	.36	.56	0.77	1.53
	Orthographic	.40	.36	.44		
	Untreated	.40	.38	.42		

The comparisons of the improvement on treated and untreated and orthographically treated compared to phonologically treated are derived from Wilcoxon two-sample tests for the change between Assessments 1 and 2 and Assessment 3.

Significance levels are one-tailed for the treated vs untreated comparison and two-tailed for the comparison of phonological and orthographic treatment (*$p < .05$ **$p < .01$) (n = 50 for the phonologically and orthographically treated sets and n = 100 for the untreated items).

eventual outcome: ranking of individuals according to naming performance is the same for the first and final therapy sessions.

Improvement in twenty words

Table 5 shows how the 20 words that each participant chose to include in treatment changed. All the participants except IK show at least some improvement with three showing significant improvement.

Relationship between background assessment and response to treatment

Table 2 (see earlier) gave each participant's score on 14 of the tests of language processing carried out during the assessment phase of the study. Performance on each of

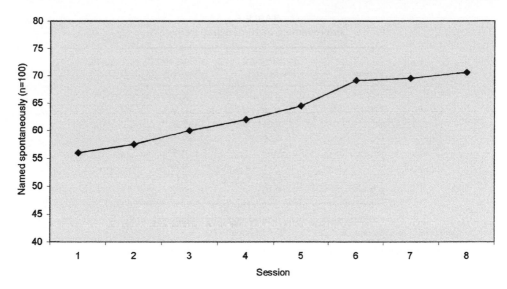

Figure 1.   Improvement in naming treated set during therapy: group results. The mean number of items from the treated set (n = 100) named spontaneously (i.e., without cueing) for eight participants across the eight therapy sessions.

these tests[2] was correlated with improvement in naming following treatment. The latter was calculated by subtracting the mean naming score on baseline assessments 1 and 2 from the naming score at assessment 3 (i.e., after Phase 1 of treatment). This was calculated for (i) naming of all 200 items, (ii) items treated using phonological cues, (iii) items treated using orthographic cues, (iv) all treated items, and (v) untreated items.[3]

Table 6 gives the results of the correlations between performance on background assessments and improvement in naming for the group as a whole. Due to the high number of correlations an α level of $p < .01$ was used to determine significance. Note that with a small number of participants, and, with the exception of SC, a limited range of treatment effect sizes (varying from 7.5 to 17%), the power of these correlational analyses is limited. Note also that because SC is an outlier in terms of the size of the treatment effect, his results are particularly influential in determining these correlations.

(i) Improvement in the complete set of 200 items is considered first. This correlates significantly with reading aloud words and the proportion of non-word reading responses where the initial phoneme was correct.

(ii) Improvement in the set of words treated using phonological cues correlates significantly only with written word to picture matching.

(iii) Improvement in items treated using orthographic cues correlates with the accuracy on the initial phoneme in reading aloud nonwords.

(iv) Improvement in the set of treated items correlates significantly with written word to picture matching and accuracy on the initial phoneme in reading aloud non-words.

---

[2] Except test 5 and 11: proportion of naming errors that were semantic and phonological respectively.

[3] In addition to being correlated with straight change in naming, the background assessments were correlated with change in naming divided by scope for change (i.e., 1 − baseline naming performance). The pattern found was very similar to that for change in naming.

TABLE 5
Improvement in 20 personal items

Patient	Assessment 2 Pre-therapy	Assessment 3 Post-therapy
HM	0.00	0.20
PH	0.20	0.85*
SC	0.00	0.20
DC	0.50	0.95*
OL	0.25	0.40
IK	0.20	0.00
NK	0.10	0.65*
KR	0.30	0.55

Proportion of items named correctly before and after therapy, n = 20. *$p < .05$ McNemar Test.

(v) None of the background variables correlates significantly with change in untreated items.

These results indicate that ability to retrieve semantic information via the written word and to retrieve output phonology from orthography relate to response to treatment. So, for example, SC does not respond to treatment and has the poorest scores in the group at both written word–picture matching and reading aloud words, and is at floor on retrieval of initial phoneme for nonwords. NK, DC, and PH all perform well on these measures and benefit from treatment.

Relationship between response to facilitation and response to treatment

There is a significant correlation between the effect of facilitation (across the four cueing conditions) and overall therapy outcome for the group as a whole ($r = 0.697$, $df = 6$, $p = .027$).

Figure 2 illustrates the response of each individual to facilitation and to therapy. The response to facilitation was calculated by subtracting the number of items named correctly in the control condition (i.e., after extra time) from the number of items named correctly after a cue, and dividing by the number of trials. Response to therapy was calculated by subtracting the number of pictures named correctly after treatment (at Assessment 3) from the mean number named correctly before therapy, i.e., at Assessments 1 and 2 (the initial naming average).

DISCUSSION

The study outlined here forms part of a larger therapy study in which there was a second phase of treatment and in which carry-over into connected speech and real-life conversation is investigated (see Osborne et al., 1998; Hickin, Herbert, Best, Howard, & Osborne, in press).

TABLE 6
Correlation of improvement in naming with performance on assessment

Test	All items	Phonologically treated items	Orthographically treated items	All treated items	Untreated items
1. Picture naming tests 1 and 2: mean percentage correct	0.568	0.387	0.385	0.408	0.373
Semantic tests:					
2. CAT Spoken word to picture matching test:	0.689	0.350	0.387	0.392	0.715
3. CAT Written word to picture matching test	0.774	0.790*	0.747	0.809*	−0.138
4. Pyramids and Palm Trees Test three-picture version	0.297	0.013	0.273	0.167	0.313
Phonological tests:					
6. ADA Auditory discrimination test	−0.137	−0.354	−0.025	−0.180	0.118
7. Short-term memory test: phoneme span	0.122	0.322	0.287	0.319	−0.512
8. Repetition of real words	0.558	0.647	0.535	0.618	−0.186
9. Repetition of non-words	−0.252	0.529	0.198	0.363	−0.301
10. Repetition of non-words: initial phoneme correct	0.429	0.592	0.430	0.529	−0.282
12. Reading real words	0.790*	0.743	0.736	0.781	−0.025
13. Reading non-words	0.458	0.508	0.645	0.617	−0.437
14. Reading non-words: initial phoneme correct	0.799*	0.732	0.8178	0.823*	−0.113

Key to tests: as in Table 4.
Df = 6, *$p < .01$, 1-tailed Pearson's r = .789 for significance.

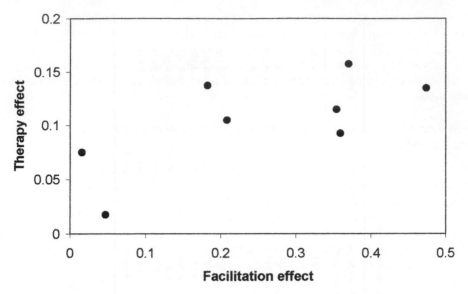

Figure 2. Relationship between response to facilitation and response to therapy.

The efficacy of treatment

For seven of the eight participants the treatment was successful, adding another tried and tested approach to the range of effective treatments for word-finding problems (for a review see Howard, 2000; Nickels & Best, 1996). In addition, treatment took place once a week for 8 weeks only. This provides an example of an effective treatment regime that is eminently practicable even within the constraints of short-term contracts of treatment. Another point with clinical significance is that progress during treatment is cumulative (see Figure 1). It would therefore seem important to persist with treatment even if it does not appear to have an immediate effect, something that can be difficult to do in the context of limited clinical resources.

The findings of this study are in line with previous results from, for example, Miceli et al. (1996), Davis and Pring (1991), and Howard et al. (1985b), showing significant benefits from phonological treatment lasting for at least a week after the end of therapy, and in most cases much longer.

One difference between this study and previous investigations of phonological treatments is that our participants were required to choose actively between different possible cues. As outlined in the introduction, this may have caused reflection upon the required form of the word, resulting in long-term changes in word retrieval (see Byng & Jones, 1993). Comments from some of the participants add weight to this argument, e.g., SC "Choice good—makes me use my head" and KR "I like it but it no easy". Basso et al. (2001) also speculate that the reason for the greater effectiveness of orthographic cueing in their study is that "the search for the correct response ... seems to be under more intentional control in the case of the orthographic cueing method than in reading or repetition" (p56). In our facilitation study, however, there was no advantage for the choice of cues over providing a single cue, so this suggestion must be tentative. Also, the design of the therapy study does not allow us to exclude the possibility that improvement of treated items was due to repeated exposure to the pictures/repeated attempts at naming. However, this seems unlikely as all of the aphasic participants in the study were noted to actively use, or attempt to use, the cues for items they could not name immediately. This is also borne out by their comments (see earlier). Howard et al.'s (1985b) finding of significantly greater improvement in phonologically treated items than in controls that were presented for naming as often as the treated items, demonstrates that the effects of similar treatments to that used here result from more than repeated exposure to hard-to-name items.

Improvement in phonologically and orthographically treated sets

All seven of the participants whose naming improved showed no significant advantage for one cue type over the other. In contrast, Basso et al. (2001) report that orthographic cueing was superior to both repetition and reading aloud with 30 normal participants learning "new" words (i.e., legal nonwords) and in treating the word-finding difficulties of two aphasic participants. Orthographic therapy may also be preferable for people with severe auditory processing problems or hearing loss (none of whom was included in this study) and is more suited to independent home practice.

Finally, the orthographic and the phonological treatments were carried out within the same sessions and therefore from the design of the present study it is not possible to be unequivocal about their independent effects. However, as the majority of the participants show item-specific effects in treatment, we wish to claim that each intervention is effective.

It is noteworthy that KR was the only person to show a trend towards benefiting more from phonological than orthographic therapy. She was also the only person who was completely unable to read non-words including the initial phoneme (with the exception of SC who showed no treatment effects). This difficulty probably severely impaired her ability to benefit from written cues.

In considering the 20 words that participants chose to include in treatment, three people improved significantly, and a further three showed a trend towards improvement. It is interesting to note that the former were the three who benefited most from treatment as a whole. Of relevance is the fact that most participants chose words that were very closely semantically related (e.g., juice and squash, brother and son, London Eye, Millennium Dome). For some participants this factor caused difficulties during therapy—for example, a semantically related target may be produced in place of the correct target.

Generalisation to untreated items

With regard to generalisation, five of the seven participants who showed significant gains from treatment demonstrated item-specific effects (DC showed significant improvement on untreated items and HM showed a tendency to improve on this set). The item-specific results are in line with the prediction (e.g., Howard, 2000) that phonological therapy will result in item-specific effects because it activates individual mappings from semantics to phonological representations. The assessment profile of the three individuals who benefited most from therapy (NK, DC, and PH) indicates that they all appear to have difficulty with mapping between semantics and phonology; i.e., they perform well on semantic tasks, are able to read and repeat words, and yet show a naming impairment that is considerably helped by cues (for a similar case see Lambon Ralph, Cipolotti, & Patterson, 1999). This adds further weight to the argument that the primary mechanism of lasting phonological cue effects may be strengthening the mapping from semantics to phonology (Howard, 2000; Nickels & Best, 1996). From a clinical perspective, generalisation of therapy to untreated items is of course the preferable outcome, representing "maximum gain for minimum effort". If, however, as Howard (2000) emphasises, the improvement is in the mapping from semantics to phonology, we should expect no generalisation, precisely because this mapping is word-specific and idiosyncratic. If we predict that therapy will not generalise, then it is even more important for aphasic clients to select which words would most usefully be targeted in treatment. (Hickin, 1997).

Relationship between assessment and therapy

As noted in the introduction, a crucial step in developing a theory of therapy will be the ability to predict response to treatment from performance on background assessment. In relation to this, examination of Table 6 reveals that there was no significant correlation between naming ability at assessment and response to treatment. This contrasts with the findings of Barry and McHattie (1991) and Bruce and Howard (1988) who both found a relationship between severity of naming impairment and ability to respond to semantic facilitation and phonemic cues respectively. However, ability to retrieve the initial phoneme on reading non-words correlates significantly with overall naming improvement and with improvement on orthographically treated items and treated items. This indicates that it is important to have at least some ability to retrieve output phonology from orthography in order to benefit from treatment. In addition, reading of words correlates significantly with overall naming improvement, while careful examination of Tables 2 and 6 reveals that word repetition and reading ability for words and non-words also tend to relate to the outcome of treatment. The shared level of processing for these tasks is phonological output processing. This relates to the finding of Raymer et al. (1993) that oral reading performance was predictive of the potential for naming improvement in three of four participants in their study. They postulate that this is because "oral reading performance may represent the potential for phonological processing available if lexical-semantics were able to access phonological output consistently in naming" (p. 50). Thus, in successful cued word retrieval, the partial activation of a representation in the phonological output lexicon appears to combine with additional activation from the cue. In relation to sublexical cueing, this explanation is compatible with interactive activation models of word production where there is feedback from the phoneme level to the word level (e.g., Dell, 1986), but is less easy to explain in terms of feedforward models of production (e.g., Levelt, Roelofs, & Meyer, 1999) without additional assumptions (see Best et al., 2002).

It is perhaps important at this point to consider SC, who did not respond to either form of treatment. SC has difficulties with semantic processing and output phonology, and severe difficulties with reading. This combination is the most likely explanation of his lack of response to therapy. This result reinforces the suggestion made earlier that this type of treatment may be most useful for those individuals who have relatively intact semantic representations and phonological representations but whose difficulty is mapping between semantics and phonology.

Relationship between facilitation and treatment

Comparison of the results of the facilitation study and the therapy study suggests that people whose word finding shows short-term gains from phonological/orthographic cues may be those who benefit from therapy involving the same kinds of cues used repeatedly:

for the group as a whole there is a significant correlation between the overall outcome of facilitation and response to therapy.

Five of the seven people who benefited from treatment also showed some benefit from facilitation (HM, PH, DC, OL, and NK: see Best et al., 2002, for details). The one person (SC) who did not respond to treatment did not respond to facilitation. The link between the outcome of facilitation and treatment suggests it may be possible to assess the appropriateness of such treatment within a single session where the effect of phonological and orthographic cues is simply compared with giving extra time for picture naming. People with anomia whose naming benefits from phonological or orthographic cues, over and above extra time, may well be those that would benefit from this treatment approach. However, these results are not conclusive because IK and KR did not show significant cue effects in facilitation but did respond to treatment. This warrants further discussion. KR showed a tendency to benefit more from phonological than orthographic treatment. A retest of her response to facilitation post-treatment showed that although she still did not benefit from orthographic facilitation, she did now benefit significantly from phonological facilitation. In other words, therapy appears to have taught her to use phonological cues. In addition, there is evidence from her progress in therapy that KR is also learning to use letters to self-cue, although this did not produce a significant improvement in naming of the orthographically treated set at Assessment 3. IK presents more of a conundrum, as he responded to both forms of treatment but did not benefit from cues in the facilitation task. This may reflect the severity of his impairment: he is poor at naming, repeating words, and repeating non-words, but has reasonably intact semantic processing and is above floor on most output tasks (see Table 2). It may be that for people with more severe aphasia, one session to measure response to cues is not sufficient as their performance may be affected more by other factors, e.g., fatigue (which is true for IK). It may be necessary to extend assessment by monitoring performance over two to three sessions.

Finally, we would like to discuss inclusion of DC and IK in the project. DC's conversation was lively and fluent and she hid her word-finding problems well, although she was aware of and frustrated by not being able to find the words she wanted in conversation. On a picture naming task, performance was 73% correct prior to treatment and we nearly excluded her on the grounds that there was relatively little room for improvement. In fact after eight sessions of treatment she reached 96% on treated and 81% on untreated items. Pre-therapy we knew that she did benefit considerably from cues. In a clinical setting this finding could be used as a pointer suggesting this type of therapy might result in change, even for someone with relatively good naming and conversational skills. Most importantly DC also showed significant change on the items she selected as relevant to her and she viewed the outcome of the treatment very positively. For someone with a milder anomia, the experience of improving on certain words can be stimulating: during treatment DC began to write down from the dictionary other words that she wanted to practise and that she could read aloud, thereby providing herself with further "self-administered treatment".

IK, on the other hand, has severe word-finding difficulties and is only able to use the occasional word during conversation, relying significantly on gesture, pointing, sometimes drawing, and on his wife's skill at interpreting his message. We debated whether to include him in the study on the basis of the severity of his difficulties, but decided to go ahead as we wanted to assess if treatment *would* work with someone with more severe difficulties. IK was also very highly motivated with the full support of his wife. IK's response to therapy vindicates his inclusion and leads us to urge caution in immediately excluding someone on the grounds of the severity of their aphasia. Finally both IK and KR are eager to continue this approach to improve their word finding.

As noted in the introduction, this study forms part of a larger project which includes a second phase of treatment aimed at improving retrieval of treated words in tasks approximating more closely to real life. The results of the treatment on word finding in connected speech and real-life conversation are reported in Herbert et al. (2002).

In conclusion, a treatment based on providing a choice of spoken or written cues improved word retrieval in seven of the eight people included in the study. The results from facilitation appear to have potential in predicting the outcome of phonological/ orthographic therapy. The possible link between the short-term and much longer-term effects of cues provides a building block in developing a theory of therapy (Byng & Black, 1995; Howard & Hatfield, 1987), and it seems possible that many techniques effective in the short term could be successfully developed into strategies to include as part of treatment for anomia. Previous research has tended to focus on short- or long-term effects and not to investigate both in the same people. Further treatment studies that attempt to make links between short- and long-term outcomes are to be welcomed, as this study has demonstrated the potential of such an approach.

REFERENCES

Barry, C., & McHattie, J. (1991). *Depth of semantic processing in picture naming facilitation in aphasic patients*. Paper presented at the British Aphasiology Society Conference. Sheffield, September.

Basso, A., Marangolo, P., Piras, F., & Galluzzi, C. (2001). Acquisition of new "words" in normal participants: A suggestion for the treatment of anomia. *Brain and Language, 77,* 45–59.

Best, W., Herbert, R., Hickin, J., Osborne, F., & Howard, D. (2002). Phonological and orthographic facilitation of word-retrieval in aphasia: Immediate and delayed effects. *Aphasiology, 16,* 151–168.

Best, W., Hickin, J., Herbert, R., Howard, D., & Osborne, F. (2000). Phonological facilitation of aphasic naming and predicting the outcome of treatment for anomia. *Brain and Language, 74,* 435–438.

Best. W., Howard, D., Bruce, C., & Gatehouse, C. (1997). Cueing the words: A single case study of treatments for anomia. *Neuropsychological Rehabilitation, 7,* 105–141.

Bird, H., & Franklin, S. (1996). Cinderella revisited: A comparison of fluent and non-fluent aphasic speech. *Journal of Neurolinguistics, 9,* 187–206.

Bruce, C., & Howard, D. (1987). Computer generated cues: An effective aid for naming in aphasia. *British Journal of Disorders of Communication, 22,* 191–201.

Bruce, C., & Howard, D. (1988). Why don't Broca's aphasics cue themselves? An investigation of phonemic cueing and tip-of-the-tongue information. *Neuropsychologia, 26,* 253–264.

Byng, S., & Black, M. (1995). What makes a therapy? Some parameters of therapeutic intervention in aphasia. *European Journal of Disorders of Communication, 30,* 303–316.

Byng, S., & Jones, E.V. (1993). *Interactions in therapy*. Paper presented at the British Aphasiology Society Conference, Warwick, September.

Caramazza, A., & Hillis, A.E. (1993). For a theory of rehabilitation. *Neuropsychological Rehabilitation, 3,* 217–234.

Davis, A., & Pring, T. (1991). Therapy for word-finding deficits: More on the effects of semantic and phonological approaches to treatment with dysphasic patients. *Neuropsychological Rehabilitation, 1* 135–145.

Dell, G.S. (1986). A spreading activation theory of retrieval in language production. *Psychological Review, 93,* 283–321.

Franklin, S., Turner, J., & Ellis, A.W. (1992). ADA (Action for Dysphasic Adults) Comprehension Battery (ADACB). London: Action for Dysphasic Adults.

Herbert, R., Best, W., Hickin, J., Howard, D., & Osborne, F. (2002) Combining lexical and conversational approaches to the treatment of word finding deficits in aphasia. Manuscript in preparation.

Hickin, J. (1997). *Not just boxes and arrows? Combining the person-centred and the cognitive neuropsychological approaches in the treatment of a person with dysphasia*. Paper presented at the British Aphasiology Society Conference, Manchester, September.

Hickin, J., Herbert, R., Best, W., Howard, D., & Osborne, F. (in press). Efficacy of treatment: Effects on word retrieval and conversation. In S. Byng, C. Pound, & J. Marshall (Eds.), *Second aphasia therapy file*. Hove, UK: Psychology Press.

Horton, S., & Byng, S. (2000). Examining interaction in language therapy. *International Journal of Language and Communication Disorders, 35*, 355–376.

Howard, D. (1986). Beyond randomised controlled trials: The case for effective case studies of the effects of treatment in aphasia. *British Journal of Disorders of Communication, 21*, 89–102.

Howard, D. (2000). *Cognitive neuropsychology and aphasia therapy: The case of word retrieval*. In I. Papathanasiou (Ed), *Acquired neurogenic communication disorders: A clinical perspective*. London: Whurr.

Howard, D., & Harding, D. (1998). Self-cueing of word-retrieval by a woman with aphasia: Why a letter-board works. *Aphasiology, 12*, 399–420.

Howard, D., & Hatfield, M.H. (1987). *Aphasia therapy*. Hove, UK: Lawrence Erlbaum Associates Ltd.

Howard, D., & Patterson, K.E. (1992). *Pyramids and Palm Trees Test: A test of semantic access from words and pictures*. Bury St Edmunds, UK: Thames Valley Test Co.

Howard, D., Patterson, K., Franklin, S., Orchard-Lisle, V., & Morton, J. (1985a). The facilitation of picture naming in aphasia. *Cognitive Neuropsychology, 2*, 49–80.

Howard, D., Patterson, K., Franklin, S., Orchard-Lisle, V., & Morton, J. (1985b). Treatment of word retrieval deficits in aphasia. A comparison of two methods. *Brain, 108*, 817–829.

Lambon Ralph, M., Cippolotti, L., & Patterson, K. (1999). Oral naming and oral reading: Do they speak the same language? *Cognitive Neuropsychology, 16*, 157–169.

Lesser, R., & Algar, L. (1995). Towards combing the cognitive neuropsychological and the pragmatic in aphasia therapy. *Neuropsychological Rehabilitation, 5*, 67–92.

Levelt, W.J.M., Roelofs, A., & Meyer, A.S. (1999). A theory of lexical access in speech production. *Behavioural and Brain Sciences, 22*, 1–38.

Marshall, J., Pound, C., White-Thomson. M., & Pring, T. (1990). The use of picture/word matching tasks to assist word-retrieval in aphasic patients. *Aphasiology, 4*, 167–184.

Miccli, G., Amitrano, A., Capasso, R., & Carramazza, A. (1996). The treatment of anomia resulting from output lexical damage: Analysis of two cases. *Brain and Language, 52*, 150–174.

Nettleton, J., & Lesser, R. (1991). Therapy for naming difficulties in aphasia: Application of a cognitive neuropsychological model. *Journal of Neurolinguistics, 6*, 139–157.

Nickels, L.A. (1992). The autocue? Self-generated phonemic cues in the treatment of a disorder of reading and naming. *Cognitive Neuropsychology, 9*, 155–182.

Nickels, L., & Best, W. (1996). Therapy for naming disorders (part II): Specifics, surprises and suggestions, *Aphasiology, 10*(1), 109–136.

Osborne, F., Hickin, J., Best, W., & Howard, D. (1998). Treating word-finding difficulties—beyond picture naming. *International Journal of Language and Communication Disorders, 33*, 208–213.

Parr, S., Byng, S., & Gilpin, S., & Ireland, C. (1997). *Talking about aphasia*. Buckingham, UK: Open University Press.

Patterson, K.E., Purell, C., & Morton, J. (1983). The facilitation of naming in aphasia. In C. Code & D.J. Muller (Eds.), *Aphasia therapy* (pp. 76–87). London: Arnold.

Raymer, A.M. Thompson, C.K., Jacobs, B., & Le Grand, H.R. (1993). Phonological treatment of naming deficits in aphasia: Model-based generalisation analysis. *Aphasiology, 7*, 27–53.

Robertson, I.H., & Murre, J.M.J. (1999). Rehabilitation of brain damage: Brain plasticity and principles of guided recovery. *Psychological Bulletin, 125*, 544–575.

Robey, R. (1998). A meta-analysis of clinical outcomes in the treatment of aphasia. *Journal of Speech, Language and Hearing Research, 41*, 172–187.

Robey, R., Schulz, M., Crawford, A., & Skinner, C. (1999). Single-subject clinical outcome research: Design, data, effect sizes, and analyses. *Aphasiology, 13*, 445–473.

Swinburn, K., Baker, G., & Howard, D. (2002). *The Comprehensive Aphasia Test*. Manuscript in preparation.

APHASIOLOGY, 2002, 16 (10/11), 1001–1030

The comparative effectiveness of gesture and verbal treatments for a specific phonologic naming impairment

Miranda Rose, Jacinta Douglas, and Thomas Matyas

La Trobe University, Australia

Background: Arm and hand gesture has been considered a potential facilitator of word production (Skelly, Schinsky, Smith, & Fust, 1974), and gesture is often considered as a therapeutic modality for the treatment of aphasia (Rao, 1994), but there is limited empirical evidence of the efficacy of gesture-based treatments. Models of the relationship between word production and gesture production have been developed (Hadar & Butterworth, 1997; Krauss & Hadar, 1999) but they are currently under-specified and provide little guidance as to whether gesture might be an efficacious treatment for word production deficits arising from particular underlying levels of impairment.

Aims: This study had two main aims: First, to examine the comparative facilitation effects of gesture production and visualisation processes on object naming skills, and second, to compare the effectiveness of three types of treatment, gesture, verbal, and combined verbal plus gesture, for word production deficits arising from impairment at the level of phonological access and encoding.

Methods & Procedures: A 68-year-old female, AB, participated in the study. AB sustained a single, left, frontoparietal, subarachnoid haemorrhage 6 months prior to the study, which resulted in a highly specific, mild, phonologic access and encoding impairment. AB initially participated in a trial comparing the relative effectiveness of gesture and visualisation processes for facilitating oral picture naming. A controlled multiple baseline single-case experiment was then carried out comparing the three naming treatments.

Outcomes & Results: The use of iconic gesture was found to significantly facilitate picture naming. Pointing, visualisation, and cued articulation produced negligible change from baseline rates. Clinically and statistically significant treatment effects were found for all three treatment conditions, with only marginal differences between conditions. Improvements made in picture naming were maintained at 1 and 3 month follow-up assessments and generalisation of enhanced object naming was found with novel stimuli and during spontaneous conversation.

Conclusions: The results supported Krauss and Hadar's (1999) model of speech and gesture production, suggesting frank interaction between the kinesic monitor of the gesture production system and the formulator of the word production system. The results caution clinicians to question the long-held axiom of the superiority of multi-modality treatments, and encourage clinicians to consider the underlying knowledge and processes generated by particular treatment protocols, rather than simply the modality in which the treatment is transmitted.

Address correspondence to: Miranda Rose, School of Human Communication Sciences, LaTrobe University, Bundoora, 3086, Victoria, Australia. Email: M.Rose@latrobe.edu.au

The authors wish to thank AB for generously giving of her time and cooperating with those long baselines. Thank you to Heather Whitney, St Vincent de Paul Centre, Melbourne for assisting in identifying AB as an appropriate participant. Sincere thanks to Robert Krauss and Uri Hadar for allowing the authors to have early access to their model, and to Lyndsey Nickels, and Brenda Rapp and Mathew Goldrick, for sharing their 'in press' works. The first author was supported by an Australian Postgraduate Award during this study.

http://www.tandf.co.uk/journals/pp/02687038.html   DOI:10.1080/02687030143000825

Treatments for specific phonological impairments in aphasia, both in terms of retrieval deficits and difficulties in phonological encoding, have received recent attention (Hillis, 1991, 1994; Raymer, Thompson, Jacobs, & LeGrand, 1993; Robson, Marshall, Pring & Chiat, 1998; Spencer et al., 2000; Thompson, Raymer, & LeGrand, 1991). Although treatments involving various forms of verbal cueing have been compared in terms of their facilitatory effect on naming, little has been written on the use of gesture as a treatment cue for phonological-level or mild naming impairments. Speech pathologists have noted the facilitatory effects of gesture cues on verbal output in aphasia (Rao, 1994; Skelly et al., 1974) but there is limited empirical evidence to direct clinicians about when and with whom to utilise gesture. Single-case design treatment efficacy studies have suggested the superiority of combined verbal and gesture treatments for word-finding deficits in aphasia (Coelho, 1991; Conlon & McNeil, 1991) and some have suggested a verbal facilitation effect with gesture use (Code & Gaunt, 1986; Hoodin & Thompson, 1983; Pashek, 1997; Ramsberger & Helm-Estabrooks, 1989; Raymer & Thompson, 1991) and with right arm pointing (Hanlon, Brown, & Gerstman, 1990). However, these studies have largely focused on severe and nonfluent types of aphasia, and have suffered from a lack of theoretical modelling to direct the research design and constrain participant selection, making generalisation from the results difficult. Furthermore, methodological flaws in the Hanlon et al. (1990) study, such as failing to balance experimental stimuli groups according to pre-stimulation individual or group error rates, limit the utility of the results.

The notion that arm and hand gestures could facilitate enhanced verbal production in aphasia rests as much in the psycholinguistic literature exploring this phenomenon with normal speakers as it does with neuropsychological studies of brain-injured speakers. When people talk they make spontaneous movements of the arms and hands called "gestures". These gestures are closely synchronised with the flow of speech and often have identical meanings or "idea units" to the speech (Kendon, 1980). McNeill, Levy, and Pedelty (1990) argued that gestures express these idea units in fundamentally different ways. Speech is realised through segments of phonemes, words, and phrases, while gesture is global and has no "language". There have been a number of attempts to classify gestures (Butterworth, Swallow & Grimston, 1981; Efron, 1972; Ekman & Friesen, 1972; McNeill, 1985) and these have carefully distinguished gestures from body-focused movements. Body-focused movements include scratching, twitching, grooming, and self-touching movements and are neither timed with speech nor reflective of speech content (Butterworth et al., 1981).

Kendon (1988) suggested that gestures could be distinguished along a continuum: Gesticulation ⟶ "Language-like" gestures ⟶ Pantomime ⟶ Emblems ⟶ Sign Languages. McNeill et al. (1990) described how changes occur from left to right along the continuum as follows: the obligatory presence of speech declines; the presence of language properties in the gesture increases; and the gestures change from idiosyncratic to socially regulated. Gesticulation consists of idiosyncratic, spontaneous movements of the hands and arms that accompany speech and almost never occur in the absence of speech. For example, the hand rises upward while the speaker says "and he climbs up the pipe". "Language-like" gestures are similar in form and appearance to gesticulation but differ in that they are linked grammatically to the utterance. For example, "the parents were all right but the kids were [gesture]", where the gesture fills the grammatical slot of an adjective. Pantomime involves the hands demonstrating objects or actions and speech is often not present. While pantomimes can be joined together to create sentence-like expressions, gesticulations do not combine. Emblems are familiar gestures specific to a given culture and are largely attempts to control the behaviour of others, for example, insults (upward rising index finger). Emblems are usually used in the absence of speech and require a degree of "well-formedness". Sign languages such as AUSLAN and ASL are fully fledged linguistic systems with segmentation, compositionality, a lexicon, a syntax, distinctiveness, arbitrariness, standards of well-formedness, and a community of users (Klima & Bellugi, 1979).

Gesticulation, henceforth termed "gesture", has been further specified by McNeill et al. (1990). They identified four major types of "gesture": iconic, in which the form, space, and movement depicts a concrete action or object; metaphoric, in which the form, space, and movement depicts an abstract idea; beats, which are small rapid movements synchronised with speech rhythms; and deictic gestures, which encompass pointing both to a physically present referent or to an abstract, missing referent. In this study we focused on the use of iconic, metaphoric, and deictic gestures (McNeill's "gesticulations" and "language-like gestures") as opposed to beats, emblems, pantomime, or sign language, and investigated their potential to enhance word production in aphasia.

While there is little disagreement in the literature that arm and hand gestures naturally occur during speech production in adults, there is controversy as to their origin and role. The major hypotheses put forward regarding their role have included the following: gesture simply reflects extraneous general arousal (Dittman, 1972); gesture is communicatively intended (Kendon, 1980; McNeill, 1992); gesture is the output of imagistic thought processes (Freedman, 1972; Kendon, 1980); gesture interferes with speech production and competes for processing resources (Feyereisen, 1997; Levelt, Richardson, & La Heij, 1985); and gesture assists in lexical retrieval (Hadar & Butterworth, 1997; Krauss & Hadar, 1999). Psycholinguistic research provides conflicting evidence for the idea that lexical gesture facilitates lexical retrieval. Researchers have studied the asynchrony between the onset of gestures and their lexical affiliates, the effects of restricting hand movements while speaking, and the information listeners extract from gesture versus speech. One group strongly supports gesture as a facilitator of lexical retrieval (Butterworth & Beattie, 1978; Frick, 1991; Frick & Guttentag, 1998; Morrel-Samuels & Krauss, 1992; Rauscher, Krauss, & Chen, 1996; Rime & Schiaratura, 1991), whereas another argues against such an account (Beattie & Aboudan, 1994; Beattie & Coughlan, 1998, 1999; Beattie & Shovelton, 1999, 2000; Feyereisen, 1997; Levelt et al., 1985). On the other hand, neuropsychological research offers considerable support for the notion that gestures facilitate word production (Butterworth & Hadar, 1989; Butterworth et al., 1981; Hadar, Burstein, Krauss, & Soroker, 1998; Hadar & Butterworth, 1997; Hadar & Krauss, 1999; Hadar, Wenkert-Olenik, Krauss, & Soroker, 1998; Hadar & Yadlin-Gedassy, 1994).

Evidence from child language development may shed some light on this issue. Goldin-Meadow (1998), Goodwyn and Acredolo (1998), and Capirci, Iverson, Pizzuto, and Volterra (1996) have presented empirical evidence indicating that young children go through a developmental stage where iconic gesture is used separately from any verbal expression, for example, to refer to objects or during a request function. The gesture alone stage precedes a stage where gesture and speech become more synchronous and a further stage where gesture and speech are synchronously related but are communicating different information. During the stage where gestures are combined with speech, it has been suggested that the gestures are acting as a transitional device, leading to the development of two-word utterances (Capirci et al., 1996). Such evidence suggests that in this early stage of development, gesture expression and verbal expression are able to operate with some degree of separation but can work cooperatively to communicate intention.

In summary, the evidence regarding the role of gesture is inconclusive at this stage. Models of gesture production have been suggested to account for gesture/speech production and possible gesture facilitation effects. These models are based on models of normal word production. While there is considerable agreement among theorists about the number of levels of processing occurring in spoken word production models, there is considerable argument regarding the degree of interaction and feedback posited to occur between the various levels (see Rapp & Goldrick, 2000, for a more detailed review). Levelt, Roelofs, and Meyer (1999) have published the most detailed model of word production in current use. They proposed a strictly feed-forward, serial account of word production where semantic and phonological aspects of word production are represented by separate and temporally distinct stages. Dell, Schwartz, Martin, Saffran, and Gagnon (1997) suggested a spreading activation model with high levels of interaction (feed-forward and feedback) throughout the system, where processing need not be complete at one level before activation is transmitted to the next. Rapp and Goldrick (2000) posed a restricted interaction model which limits the amount of feed-forward and feedback between the various levels of processing in the system (see Nickels, 2001, for a full discussion). These models have implications for the understanding of the processes involved in the facilitation and treatment effects occurring in the remediation of aphasic word production. Of particular interest when investigating post semantic level impairments is the nature of processing proposed at the phonological level. Levelt et al. (1999) specified three types of information that must be acquired in order to generate a phonological word that optimises pronounceability in the prosodic context in which it will be spoken. First, the morphological make-up of the word must be accessed, then its metrical shape in terms of the numbers of syllables and syllable stress, and finally the actual segmental make-up. This phonological word must then be syllabified to take into account the phonology of its neighbours, so that the final phonological output is maximally pronounceable. A metrical frame specifies the number of syllables and syllable stress, with regularly stressed words being constructed "on line" by a default mechanism and irregularly stressed words being constructed from units stored in a syllabary.

Recently, Krauss and Hadar (1999) proposed a model of lexical gesture and word production based on Levelt's (1989) model of speech production (see Figure 1). In their model, gesture is thought to arise from imagistic thinking processes prior to the conceptualisation of an intended message. The spatial and dynamic features of the image are translated into a set of spatial/dynamic specifications containing the abstract descriptions of the speed, direction, and contour of the movement. These specifications are then processed by a motor planner which constructs a motor plan and passes this on to the motor system for production of the gesture. Facilitation of lexical retrieval is proposed to occur via cross-modal priming, where the gesturely represented features of the concept help to activate the lexical features that were previously unavailable. The model is at present under-specified and is not able to specifically identify at what level/s lexical gesture processes interact with word production processes. However, Krauss and Hadar have suggested a direct route from the kinesic monitor to the formulator phase of word production.

An alternative account of how lexical gesture could facilitate word production has been presented by Hadar and Butterworth (1997) (see Figure 2). In their model, there are three suggested sources of imagistic/gesture assistance for lexical retrieval. The model assumes that conceptual processing automatically activates visual imagery to the extent that the concepts in mind are imageable. A second assumption is that a visual image mediates between conceptual processing and the generation of iconic gesture. The visual image is then able to facilitate word finding in three different ways: via a preverbal route,

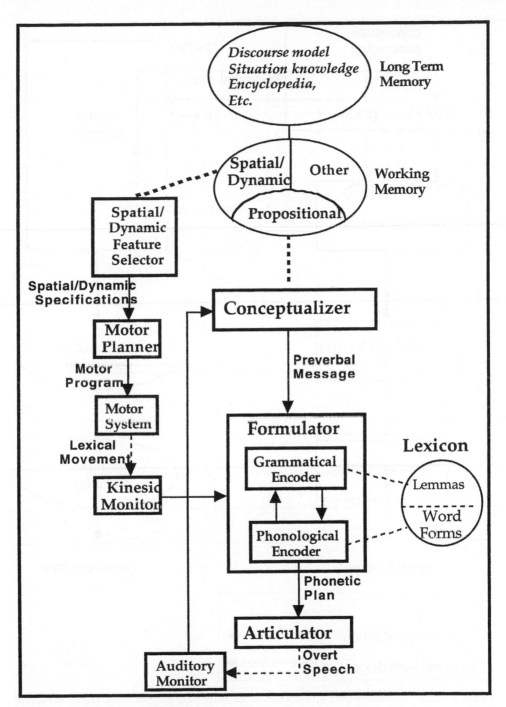

Figure 1. Krauss and Hadar's model of the interaction of the speech and gesture system. From *Gesture, speech and sign*, by R. Campbell and L. Messing (1999), p. 106, Oxford: Oxford University Press. Copyright by Oxford University Press. Reprinted with permission.

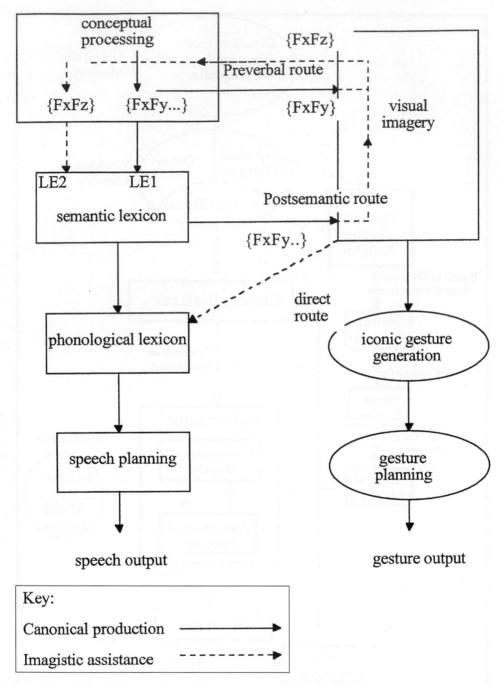

Figure 2. Hadar and Butterworth's (1997) model of the relationship between iconic gesture and speech production. From "Iconic gestures, imagery, and word retrieval in speech" by U. Hadar and B. Butterworth (1997), *Semiotica*, *115*, p.163. Copyright 1997 by Walter de Gruyter. Adapted with permission.

by refocusing conceptual processing; via a post semantic route, by holding core features during semantic reselection; and via a direct route, by directly activating word forms in the phonological lexicon. A direct route has only indirect empirical support but it may be the source of demonstrated imageability effects in a variety of lexical tasks.

Neither model specifically predicts how effective gesture could be at facilitating naming ability with respect to impairment at various stages in the word production process, for example, lexical-semantic, lexical-phonologic, or phonological encoding impairments. However, one might reason that increased activation at earlier, unimpaired levels of processing might enhance processing at later, damaged levels, particularly for access rather than storage deficits. Such information is vital for speech pathologists interested in remediating naming abilities in aphasia and for theorists attempting to further specify speech and gesture production models.

PURPOSE OF THE STUDY

The present study had two main aims. First, the study aimed to contribute to the development of a more specified model of speech and gesture production, by examining the comparative facilitation effects of gesture production and visualising processes on object naming skills. Due to the positive effects of iconic gesture on speech previously reported in treatment studies (Code & Gaunt, 1986; Hoodin & Thompson, 1983; Pashek, 1997; Skelly et al., 1974), it was hypothesised that the use of iconic gesture would significantly enhance object naming skills in the presence of a phonological-level naming impairment. Second, the study aimed to investigate the relative efficacy of gesture and verbal treatments for a mild phonological-level word production impairment. On the basis of the findings of previous treatment studies (Code & Gaunt, 1986; Hoodin & Thompson, 1983; Pashek, 1997; Skelly et al., 1974), it was hypothesised that a combined gesture and verbal treatment would be more efficacious than either verbal or gesture treatments alone. Further, other work (Raymer et al., 1993; Robson et al., 1998; Spencer et al., 2000) suggested that the model-driven treatment utilised in this study would lead to improvements in picture naming for trained items, as well as generalisation to untrained items and contexts.

METHOD

A cognitive neuropsychological approach was utilised in this single-case experiment which employed a multiple-baseline design. The study had three distinct phases. Phase one involved the detailed analysis of naming error data in the light of current models of word production (Dell et al., 1997; Levelt et al., 1999; Rapp & Goldrick, 2000). Phase two consisted of a controlled facilitation trial which aimed to investigate whether the participant would respond to gesture or visual facilitation, and if so which type of gesture (pointing or iconic) or visualisation process (visualising static objects or visualising the object being utilised) produced the maximum facilitation effects. Phase three consisted of a multiple-baseline across-conditions treatment study investigating the relative efficacy of gesture and verbal naming treatments.

Participant

AB was a 68-year-old female who sustained a left frontoparietal subarachnoid haemorrhage 6 months prior to the study commencing. She was selected on the basis of several inclusion criteria including no history of other neurological disease, psychiatric illness, alcohol abuse, or uncorrected auditory or visual deficits. She was right handed premorbidly as established from responses to the Simplified Hand Preference Questionnaire (Bryden, 1982), English was her first and only language, and there was no history of gesture communication training during previous speech-language pathology intervention. AB left school at age 15, became a mother of five children and worked as a sewing machinist and company tea lady. Premorbidly, she enjoyed reading and took a great interest in China, world events, and religion.

Initial assessment

On initial assessment AB demonstrated a mild conduction type aphasia (Western Aphasia Battery [WAB]: Aphasia Quotient 84.4, Kertesz, 1982), no oral or limb apraxia (Test of Oral and Limb Apraxia, Helm-Estabrooks, 1992; Adult Apraxia Battery, Dabul, 1979), normal oro-facial sensation and motor skills (cranial nerve assessment), and normal visuospatial and visuoconstructive skills (line bisection, shape and figure drawing, block design from WAB, early items from the Raven's Coloured Progressive Matrices, Raven, Court, & Raven, 1995). Auditory comprehension was normal within a reduced auditory verbal memory span (4 digits forward) and reading comprehension was mildly impaired at the paragraph level (WAB Reading Score: 84/100 prorated). Oral expression was largely fluent and grammatically correct until a word-finding error occurred, where paraphasia, successive approximation, and/or pausing ensued. Errors occurred on nouns and occasionally on verbs, and sentence revision was required to overcome these word-finding problems. Written naming also contained phonologically plausible errors with some inability to find particular written word forms, although these errors were less prevalent than in oral naming tasks.

PHASE ONE: ANALYSIS OF NAMING ERRORS

Procedure

A detailed assessment of AB's naming abilities was carried out over five 1-hour sessions. All sessions were videotaped so that responses could be transcribed and scored at a later date. Naming ability was measured on the Psycholinguistic Assessment of Language Processing in Aphasia (PALPA) (Kay, Lesser, & Coltheart, 1992), a corpus of 180 low-frequency nouns, and in a 20-minute semi-structured conversation with the first author.

Data analysis

Naming errors were categorised according to guidelines suggested by Rapp and Goldrick (2000) as follows: ''Semantic'': if the error clearly shared a semantic relationship with the target (further specified as coordinate, subordinate, or description); ''Nonword'': error did not correspond to the words of English, including phonologically related errors; ''Similar word'': a real word not semantically related but sharing at least 50% of the target's phonemes; ''Don't know'': no response given; ''Other'': neither phonologically nor semantically related to the target. In addition, the ''successive approximation'' category was added to capture AB's frequent use of ''conduite d'approche'' responses. Examples are provided in Appendix 1. Error patterns were examined in terms of the stages of phonological processing proposed by Levelt et al. (1999).

Results

Results of language assessments are provided in Table 1. AB demonstrated impaired picture naming, hypothesised to result from occasionally impaired access to the phonological output lexicon (22% of errors were no response, 22% descriptions or noun coordinates) and frequent difficulty with phonological encoding. Of AB's naming errors, 54% were phonological, including sound transpositions, syllable order and stress errors with some neologism and successive approximation to the target, "conduite d'approche". AB was always aware of her errors and either attempted to self-correct

TABLE 1
Results of selected language assessments and analysis of naming errors

Task	Correct	Semantic	Similar word	Non word	Successive approximation	Other word	No response
PALPA 47: Spoken Word Picture Match	100%						
PALPA 48: Written Word Pict Match	100%						
Pyramids and Palm Trees: 3 pictures	100%						
PALPA 49: Auditory Synonym Judgement	98%						
PALPA 50: Written Synonym Judgement	100%						
Oral naming in conversation n = 208	73%	0.5%	1.5%	6.3%	0.5%	14.4%	3.8%
Oral naming WAB picture description	60%	0%	5%	0%	20%	10%	5%
PALPA 53: Oral Picture Naming	85%	2.5%	2.5%	2.5%	5%	0%	2.5%
PALPA 53: Written Picture Naming	97.5%	0%	2.5%	0%	0%	0%	0%
PALPA 53: Oral Reading	92.5%	0%	7.5%	0%	0%	0%	0%
PALPA 53: Picture Name Repetition	95%	0%	0%	2.5%	0%	2.5%	0%
PALPA 53: Writing Names to Dictation	87.5%	0%	0%	12.5%	0%	0%	0%
PALPA 54:							
Low frequency	65%	0%	10%	5%	0%	0%	20%
Medium frequency	100%	0%	0%	0%	0%	0%	0%
High frequency	100%	0%	0%	0%	0%	0%	0%
Low Frequency Picture Name n = 180	54.4%	4.5%	3.8%	12.2%	8.9%	6.2%	10%
PALPA 28: Homophone Decision	100%						

or recognised her inability and moved on to the next utterance. When noun coordinates were uttered, they were knowingly offered as best alternatives to the unavailable target. Phonemic cues frequently led to correct productions for phonologically simple targets but were unsuccessful for more complex targets. Both conceptual and lexical semantics were intact (Pyramid and Palm Trees Test, Howard & Patterson, 1992; PALPA 47 Spoken word picture matching and 48 Written word picture matching; 49 Auditory synonym judgements, 50 Written synonym judgements). A strong frequency effect in picture naming was evident (PALPA 54; a corpus of 180 low-frequency words produced errors for targets below 30 per million, Francis & Kucera, 1982) but silent homophone decision skills were intact (PALPA 28). Error rates increased with word length (one-syllable: 71.4% correct; two-syllable: 54.2% correct; three-syllable: 43.9% correct; four-syllable: 9.9% correct). Repetition of picture names, reading aloud picture names, and writing picture names were mildly impaired with all errors being phonological in nature. As reading aloud was less impaired than picture naming, AB may have utilised sub-word level orthographic-to-phonological conversion routines for reading some words and/or the orthographic information provided better access to phonological forms than did picture information. Single word repetition was also better than picture naming.

AB appeared to have no phonological information at all on about 20% of naming occasions, resulting in a no response. However, when AB did make an attempt at a target her performance was interesting. Her errors on both regularly stressed words (that is, words that show stress on the first syllable with a full vowel) (e.g., 'skeleton —→ 'skeles.. 'skelestən) and irregularly stressed words (e.g., mo 'squito —→ 'moz..kæt.. 'mozkoti.. 'mozkæti. .. 'moskousits... 'moskwi:tou) occurred at approximately the same rate (65% error on regular words, 64% error on irregular words) (see Appendix 1). However, the stress produced in her nonwords and successive approximation errors was frequently incorrect and did not conform to a regular stress default setting (i.e., stress the first syllable containing a whole vowel). Of the 21 nonword errors made on regularly stressed targets, 81% were realised with regular stress, while seven of the eight nonword errors made on irregularly stressed targets were regularised on initial attempts. Following the predictions made by Levelt et al. (1999), we suggest that AB's use of the regular stress pattern on nonword productions results from breakdown in the use of on-line computation processes for irregularly stressed targets and the subsequent reversion to a default mechanism. The number of syllables in the erroneous productions was correct on 75% of occasions, showing that she had considerable information about the metrical shape of targets. Furthermore, there was substantial phonological overlap between targets and errors, with often one syllable being entirely correct. It appears that, when AB made an attempt at naming, she often had considerable phonological knowledge regarding the number of syllables and the individual segmental items but lacked syllable stress information and the complete segmental spell out.

Discussion

AB's stress assignment errors are inconsistent with a previous report (Nickels & Howard, 1999) where a subgroup of aphasic participants were found to omit unstressed syllables but not to make stress assignment errors. We suggest that AB demonstrates a specific deficit in stress allocation processes, similar to that reported by Cappa, Nespor, Ielasi, and Miozzo (1997) and that such a deficit adds evidence to the notion of a separate computational stage for stress assignment. Caution is required in interpreting these results however, as the analyses were made post-hoc and hence there was no deliberate attempt to balance groups of regular and irregular stressed words on variables such as word length or phonetic complexity. Having analysed AB's error data and verified a deficit in word production resulting from phonological access and encoding impairment, we then examined how successful various gesture and visualisation processes were at facilitating AB's spoken naming abilities.

PHASE TWO: FACILITATION TRIAL

Procedure

AB named 100, 12 × 15 cm black and white line-drawn objects on three separate occasions in order to measure pre-facilitation trial naming accuracy. No instructions were given during the three baseline trials regarding arm and hand movements. Stability was demonstrated across the three trials with accuracy measured at 55%, 55%, and 60% respectively. Where possible the pictures were selected from a standardised set published by Snodgrass and Vanderwart (1980). Where this was not possible, stereotypical black and white line drawings were chosen. The 100 pictures were then divided into five groups of twenty items, each group balanced for imageability, word frequency, word length, syllable length, phonetic complexity, and AB's pre-trial error rates. Each group was then assigned to one of five experimental conditions. Pointing, cued articulation (Passy, 1990), iconic gesture, visualising the object, and visualising the action associated with the object were compared as potential facilitators. AB was asked to name the pictures following an instruction to either point with the right hand, make an iconic gesture of the object, shut her eyes and visualise the object, shut her eyes and visualise using the object, or make a cued articulation gesture of the first phoneme of the object's name.[1] The facilitation trials were conducted on five separate days, with the order of presentation of conditions being rotated each time to minimise possible order effects. Full details of the procedure of the facilitation trial are presented in Rose and Douglas (2001).

Data analysis

In order to ascertain whether any experimental condition produced a significant improvement in naming, a Wilcoxon Matched-Pairs Signed-Ranks test (Siegel, 1956) was performed. The proportion of items correctly named in each condition during the pre-facilitation phase was compared to the proportion of items correctly named in each condition during the first three facilitation trials. Comparisons were performed with the three pre-facilitation trials and the first three facilitation trials rather than the full five facilitation trials, in order to reduce the chance of type 1 errors that could occur from entering unequal proportions into the statistical comparisons (e.g., 1/3 or .33 versus 1/5 or .2, 2/3 or .67 versus 2/5 or .4 etc.). Further, the first three facilitation trials were chosen rather than the last three in order to minimise potential practice effects.[2]

---

[1] AB was required to learn a series of cued articulation gestures (Passy, 1990) prior to the baseline and facilitation trials. Training involved learning to pair a given phoneme with a hand posture that represented aspects of phoneme production such as place, manner, and voice. AB demonstrated acquisition of 4 vowel and 16 consonant cued articulation gestures. Acquisition required three, 45-minute practice sessions.

[2] In our previous paper (Rose & Douglas, 2001) we utilised an alternative statistical analysis (comparing a single pre-facilitation trial with a single facilitation trial that best matched the respective means of those trials, in a binomial comparison). The same findings resulted from both analyses.

Results

A speech pathologist who was unaware of the aims and hypotheses of the study transcribed and scored the responses from 20% of the pre-facilitation and facilitation sessions. Point to point inter-rater agreement was calculated to be 100%.

The raw scores obtained in pre-facilitation and facilitation trials for each condition are presented in Table 2. The presence of a significant degree of facilitation for each condition was ascertained by the use of the Wilcoxon Matched-Pairs Signed-Ranks Test. The results from the three pre-facilitation trials were compared to the results from the three facilitation trials. AB responded well to the gesture facilitation trial, showing a strong and statistically significant effect for iconic gesture ($N = 10$, $T = 0$, $p < .005$, one-tailed) and a moderate but statistically insignificant improvement with cued articulation ($N = 7$, $T = 9$, $p > .05$, two-tailed), that is, when AB made an iconic gesture of the object she was trying to name, her naming accuracy improved. This improvement could not be accounted for by differences among the five groups of words which were matched on psycholinguistic variables and AB's individual error rates. The remaining three conditions, pointing ($N = 9$, $T = 7$, $p > .05$, two-tailed), visualising the object ($N = 7$, $T = 8$, $p > .05$, two-tailed), and visualising the use of the object ($N = 9$, $T = 18$, $p > .05$, two-tailed) were associated with negligible change from pre-facilitation scores.

Discussion

As predicted, AB showed significant facilitation effects on picture naming following the use of iconic gesture, whereas the use of cued articulation, pointing, and visualising processes did not significantly enhance naming scores. Our understanding of the relationship between gesture and word production has been greatly enhanced in recent years by research attempting to clarify models of speech and arm/hand gesture. One part of the model proposed by Krauss and Hadar (1999) (see Figure 1) which at present is under-specified, is the point where frank interaction between the speech and gesture production systems is hypothesised to occur. Krauss and Hadar suggested that the most likely point of interaction is at the level where facilitation effects are demonstrated and we have argued in a separate paper (Rose & Douglas, 2001) that such interactions are likely to occur between the kinesic monitor of the gesture production system and the formulator of the word production system. AB's phase one results shed some light on this issue.

If interaction was occurring earlier in the production processes of both systems, that is prior to actual execution of the gesture, significant facilitation effects should have been

TABLE 2
Raw scores of baseline and facilitation trials according to condition

Condition	Baseline trial				Facilitation trial					
	1	2	3	M	1	2	3	4	5	M
Iconic	11	11	12	11.3	16	19	19	19	18	18.2
Cued articulation	11	11	13	11.7	15	14	14	17	18	15.6
Pointing	11	10	12	11	14	15	15	16	14	14.8
Visualising object	11	10	14	11.6	15	13	14	16	15	14.6
Visualising using	11	13	12	12	13	13	13	14	15	13.6

found with the visualising conditions. However, significant facilitation effects were only found for the iconic gesture condition. This result does not support Hadar and Butterworth's (1997) ''direct route'' hypothesis, as their model predicts facilitation effects from visualising objects and their functions. Furthermore, the significant facilitation effect demonstrated for iconic gesture cannot be seen as a result of general increased motor activity and subsequent stimulation of the anterior action microgeny, as has been suggested by others (Hanlon et al., 1990). If this were the case, there should also have been significant facilitation effects with the pointing and cued articulation conditions which involve proximal limb movement. We therefore concluded that there is likely to be significant interaction between systems supporting the execution of iconic gestures and the processes involved in the formulator mechanism of the speech production process. In particular, AB's results suggested that such interaction may be operative at the level of phonological access rather than than phonological encoding, a point to be further elaborated later in this paper.

PHASE THREE: TREATMENT STUDY

Procedure

A treatment study was then commenced utilising the findings from the facilitation trial to direct the type of gesture intervention to be examined. All sessions were carried out by the first author in the participant's home. Baseline naming rates were obtained by having AB name 80 object pictures on 10 separate occasions over a period of 3 weeks. This baseline length is in line with Gorman and Allison's (1996) recommendation for sufficient length of baseline where statistical tests of significance are to be applied in interrupted time series analysis. While naming the items, AB was asked to keep her arms and hands at rest on her lap so that any attempts at gesturing while naming could be minimised.

Stimuli

As the participant was required to complete 10 baseline naming trials prior to any intervention, stimuli were chosen in order to achieve a baseline success rate of approximately 50% so that participant motivation would be maintained through the baseline phase and frustration could be kept at acceptable levels. Due to AB's mild level of deficit, it was necessary to include low-frequency (below 60 per million, Francis & Kucera, 1982) and multisyllable items in order to achieve a 50% error rate. Although it was the intention to select items on the basis of the participant's daily needs and personal preferences, the mild nature of her impairment necessitated the investigators directing most of the item selection, but where possible items were selected that were anticipated to be items of her conversational vocabulary.

Following the baseline naming phase, the 80 items were divided into four groups (groups A to D) of 20 items each, balanced for word frequency, imageability, number of syllables, number of phonemes, phonetic complexity, and AB's error rates and types during the baseline phase. The stimuli are presented in Appendix 2. Group B was assigned to the verbal treatment condition, group C to the gesture treatment condition and group D to the combined verbal and gesture treatment condition. Initially, group A was assigned to the control condition. An additional control task, thought to be unrelated to the naming tasks but sensitive to improvements in speed of processing and self-monitoring, the d2 Test of Attention (Brickenkamp, 1981) was administered every third session, to measure improvement that may have occurred as a result of spontaneous recovery or general therapeutic stimulation. The d2 consists of 14 lines each comprising 47 characters. The characters are either "d"'s or "p"'s with one to four dashes. The participant is required to scan across each line to identify and cross out all the "d"'s with two dashes. A maximum of 20 seconds per line is allowed. Three, 45-minute treatment sessions were held per week. Every third session commenced with the d2 task, followed by naming the items from Group A (control probe measure). Sessions without the d2 task commenced with naming items from Group A. Items from groups B to D were then trained in three different conditions. The order of conditions was rotated every session, with a repeated cycle every three sessions.

Therapy protocols

Training was applied to any item in sets B to D that was not spontaneously named within 20 seconds of presentation. Training was not commenced until 20 seconds had elapsed from the point of presentation of the stimuli. Training continued in this way until one set reached 90% correct on three out of four consecutive sessions, at which time the condition applied to that successful set was then applied to the control set A. The remaining two sets continued to receive their respective treatment conditions and all training continued until one set reached 90% correct on three consecutive occasions or 20 sessions were completed, whichever came first.

The treatment protocols consisted of 10 to 12 steps depending on the condition, organised into a behavioural hierarchy involving imitation, discrimination, and reinforcement based on methods used by Code and Gaunt (1986), Coelho (1991), Raymer and Thompson (1991), and Robson et al. (1998). Verbal treatment consisted of AB identifying the number of syllables in the target, the first phonemes of syllables in error, rearranging written syllable anagrams of the target, identifying which syllables contained the primary stress, and finally copying a verbal model if required. The gesture types selected to use in the gesture conditions were iconic gesture and cued articulation, as they were shown to be the most facilitative during the facilitation trials. The iconic gestures used in training were those spontaneously generated by AB when asked to "show how you could represent this object with your hands", except for four items (alley, aquarium, alphabet, and pyramid) where her spontaneous gestures were deemed to be ambiguous and potentially confusable with other gestures she had generated. From a clinical point of view, we were keen for her to use unambiguous and iconic forms, so that in the event that she failed to develop the verbal form, she could utilise the gesture form as a communicative symbol. For those four items, the investigator modelled the preferred gesture and gained AB's agreement that the latter gesture was a better representation of the target. Gesture treatment consisted of AB using an iconic gesture before naming the target and if unsuccessful, making the cued articulation gesture of the first phoneme of the first and successive syllables in error, indicating on her fingers the number of syllables in the target, and finally copying a verbal model if required. Combined verbal and gesture treatment consisted of combining the steps in the verbal and gesture conditions and alternating the order of the steps across items. In each condition, the therapy protocol was abandoned at the point where AB correctly named the target. AB was simply asked to name items from the control group on each occasion, with no specific feedback from the researcher other than general encouragement. A full description of the treatment protocol for each condition is provided in Appendix 3.

Data analysis

All treatment sessions were videotaped with participant permission for later transcription and analysis. Items were scored as correct if the name was produced without error and without assistance from the researcher, within 20 seconds of presentation of the stimuli. Correct attempts at naming after any therapeutic intervention for an item were not scored as correct in that session. An independent speech pathologist transcribed and rated the responses from 20% of the baseline and treatment sessions. Inter-rater agreement was 99.3%. In addition, the independent rater checked for adherence to the therapy protocols on the same 20% of sessions and found adherence 98% of the time.

Consistent with recent recommendations by Robey, Schultz, Crawford, and Sinner (1999), and Matyas and Greenwood (1996) visual inspection of the plots of performance in baseline and treatment conditions was rejected as the sole means of assessing the occurrence of significant treatment effects, due to the high degree of unreliability of such analyses. Rather, a statistical analysis of the interrupted time series was carried out (Gorman & Allison, 1996). First, a standard case chart was constructed and is presented in Figure 3. Visual inspection of the data for each variable, in baseline and intervention phases, suggested that two separate curvilinear functions of the number of the sessions might more adequately describe the data for each variable than a single overall curvilinear function. A mathematical model was then identified that best described the data in the baseline and intervention phases of each variable. Consistent with reports on behavioural change in humans (Anderson, 1990), a power function was found to account for more variance than a logarithmic or growth function (see Table 3).

In order to demonstrate significant treatment effects, two analyses were completed. First, continuous and piecewise regression models were compared for goodness of fit. If there had been no significant change from baseline levels as a result of treatment, a single continuous power function should have adequately described the overall baseline and treatment data. Conversely, if significant treatment effects were present, a second power function should begin from where the baseline ended, that is, a continuous power model would be superseded by a piecewise regression model. The presence of serial dependency in the data was examined by calculating the degree of autocorrelation in the residuals obtained from the piecewise regression curve constructed by fitting two separate power functions to the baseline and intervention phases and comparing these to the residuals obtained from fitting the single overall power curve. It was anticipated that there would be no significant autocorrelation in the residuals from the piecewise regression model, but significant autocorrelation would be found in the residuals from the single power model, thereby confirming the superiority of the piecewise model in describing the data. Second,

TABLE 3

Variance accounted for by three mathematical functions for each dependent variable in baseline and intervention phases

Variables	Power		Logarithmic		Growth	
	Baseline	Intervention	Baseline	Intervention	Baseline	Intervention
Control	.599	.924	.588	.883	.40	.77
Verbal	.804	.705	.754	.689	.824	.504
Gesture	.877	.785	.858	.752	.746	.62
Verbal + Gesture	.576	.719	.528	.749	.393	.437

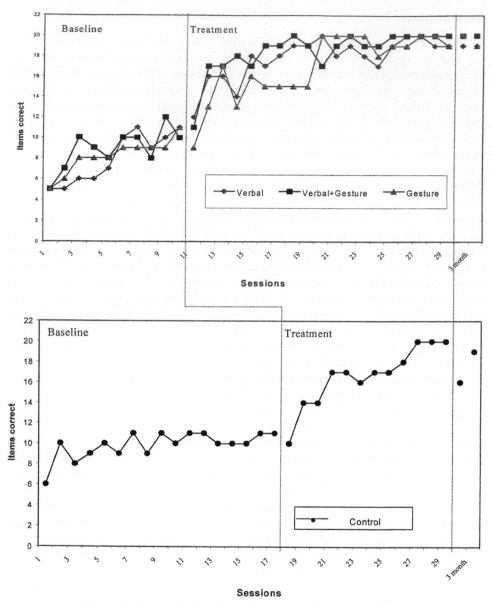

Figure 3. Comparative baseline and treatment results across conditions.

to satisfactorily demonstrate statistically significant treatment effects, the residual variances from both models were analysed with an F test. It was anticipated that there would be a significantly greater variance in the single power model, representing the null hypothesis, than that found in the piecewise model, representing positive effects of intervention.

Furthermore, in order to ascertain whether one treatment condition was more effective than another, two further analyses were completed. First, the rate of item acquisition was examined by comparing the slopes of the power model curves for the three intervention series. A logarithmic transformation of the intervention data was performed so that linear regression curves could be constructed. The presence of significant differences in slope parameters were then examined using Student's *t* tests. It was hypothesised that the slope of the combined verbal plus gesture condition would be significantly greater than the gesture or verbal alone. Secondly, the degree of stability in the learning curves was ascertained by calculating F ratios of the variance in the residuals from the power curves of the three treatment conditions. It was hypothesised that there would be greater stability in the combined gesture plus verbal condition as compared to the gesture or verbal alone.

A further simple analysis was carried out on the amount of intervention required to produce criterion levels of naming across the three conditions, by comparing the number of occasions that intervention was required in each set.

Results

Visual inspection of Figure 3 indicates a clear difference between baseline and intervention phases. Treatment led to marked improvements in all three treatment conditions, while the control condition rose initially and then plateaued from baseline session 7. After seven treatments (session 17), Set D (combined verbal plus gesture) reached the pre-established criteria of 90% correct on three out of four consecutive sessions, only just prior to treatment Set B (verbal) which reached criterion with eight treatments (session 18). Set C (gesture) reached criterion with 12 treatments (session 22). As the control Set A scores stayed consistent with the baseline scores until a treatment condition was applied, the improvement achieved in the treatment sets (B–D) can be attributed specifically to the treatments and not to general therapeutic stimulation or spontaneous recovery. Furthermore, the results of an additional control task, the d2, also remained stable across the entire investigation, adding support to positive treatment effects (Total scores – Error scores deviated by less than 5% across all trials). When the marginally superior condition, combined verbal and gesture treatment, was applied to the control set (A) from session 18, there was rapid improvement with criterion being reached by session 29, at which time the treatment ceased.

Visual inspection of the baseline curves for each condition reveals an increase in naming accuracy from session 1 through to session 10. The control condition shows plateauing occurring from session 9. The importance and likely source of such "untreated" improvement will be highlighted in the discussion.

The number of steps of the treatment protocol required to generate a correct picture name was recorded for each condition. The data are reported in Table 4. Overall, the combined verbal plus gesture condition set required significantly fewer occasions of intervention as compared to the gesture condition set, $\chi^2 = 7.35$, df(1), $p < .01$). However, there was no significant difference between the number of occasions of intervention applied to the combined condition set and the verbal condition set, $\chi^2 = 3.06$, df(1), $p > .05$). Furthermore, it can be seen that the required level of treatment varied across the occasions of intervention and did not simply regress to a repetition of the target, that is the final step in the protocols, each time. Rather, AB required information regarding the initial phoneme, number of syllables in the target, and/or syllable stress, and these requirements varied across trials.

Statistical analyses, using the $Y = aX^b$ model (Power Function), which accounted for most of the variance in the baseline and intervention phases for each condition, were carried out for the null hypothesis using a curve estimated from the baseline data and for the alternative hypothesis using a piecewise curve constructed from both the actual baseline and treatment data (see Figure 4). Significant autocorrelation was found in the residuals from the curves constructed under the null hypothesis, whereas there was no significant autocorrelation found in the residuals from the piecewise regression models (see Table 5). In addition, there was significantly more variance found in the residuals from the overall curve than the piecewise curve (see Table 6) suggesting statistically significant treatment effects for all three conditions.

The relative effectiveness of the three treatment conditions was examined in terms of the rate of item acquisition (slope parameters) and stability of item acquisition (variance

TABLE 4

Number of required treatment steps prior to items uttered correctly for each condition and the total number of treatments given per condition

Protocol step	Verbal	Gesture	Verbal + Gesture
2	2	2	3
3	0	2	1
4	1	4	2
5	0	1	1
6	7	12	7
7	0	1	1
8	7	6	1
9	1	6	1
10	10	19	4
11	0	NA	0
12	9	NA	8
Total treatments	37	53	29

Step 1 removed from analysis as it does not involve treatment.

TABLE 5

Autocorrelation of the residuals at lags 1–5 from fitting a power curve to the overall data and from the creation of a piecewise curve

	Piecewise					Overall				
	Lag 1	Lag 2	Lag 3	Lag 4	Lag 5	Lag 1	Lag 2	Lag 3	Lag 4	Lag 5
Verbal	−.015	−.205	.072	−.338	−.019	*.468	.236	.268	.098	.176
Gesture	.118	−.008	−.081	−.053	−.117	*.512	.370	.283	.030	.123
Verbal + Gesture	−.153	−.300	.227	−.045	.016	*.515	*.309	*.360	.061	−.101
Control	−.244	−.017	−.065	−.255	.190	*.760	*.660	*.490	.350	.300

*Significant autocorrelation.

TABLE 6

Variance of residuals from overall model as compared to piecewise regression model, expressed as an F ratio, degrees of freedom and significance values for each variable

Variable	F ratio	Degrees of Freedom	P value
Control	7.97	27, 25	0.001
Verbal	2.12	27, 25	0.05
Gesture	2.18	27, 25	0.01
Verbal + Gesture	2.73	27, 25	0.005

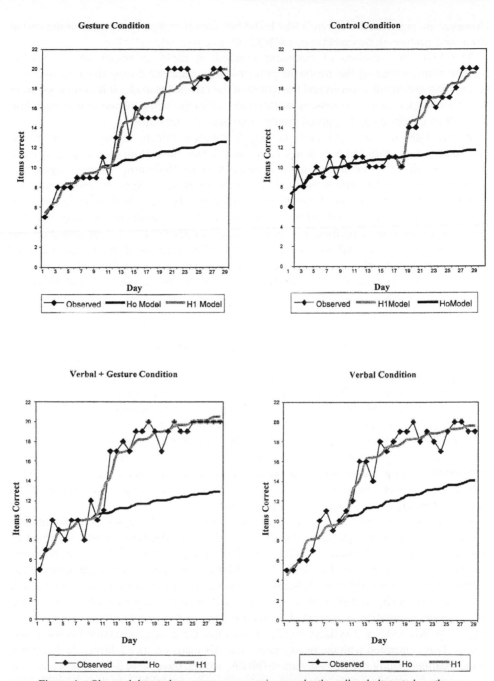

Figure 4.   Observed data and power curve comparisons under the null and alternate hypotheses.

in power curve residuals). There were no statistically significant differences found between conditions in terms of their relative variances: Combined Verbal plus Gesture vs Verbal, $F = 1.127$, df(17,17), $p > .05$; Combined Verbal plus Gesture vs Gesture, $F = 1.524$, df(17,17), $p > .05$; Verbal vs Gesture, $F = 1.714$, df(17,17), $p > .05$. As predicted, the slope of the combined condition was significantly greater than the gesture condition, $t = 2.36$, df(34), $p < .01$, and the verbal condition, $t = 2.66$, df(34), $p < .01$.

However, no significant difference was found between the slope parameters of the verbal alone and gesture alone conditions, $t = 0.32$, df(34), $p > .05$.

The first four sessions of treatment resulted in rapid improvements in naming accuracy. In comparing the treatment protocol steps required during the first four and second four treatment sessions and the nature of the errors AB made, it becomes apparent that phonological access problems were remedied early, while phonological encoding difficulties continued and required greater amounts of intervention.

In the light of the significant naming facilitation effects found for AB in the facilitation study with the use of iconic gesture, it was interesting to examine in more detail how effective the use of iconic gesture was in facilitating naming during the treatment study. In the gesture condition, there were instances where the production of a gesture clearly led to the production of the picture name, but equally there were instances where this did not happen and AB then required further steps of the treatment protocol in order for the name to be realised. It is important to identify the factors that contributed to successful naming as a result of gesture facilitation. Given the two distinct components of her naming deficit—first, a phonological access impairment usually leading to a no response or production of a coordinate noun, and second, a phonological encoding impairment resulting in successive approximations and nonword responses—we hypothesised that the facilitation effects demonstrated in this study may have been more related to one of these stages than the other. Hence, we examined AB's baseline error types with the expectation that targets that elicited one type of error, for example, phonological access errors, might have responded better to gesture facilitation in the treatment study than targets that elicited phonological encoding errors.

The errors elicited in the iconic gesture condition of the baseline sessions of the facilitation study were 50% phonological encoding and 50% phonological access errors and both types responded equally well to iconic facilitation. For the gesture set (set C) of the treatment study however, 80% of the baseline errors were realised as partial approximations to the target and therefore considered to be phonological encoding errors rather than straight phonological access errors. Gesture facilitation was successful for only 25% of targets, substantially less than in the phase two trials. We examined the nature of the targets to try to explain this discrepancy.

First, a potential word frequency effect was investigated: Perhaps gesture facilitation is not possible beyond a particular frequency level. This hypothesis proved incorrect as AB demonstrated facilitation on targets with frequencies as low as 2 and not on some targets with higher frequencies. Second, word length and phonologic complexity were examined and this proved fruitful. Items selected in the treatment study were longer and more phonologically complex than those selected in the facilitation phase. The nine targets in the facilitation phase that elicited error consisted of one 4-syllable word, two 3-syllable words and six 2-syllable words, while only three items contained consonantal blends. This contrasted with the twelve items that AB made errors on during the baselines of the treatment study, where two were 4-syllable words, three were 3-syllable words and seven were 2-syllable words, while six contained consonantal blends. It is possible that the increased phonologic complexity in the targets of the treatment study made it less likely that a gesture facilitation effect would be successful, due to the greater opportunity for encoding errors to occur. From this perspective, we are suggesting for AB that the prime facilitation effect of iconic gesture was achieved by enhancing phonological access processes rather than phonological encoding processes. Clearly, further investigation of this hypothesis is required.

Maintenance and generalisation

Follow-up naming trials were conducted at 1 month and 3 months from the date of the last treatment session and revealed maintenance of the accuracy levels achieved during the treatment phases (see Figure 3).

In order to assess potential generalisation effects a formal reassessment was carried out following the completion of the treatment phases on the same battery of tests utilised in the initial assessment. The semi-structured conversation was repeated at 1 and 3 months following the cessation of treatment. The same set of questions were used to elicit a connected speech sample on each occasion and are provided in Appendix 4. The full 20-minute conversation was transcribed in broad phonetic transciption following each taping session and the occasions of word production error on nouns counted. The results of the reassessments are presented in Table 7. AB demonstrated improvement on measures that had initially shown impairments, both on standardised measures such as the WAB Aphasia Quotient and on more functional measures of communication such as noun error rates in spontaneous conversation. Items that improved did not specifically receive training in the treatment study, thus a deficit-specific rather than item-specific treatment effect appears to have been demonstrated. Furthermore, the frequency of phonologically related naming errors (similar words, nonwords, and successive approximations) demonstrated in the 20-minute conversation sample reduced from 17 errors pre-treatment to 6 errors post-treatment, suggesting a more intact word production system post-treatment. It is noteworthy that generalisation of improved naming did not occur to the control set during the treatment phase. The control set only improved when treatment was applied to it from session 18 (treatment session 8) onwards (see Figure 3). Further, three non-linguistic measures showed no post-treatment change: the d2 Test, the Coloured Progressive Matrices, and digit span forwards.

TABLE 7
A comparison of pre- and post-treatment linguistic abilities

Test	Pre-treatment	Post-treatment	3 month follow-up
WAB Aphasia Quotient	84.4	91.4	
WAB Spontaneous Speech Information	9/10	10/10 ([a]3)	
WAB Spontaneous Speech Fluency	9/10	9/10	
WAB Object Naming	15/20	19/20 ([a]4)	
PALPA Spoken Word Picture Matching	40/40	40/40	
PALPA Written Word Picture Matching	40/40	40/40	
PALPA Spoken Picture Name	34/40	39/40 ([a]5)	
PALPA Picture Naming Low Frequency	13/20	20/20 ([a]7)*	
PALPA Reading Picture Names Aloud	37/40	40/40 ([a]3)	
PALPA Repeating Picture Names	40/40	40/40	
PALPA Written Picture Naming	39/40	39/40	
PALPA Written Picture Spelling	35/40	37/40 ([a]2)	
Naming errors in conversaion sample	27%	5.4% ([a]6) ([b]1)	5% ([a]5)
Name error rate in conversation sample	3.46/minute	0.62/minute	0.48/minute

[a] Specifies number of items in brackets improved from pre-treatment performance to post-treatment performance that were not direct targets during the treatment phases.

[b] Specifies number of items in brackets improved from pre-treatment performance to post-treatment performance that were direct targets during the treatment phases.

* Specifies significantly different binomial test ($p = .008$).

Discussion

As predicted, results from phase three of this study provided clear evidence as to the efficacy of phonological and gesture treatments for a word production impairment arising from phonological access and encoding deficits. The treatments produced significantly improved naming within seven treatment sessions but required eleven treatments to show stability. Clear generalisation effects were demonstrated by improved naming skills in picture description, picture naming, and naming in conversation, for targets not specifically addressed by the treatment stimuli. Improved naming skills did not appear to reflect a spontaneous recovery or generalised therapeutic stimulation effect. Furthermore, maintenance of the improved naming ability was demonstrated at 1 and 3 months after the treatments ceased, suggesting that there had been a permanent change to the word production system, rather than temporary changes as a result of stimulation or concentrated therapeutic activity. AB described a greater sense of confidence about her communicative skills post-treatment. At the 3 month follow-up session she recounted her recent unaccompanied trip to China, where she managed all communicative acts associated with international travel without difficulty.

An important consideration in the data emerging from this treatment phase concerns the naming improvements demonstrated during the baseline phase. The lack of stability in AB's baselines adds weight to the arguments made by advocates of the use of statistical analysis in single-case-design experiments. Relying on visual inspection of plots with rising baselines for the evaluation of treatment effects has been shown to be grossly inadequate (Matyas & Greenwood, 1990). One can see the error that would have been made had there been three baseline trials, being the most frequently reported number (Robey et al., 1999), rather than the 10 used here. Treatment effects would have been grossly over-estimated. We speculate regarding the source of such ''untreated'' improvement, noticing the reduced number of phonological access difficulties and the increased number of phonological encoding difficulties as the baseline naming trials progressed. Such behaviour may result from repeated exposure to picture stimuli such that signal strength improves from semantic stores to the phonological output lexicon, thereby reducing the number of phonological access difficulties but leaving phonological encoding deficits more exposed (see Nickels, in this special issue, for an account of such behaviour).

GENERAL DISCUSSION

As predicted, results from phase two of this study provided support for the superiority of iconic gesture as a facilitator of object naming for a participant with a phonologic access and encoding-level naming impairment. Pointing, cued articulation, and visualising processes were not found to significantly enhance picture naming. Further, results from phase three of this study supported the efficacy of phonological and gesture treatments for naming deficits resulting from phonologic access and encoding impairments, while failing to support the expected superiority of multi-modality intervention over single-modality interventions. In terms of the level at which iconic gesture is interacting with the word production system, we have argued in agreement with Krauss and Hadar (1999) that there must be frank interaction between end stage gesture production processes and some level of word production. Krauss and Hadar have suggested that the most likely point of interaction is the level at which facilitation effects are demonstrated, and we have argued in a separate paper (Rose & Douglas, 2001) that such interactions are likely between the kinesic monitor of the gesture production system and the formulator of the word production system. The results from phase three of this study shed further light on this issue. The results suggested that interaction may be greater between gesture production processes and phonological access processes rather than phonological encoding processes. Although there was no apparent effect of word frequency on the degree of gesture facilitation demonstrated, less facilitation was found on longer and more phonetically complex targets. Thus, it is possible that increased phonologic complexity made it less likely that a gesture facilitation effect would be successful, due to the greater opportunity for encoding errors to occur. From this perspective, we tentatively suggest that for AB, the prime facilitation effect of iconic gesture was achieved by enhancing phonological access processes rather than phonological encoding processes. Clearly, detailed investigation of this hypothesis is required in future study. Such interaction may have ontological foundations in behaviours and by implication, neuronal networks established in early childhood as discussed by Goldin-Meadow (1998), Goodwyn and Acredolo (1998), and Capirci et al. (1996).

The lack of substantial clinical and statistical differences between the overall success of the gesture, verbal, or combined treatments in phase three of this study is of interest and contrary to initial predictions. First, this finding is inconsistent with several other published studies to date which have shown a superiority for combined gesture and verbal treatments (Code & Gaunt, 1986; Hoodin & Thompson, 1983; Schneider, Thompson, & Luring, 1996). In the current study, it is possible that the underlying treatment strategy was a more salient feature in predicting treatment success than the modality in which it was carried out. In the current study, information regarding phonological make-up, syllable length, and syllable stress was utilised to restore phonological access and encoding mechanisms, in all treatment conditions, albeit through different modalities (gesture versus verbal). Previous studies investigating the relative efficacy of combined or single modality treatments have confounded the variables of treatment modality and treatment strategy. For example, Hoodin and Thompson (1983) compared verbal, combined, and gesture treatments for word production deficits, where the gesture treatment consisted of simply pairing an iconic gesture with the target. This contrasts with the method utilised in the current study whereby the gesture condition contained the same underlying phonologic components of syllable number, syllable stress, etc but presented in the gesture modality through cued articulation gestures. Our results suggested that for a mild, phonologic access and encoding word production impairment, the modality of instruction is less important than the technique *per se*. Obviously, this finding requires replication and comparison to spoken word production impairments of differing underlying origins and severities. We are currently undertaking such study and aim to report the results in the near future.

Another finding of interest from phase three concerns the demonstrated generalisation of treatment effects to untreated items and untreated contexts, a result inconsistent with many of the previous reports of phonological-level treatments (Howard, Patterson, Franklin, Orchard-Lisle & Morton, 1985a,b; Marshall, Pound, White-Thompson, & Pring, 1990; Miceli, Amitrano, Capasso, & Caramazza, 1996; Pring, Hamilton, Harwood, & Macbride, 1993) that have demonstrated item-specific improvements. AB's results are more consistent with results obtained by Best, Howard, Bruce, and Gatehouse (1997), Robson et al. (1998), and Spencer et al. (2000), where system-level changes were hypothesised to be the underlying cause of improved naming, rather than patients consciously applying therapeutic strategies. In the current study, the fact that the untreated "control" items remained stable until treatment was applied to them (from treatment session 8) argued against the post-treatment generalisation being simply the result of overall improvements to general functioning, for example, as a result of spontaneous recovery. Rather, we speculated that a certain amount of treatment was required before system-level changes were effected. Just what this certain "threshold" is remains obscured in our data. In hindsight, a second "untreated" control group would have been useful in terms of demonstrating at what point during the therapy such hypothesised system-level changes and generalisation began to occur.

REFERENCES

Anderson, J. (1990). *Cognitive psychology and its implications: Development of expertise* (3rd ed., pp. 256–288). New York: W. Freeman & Co.

Beattie, G., & Aboudan, R. (1994). Gestures, pauses and speech: An experimental investigation of the effects of changing social context on their precise temporal relationships. *Semiotica, 99*(3/4), 239–272.

Beattie, G., & Coughlan, J. (1998). Do iconic gestures have a functional role in lexical access? An experimental study of the effects of repeating a verbal message on gesture production. *Semiotica, 119*(3/4), 221–249.

Beattie, G., & Coughlan, J. (1999). An experimental investigation of the role of iconic gestures in lexical access using the tip-of-the-tongue phenomenon. *British Journal of Psychology, 90*, 35–56.

Beattie, G., & Shovelton, H. (1999). Do iconic gestures really contribute anything to the semantic information conveyed by speech? An experimental investigation. *Semiotica, 123*(1/2), 1–30.

Beattie, G., & Shovelton, H. (2000). Iconic hand gestures and the predictability of words in context in spontaneous speech. *British Journal of Psychology, 91*, 473–491.

Best, W., Howard, D., Bruce, C., & Gatehouse, C. (1997). A treatment for anomia combining semantics, phonology, and orthography. In S. Chiat, J. Law, & J. Marshall (Eds.), *Language disorders in children and adults* (pp. 102–129). London: Whurr.

Brickenkamp, R. (1981). *Test d2. Concentration–endurance test: Manual* (5th ed.). Gottingen: Verlag für Psychologie.

Bryden, M. (1982). Handedness and its relation to cerebral function. In M. Bryden (Ed.), *Laterality: Functional asymmetry in the intact brain* (pp. 157–179). New York: Academic Press.

Butterworth, B., & Beattie, G. (1978). Gesture and silence as indicators of planning in speech. In R. Campbell & P. Smith (Eds.), *Recent advances in the psychology of language* (pp. 347–360). New York: Plenum Press.

Butterworth, B., & Hadar, U. (1989). Gesture, speech, and computational stages: A reply to McNeill. *Psychological Review, 96*, 168–174.

Butterworth, B., Swallow, J., & Grimston, M. (1981). Gestures and lexical processes in jargonaphasia. In J. Brown (Ed.), *Jargonaphasia* (pp. 113–124). New York: Academic Press.

Capirci, O., Iverson, J., Pizzuto, E., & Volterra, V. (1996). Gestures and words during the transition to two word speech. *Journal of Child Language, 23*(3), 645–673.

Cappa, S., Nespor, M., Ielasi, W., & Miozzo, A. (1997). The representation of stress: Evidence from an aphasic patient. *Cognition, 65*, 1–13.

Code, C., & Gaunt, C. (1986). Treating severe speech and limb apraxia in a case of aphasia. *British Journal of Disorders of Communication, 21*, 11–20.

Coelho, C. (1991). Manual sign acquisition and use in two aphasic subjects. In T. Prescott (Ed.), *Clinical aphasiology* (Vol. 19, pp. 209–218). Texas: Pro-Ed.

Conlon, C., & McNeil, M. (1991). The efficacy of treatment for two globally aphasic adults using visual action therapy. In T. Prescott (Ed.), *Clinical aphasiology* (Vol. 19, pp. 185–194). Texas: Pro-Ed.

Dabul, B. (1979). *Apraxia battery for adults.* Oregon: C.C. Publications.

Dell, G., Schwartz, M., Martin, N., Saffran, E., & Gagnon, D. (1997). Lexical access in normal and aphasic speech. *Psychological Review, 104*, 801–838.

Dittman, A. (1972). The body movement–speech rhythm relationship as a cue to speech encoding. In A. Siegman & B. Pope (Eds.), *Studies in dyadic communication* (pp. 135–152). New York: Pergamon Press.

Efron, D. (1972). *Gesture, race and culture.* The Hague: Mouton.

Ekman, P., & Friesen, W. (1972). Hand movements. *Journal of Communication, 22*, 353–374.

Feyereisen, P. (1997). The competition between gesture and speech production in dual-task paradigms. *Journal of Memory and Language, 36*, 13–33.

Francis, N., & Kucera, H. (1982). *Frequency analysis of English usage.* Boston: Houghton Mifflin.

Freedman, N. (1972). The analysis of movement behaviour during the clinical interview. In A. Siegman & B. Pope (Eds.), *Studies in dyadic communication* (pp. 153–175). New York: Pergamon Press.

Frick, D. (1991). *The use of hand gestures as self-generated cues.* Unpublished Doctoral Thesis, University of North Carolina, Greensboro, USA.

Frick, D., & Guttentag, R. (1998). The effects of restricting hand gesture production on lexical retrieval and free recall. *American Journal of Psychology, 3*(1), 43–62.

Goldin-Meadow, S. (1998). The development of gesture and speech as an integrated system. *New Directions for Child Development, 79*, 29–42.

Goodwyn, S., & Acredolo, L. (1998). Encouraging symbolic gestures: A new perspective on the relationship between gesture and speech. *New Directions for Child Development, 79*, 61–73.

Gorman, B., & Allison, D. (1996). Statistical alternatives for single-case designs. In R. Franklin, D. Allison, & B. Gorman (Eds.), *Design and analysis of single-case research* (pp. 159–214). Hillsdale, NJ: Lawrence Erlbaum Associates Inc.

Hadar, U., Burstein, A., Krauss, R., & Soroker, N. (1998). Ideational gestures and speech in brain damaged subjects. *Language and Cognitive Processes, 13*(1), 59–76.

Hadar, U., & Butterworth, B. (1997). Iconic gestures, imagery, and word retrieval in speech. *Semiotica, 115*, 147–172.

Hadar, U., & Krauss, R. (1999). Iconic gestures: The grammatical categories of lexical affiliates. *Journal of Neurolinguistics, 12*(1), 1–12.

Hadar, U., Wenkert-Olenik, D., Krauss, R., & Soroker, N. (1998). Gesture and the processing of speech: Neuropsychological evidence. *Brain and Language, 62*, 107–126.

Hadar, U., & Yadlin-Gedassy, S. (1994). Conceptual and lexical aspects of gesture: Evidence from aphasia. *Journal of Neurolinguistics, 8*, 57–65.

Hanlon, R., Brown, J., & Gerstman, L. (1990). Enhancement of naming in nonfluent aphasia through gesture. *Brain and Language, 38*, 298–314.

Helm-Estabrooks, N. (1992). *Test of oral and limb apraxia.* Chicago: The Riverside Publishing Company.

Hillis, A. (1991). Effects of separate treatments for distinct impairments within the naming process. *Clinical Aphasiology, 19*, 255–266.

Hillis, A. (1994). Contributions from cognitive analyses. In R. Chapey (Ed.), *Language intervention strategies in adult aphasia* (pp. 207–219). Baltimore: Williams & Wilkins.

Hoodin, R., & Thompson, C. (1983). Facilitation of verbal labeling in adult aphasia by gesture, verbal or verbal plus gesture training. In R.H. Brookshire (Ed.), *Clinical aphasiology* (pp. 62–64). Minneapolis: BRK.

Howard, D., & Patterson, K. (1992). *The pyramids and palm trees test.* Bury St. Edmunds, UK: Thames Valley Test Company.

Howard, D., Patterson, K., Franklin, S., Orchard-Lisle, V., & Morton, J. (1985a). The facilitation of picture naming in aphasia. *Cognitive Neuropsychology, 2*, 49–80.

Howard, D., Patterson, K., Franklin, S., Orchard-Lisle, V., & Morton, J. (1985b). The treatment of word retrieval deficits in aphasia: A comparison of two therapy methods. *Brain, 108*, 817–829.

Kay, J., Lesser, R., & Coltheart, M. (1992). *Psycholinguistic Assessments of Language Processing in Aphasia.* Hove, UK: Lawrence Erlbaum Associates Ltd.

Kendon, A. (1980). Gesticulation and speech: Two aspects of the process of utterance. In M. Key (Ed.), *The relationship of verbal and nonverbal communication* (pp. 207–227). The Hague: Mouton.

Kendon, A. (1988). How gestures can become like words. In F. Poyatos (Ed.), *Cross cultural perspectives in nonverbal communication* (pp. 131–141). Toronto: Hogrefe Publishers.

Kertesz, A. (1982). *Western aphasia battery.* New York: Grune & Stratton.

Klima, E., & Bellugi, U. (1979). *The signs of language.* Cambridge, MA: Harvard University Press.

Krauss, R., & Hadar, U. (1999). The role of speech-related arm/hand gestures in word retrieval. In R. Campbell & L. Messing (Eds.), *Gesture, speech, and sign* (pp. 63–116). Oxford: Oxford University Press.

Levelt, W. (1989). *Speaking–From intention to articulation.* Cambridge, MA: MIT Press.

Levelt, W., Richardson, G., & La Heij, W. (1985). Pointing and voicing in deitic expressions. *Journal of Memory and Language, 24*, 133–164.

Levelt, W., Roelfs, A., & Meyer, A. (1999). A theory of lexical access in speech production. *Behavioural and Brain Sciences, 22*, 1–75.

Marshall, J., Pound, C., White-Thompson, M., & Pring, T. (1990). The use of picture/word matching tasks to assist word retrieval in aphasic patients. *Aphasiology, 4*, 167–184.

Matyas, T., & Greenwood, K. (1990). Visual analysis of single-case time series: Effects of variability, serial dependence, and magnitude of intervention effects. *Journal of Applied Behavior Analysis, 23*, 341–351.

Matyas, T., & Greenwood, K. (1996). Serial dependency in single-case time series. In R. Franklin, D. Allison, & B. Gorman (Eds.), *Design and analysis of single-case research* (pp. 215–244). Hillsdale, NJ: Lawrence Erlbaum Associates Inc.

McNeill, D. (1985). So you think gestures are nonverbal. *Psychological Review*, *92*(3), 350–371.

McNeill, D. (1992). *Hand and mind: What gesture reveals about thought*. Chicago: University of Chicago Press.

McNeill, D., Levy, E., & Pedelty, L. (1990). Speech and gesture. In G. Hammond (Ed.), *Cerebral control of speech and limb movements* (pp. 203–256). North Holland: Elsevier.

Miceli, G., Amitrano, A., Capasso, R., & Caramazza, A. (1996). The treatment of anomia resulting from output lexical damage: Analysis of two cases. *Brain and Language*, *52*, 150–174.

Morrel-Samuels, P., & Krauss, R. (1992). Word familiarity predicts temporal asynchrony of hand gestures and speech. *Journal of Experimental Psychology: Learning, Memory and Cognition*, *18*(2), 615–622.

Nickels, L. (2001). Producing spoken words. In B. Rapp (Ed.), *A handbook of cognitive neuropsychology* (pp. 291–320). New York: Psychology Press.

Nickels, L., & Howard, D. (1995). Aphasic naming: What matters? *Neuropsychologia*, *33*(10), 1281–1303.

Nickels, L., & Howard, D. (1999). Effects of lexical stress on aphasic word production. *Clinical Linguistics and Phonetics*, *13*(4), 269–294.

Pashek, G. (1997). A case study of gesturely cued naming in aphasia: Dominant versus nondominant hand training. *Journal of Communication Disorders*, *30*, 349–366.

Passy, J. (1990). *Cued articulation*. Melbourne: Australian Council of Educational Research.

Pring, T., Hamilton, A., Harwood, A., & Macbride, L. (1993). Generalization of naming after picture/word matching tasks: Only items appearing in therapy benefit. *Aphasiology*, *7*(4), 383–394.

Ramsberger, G., & Helm-Estabrooks, N. (1989). Visual action therapy for bucco-facial apraxia. In T. Prescott (Ed.), *Clinical aphasiology* (Vol. 18, pp. 395–406). Cambridge, MA: College-Hill.

Rao, P. (1994). Use of amer-ind code by persons with aphasia. In R. Chapey (Ed.), *Language intervention strategies in adult aphasia* (3rd Edn., pp. 358–367). Baltimore: Williams & Wilkins.

Rapp, B., & Goldrick, M. (2000). Discreteness and interactivity in spoken word production. *Psychological Review*, *107*(3), 460–499.

Rauscher, F., Krauss, R., & Chen, Y. (1996). Speech and lexical access: The role of lexical movements in speech production. *Psychological Science*, *7*(4), 226–231.

Raven, J.C., Court, J., & Raven, J. (1995). *Coloured progressive matrices*. Oxford: Oxford Psychologists Press.

Raymer, A., & Thompson, C. (1991). Effects of verbal plus gesture treatment in a patient with aphasia and severe apraxia of speech. In T. Prescott (Ed.), *Clinical aphasiology* (Vol. 20, pp. 285–297). Texas: Pro-Ed.

Raymer, A., Thompson, C., Jacobs, B., & LeGrand, H. (1993). Phonological treatments of naming deficits in aphasia: Model-based generalisation analysis. *Aphasiology*, *7*, 27–53.

Rime, B., & Schiaratura, L. (1991). Gesture and speech. In R. Feldman & B. Rime (Eds.), *Fundamentals of nonverbal behaviour* (pp. 239–284). Cambridge: Cambridge University Press.

Robey, R., Schultz, M., Crawford, A., & Sinner, C. (1999). Single-subject clinical-outcome research: Designs, data, effect sizes, and analyses. *Aphasiology*, *13*, 445–473.

Robson, J., Marshall, J., Pring, T., & Chiat, S. (1998). Phonological naming therapy in jargon aphasia: Positive but paradoxical effects. *Journal of the International Neuropsychological Society*, *4*, 675–686.

Rose, M., & Douglas, J. (2001). The differential facilitatory effects of gesture and visualisation processes on object naming in aphasia. *Aphasiology*, *15*(10), 977–990.

Schneider, S., Thompson, C., & Luring, B. (1996). Effects of verbal plus gesture matrix training on sentence production in a patient with primary progressive aphasia. *Aphasiology*, *10*(3), 297–317.

Siegel, S. (1956). *Nonparametric statistics for the behavioral sciences*.Tokyo: McGraw-Hill Book Company.

Skelly, M., Schinsky, L., Smith, R., & Fust, R. (1974). American Indian sign (Amer-Ind) as a facilitator of verbalisation for the oral verbal apraxic. *Journal of Speech and Hearing Disorders*, *34*, 445–455.

Snodgrass, J., & Vanderwart, M. (1980). A standardised set of 260 pictures: Norms for name agreement, image agreement, familiarity, and visual complexity. *Journal of Experimental Psychology: Human Learning and Memory*, *6*, 174–215.

Spencer, C., Doyle, P., McNeil, M., Wambaugh, J., Park, G., & Carrol, B. (2000). Examining the facilitative effects of rhyme in a patient with output lexicon damage. *Aphasiology*, *14*, 567–584.

Thompson, C., Raymer, A., & LeGrand, H. (1991). Effects of phonologically based treatment on aphasic naming deficits: A model driven approach. In T. Prescott (Ed.), *Clinical aphasiology* (Vol. 20, pp. 239–261). Austin, Texas: Pro-Ed.

APPENDIX 1

Stress regularity and error type on 180 low-frequency words

Target	Stress type	Response	Error type
'skeleton	R	'skeles...'skelestən	successive approx
'athlete	R	æ'θʌlit..θæ'θlit..æ'θlet	successive approx
guitar	R	g..gaza..gazi	successive approx
'nozzle	R	'nozʌlen.. 'snozəlz.. 'nozlʌ	successive approx
'secretary	R	'grekɑt. 'grekʌtariʌ'sekredriʌ	successive approx
'dinosaur	R	'daisən.. 'dinæn.. 'dindænɔ	successive approx
'parachute	R	'pærʌ.. 'paramount	successive approx
'handkerchief	R	'hanky.. 'hander	successive approx
'ashtray	R	'sash.. 'ashed	successive approx
'helicopter	R	e'li..he'licopsʌ	successive approx
'artichoke	R	'ælʌtok... 'arti.. 'ai.. 'artru	successive approx
'saddle	R	'pridəl	nonword
asparagus	R	æspagus..æspu..	nonword
'tissue	R	'diʃjus	nonword
'venom	R	fi'næm	nonword
'clarinet	R	'flɔntəst	nonword
'typewriter	R	'night-tiprʌ	nonword
'telescope	R	'θɛmomʌbʌ	nonword
'banjo	R	'mæindolin	nonword
'artist	R	oi'lest	nonword
'statue	R	'bedʌstɔl.. 'pedastal	nonword/semantic
'mixer	R	food..meters	similar word
'seesaw	R	see-sword	similar word
'shaving brush	R	sh..brush	similar word
'screwdriver	R	ɛcrew...traivʌ	similar word
'instrument	R	tambourine	subordinate
'alley	R	lane....kʌl..də..kʌlt	coordinate/nonword
'pyramid	R	cubit thing	coordinate
'burglar	R	bank robber	coordinate
'crucifix	R	cross	coordinate
'bristle	R	brush	coordinate
'transport	R	motor	coordinate
'walrus	R	seal	coordinate
'moccasin	R	shoe	coordinate
'tulip	R	grows in Holland	description
'beater	R	egg white thingy	description
'rocket	R	space thing	description
'flippers	R	f......help you swim	description
'dustpan	R	go with a brush	description
'grasshopper	R	no response	no response
'caterpillar	R	no response	no response
'clipboard	R	no response	no response
'astronaut	R	no response	no response
'carpenter	R	no response	no response
'puzzle	R	no response	no response
'watermelon	R	no response	no response
'pulpit	R	no response	no response
'bison	R	no response	no response
'garlic	R	no response	no response
'planet	R	no response	no response
ma'scara	I	'mæskala.. 'mækaris.. 'mæskari	successive approx

(Continued)

Stress regularity and error type on 180 low-frequency words (Continued)

Target	Stress type	Response	Error type
spee'dometer	I	'speed...'speedo..'spidomenʌ	successive approx
mo'squito	I	'moz..kæt.. 'mozkoti. . 'mozkæti.. 'moskausits. .. 'moskwito	successive approx
sy'ringe	I	'serʌ	nonword
vio'lin	I	'triafa.. 'vaiʌ.. 'vilʌfaun	nonword
balle'rina	I	'bælatin.. 'bælʌlost	nonword
har'monica	I	'maust..nɔg	nonword
ex'haust	I	'funeli..hose thing	nonword/coordinate
mu'sician	I	trumpeter	coordinate
pho'tographer	I	uses a camera	description
refe'ree	I	punching	description
a'ccordion	I	whisker box	other
me'chanic	I	no response	no response
gi'raffe	I	no response	no response
ca'noe	I	no response	no response
cer'tificate	I	no response	no response
prong		poŋ.. spoŋ	successive approx
crutch		k..krʌntʃ..ʌnk..ʌtʃəs	successive approx
vase		vaiz	nonword
bat		baitsbɔl	nonword
flute		lu..flɔnt	nonword
slide		sliniŋ..liniŋ	nonword
globe		klaub	nonword
bunk		punk..bonk	similar word
drill		driller	similar word
deer		ear	similar word
slide		lifts	description
coin		silver money	description
truck		dumper	description
dart		no response	no response
dice		no response	no response
flask		no response	no response

R = regular stress, I = irregular stress.

APPENDIX 2

Word stimuli for phase three, treatment study

Set A: Control	Set B: Verbal	Set C: Gesture	Set D: Verbal + Gesture
cave	pet	curb	film
rung	pier	wick	prong
bunk	flask	vase	spire
coin	crutch	tusk	slip
mortar	stopper	slide	puddle
pattern	ankle	cigar	muffin
bouquet	record	artist	tulip
parade	siren	nozzle	garlic
burglar	banjo	alley	cooler
tissue	buckle	planet	venom
clipboard	airport	pulpit	puzzle
scraper	exhaust	tombstone	transport
shadow	statue	athlete	bristle
artichoke	archery	instrument	crockery
appliance	waterfall	canary	referee
container	mosquito	alphabet	conductor
skeleton	musician	pyramid	receiver
astronaut	carpenter	crucifix	dinosaur
caterpillar	speedometer	aquarium	secretary
asparagus	certificate	photographer	watermelon

Bold phonemes indicate consonantal blends.

APPENDIX 3

Phase three therapy protocols

Verbal condition
1. Ask participant to name the picture. If incorrect go to step 2.
2. Ask participant how many syllables are in the target. If correct go to step 4, if not step 3.
3. Tell participant how many syllables are in the target.
4. Ask participant for the first sound of the first syllable in error. If correct go to step 6, if not step 5.
5. Tell participant first sound of the first syllable in error.
6. Ask participant to say the syllables. If correct go to step 8, if incorrect go to step 7.
7. Ask participant for the first sounds of remaining syllables in error. Go to step 8.
8. Provide participant with syllables written phonetically in incorrect order. Ask participant to arrange correctly and say the word. If correct go to step 10, if incorrect step 9.
9. Provide participant with the correct arrangement of the syllables.
10. Ask participant to name picture. If incorrect stress, go to step 11.
11. Ask participant which syllable should be stressed and provide model if incorrect.
12. Tell participant the name and ask her to copy.

Gesture condition
1. Participant names picture. If incorrect go to step 2.
2. Ask participant to make an iconic gesture of the target. If correct go to step 4, if incorrect go to step 3.
3. Provide model of gesture for participant to copy.
4. Ask participant to make a cued articulation gesture of the first sound of the first syllable in error and then remaining syllables in error. If correct go to step 6, if incorrect go to step 5.
5. Provide models of cued articulation gestures for participant to copy.
6. Ask participant to show the number of syllables in the word on her fingers. If correct go to step 8, if incorrect go to step 7.
7. Simultaneously show the number of syllables on fingers and say number aloud.

8. Ask participant to name the picture.
9. If incorrect stress, ask participant to indicate on her fingers which syllable should be stressed.
10. Tell participant the name and ask her to copy.

Verbal and gesture condition
1. Participant names picture. If incorrect go to step 2.
2. Ask participant to make an iconic gesture of the target. If correct go to step 4, incorrect go to step 3.
3. Provide an iconic gesture model for participant to copy.
4. Ask participant how many syllables are in the target. If correct go to step 6, if incorrect step 5.
5. Tell participant the number of syllables.
6. Ask participant to make a cued articulation gesture of first sound of the first and remaining syllables in error. If correct go to step 8.
7. Provide the cued articulation gestures of the first phonemes of the syllables in error for participant to copy.
8. Ask participant to say the syllables of the target. If correct go to step 10, if incorrect step 9.
9. Provide the participant with the written syllables in the incorrect order for her to rearrange.
10. Ask participant to name the picture.
11. If incorrect stress ask participant to indicate on her fingers and by moving the printed syllable, which syllable should be stressed.
12. Tell participant the name and ask her to copy.

Order of gesture and verbal steps in the combined condition are rotated on every alternate item.

APPENDIX 4

Questions used to elicit conversation pre-treatment, post-treatment, and at 3-month follow-up

What have you been doing today?
Can you tell me about your stroke?
What sort of work have you done in your life?
Can you tell me about your family?

APHASIOLOGY, 2002, *16* (10/11), 1031–1045

Response to contrasting verb retrieval treatments: A case study

Anastasia M. Raymer

Old Dominion University, Norfolk, VA, and
VA RR&D Brain Rehabilitation Research Center, Gainesville, FL, USA

Tina A. Ellsworth

Old Dominion University, Norfolk, VA, USA

Verb retrieval treatments for individuals with aphasia that have led to greater improvements in sentence production typically have incorporated semantic as compared to repetition treatments. However, studies have not contrasted treatments within subjects to compare treatment effectiveness. We compared effects of sequential verb retrieval treatments in one participant and analysed effects on sentence production. We tested one woman, WR, with nonfluent aphasia and mild verb retrieval impairment related to semantic dysfunction. She participated in three phases of verb retrieval treatment, semantic, phonologic, and rehearsal, in a multiple baseline crossover design. We examined accuracy of picture naming and sentence production for trained and untrained verbs. All treatments resulted in significantly improved naming of trained verbs, some generalised sentence production, and no improvement for untrained verbs. No difference was evident in effects across treatments. Unlike earlier studies, the repetition and phonologic treatments were as effective as semantic treatment for improving sentence production. These positive findings for all three treatments may relate to semantic activation that occurs whenever a word is retrieved in the context of picture presentation, thereby fundamentally altering semantic activation patterns and making the word more easily accessible in subsequent retrieval attempts, whether in isolation or in sentences.

Impairments of word retrieval, as often assessed using confrontation picture-naming tasks, are pervasive among individuals with aphasia (Goodglass & Kaplan, 1983). Whereas the majority of studies of word retrieval disturbances have concentrated on noun retrieval, many recent investigations have examined impairments affecting verb retrieval as well. Although many individuals are impaired in retrieval of both nouns and verbs, greater difficulties with verbs have been reported particularly (though not exclusively) in individuals with nonfluent aphasia and in association with lesions of the left frontal operculum (Caramazza & Hillis, 1991; Damasio & Tranel, 1993; Miceli, Silveri, Villa, & Caramazza, 1984; Zingeser & Berndt, 1990). Verb retrieval is influenced by factors such

Address correspondence to: Anastasia M. Raymer, Child Study Center, Old Dominion University, 45th St & Hampton Blvd, Norfolk, VA 23529-0136, USA. Email: sraymer@odu.edu

We are grateful to WR for her participation in this study and to Rita Berndt for sharing the noun–verb battery stimuli. This research was supported by a grant from the American Speech-Language-Hearing Foundation and a programme project grant from the NIH (NIDCD) (P50 DC03888-01A1). An earlier version of the paper was presented at the 1998 annual meeting of the American Speech-Language-Hearing Association.

http://www.tandf.co.uk/journals/pp/02687038.html   DOI:10.1080/026870401430000609

as familiarity (Kemmerer & Tranel, 2000), semantic complexity (Breedin, Saffran, & Schwartz, 1998), and argument structure complexity (Kim & Thompson, 2000; Thompson, Lange, Schneider, & Shapiro, 1997). In some individuals, it is the verb retrieval failure that may undermine the whole process of sentence formulation leading to nonfluent verbal output (Berndt, Mitchum, Haendiges, & Sandson, 1997, Mitchum & Berndt, 2001).

As investigations of word retrieval impairments have moved their focus from nouns to verbs, so too have investigations of word retrieval treatments. Some recent treatment investigations have been influenced by cognitive neuropsychological models that recognise that word retrieval, whether considered in lexical or sentence production models, involves a complex series of processes and representations. Although models vary in their details (Hillis, 2001; Nickels, 2001), researchers generally acknowledge that retrieval of familiar words requires, at a minimum, semantic and phonologic lexical mechanisms whereby word meanings and corresponding spoken forms are activated for familiar words. Some word retrieval treatment studies, developed with neuropsychological models as a theoretical backdrop, have incorporated methods that integrate either semantic or phonologic aspects of processing in an attempt to improve word retrieval abilities. Whereas most earlier treatment studies investigated effects for noun retrieval impairments (see Raymer & Rothi, 2000, 2001, for recent reviews), a number of recent studies have examined lexical treatments for verb retrieval impairments as well.

Word repetition and oral reading presumably activate the same phonologic representations accessed in the process of word retrieval during picture naming. Therefore, some researchers have used practice with repetition (Mitchum & Berndt, 1994; Reichmann-Novak & Rochon, 1997) and oral reading (Hillis, 1989) with some success to improve verb retrieval in picture naming. Little change in sentence production was reported in relation to improved verb retrieval abilities in these studies. Other researchers have trained verb naming by using tasks that exploit semantic processing. Word–picture matching or yes–no verification, which require activation of semantic information for correct performance, were paired with repetition or oral reading to improve verb retrieval abilities in some individuals with aphasia (Fink, Schwartz, Sobel, & Myers, 1997; Marshall, 1999; Marshall, Pring, & Chiat, 1998). Marshall and colleagues (1998) noted that their subject improved not only in verb naming, but also in the use of grammatical sentences incorporating trained verbs. Mitchum and Berndt (2001) suggested that improved sentence production may occur if verb treatment tasks engage information pertinent to the verb argument structure implicated in sentence production, as may occur in semantic treatments in which verbs are retrieved in relation to noun information.

Because word retrieval failure can stem from either phonologic or semantic stages of lexical processing, it is of interest to examine whether treatments that target purported stages of lexical dysfunction have greater influence on word retrieval recovery. However, Hillis (1993) noted that in her series of studies of noun retrieval treatments across subjects there was no clear one-to-one relationship between type of impairment and treatment effectiveness. Another means to address this issue is to contrast different treatments within the same subjects.

The direct comparison of semantic and phonologic treatment has been reported for studies of noun retrieval. Howard, Patterson, Franklin, Orchard-Lisle, and Morton (1985) reported greater improvement for noun retrieval in their group of individuals with aphasia following semantic treatment (matching and verification tasks about target pictures) than phonological treatment (making judgements about phonologic aspects of target words).

In a series of four single-subject investigations contrasting semantic and phonologic treatments modeled after the Howard et al. study, Ennis (1999) reported no consistent relationship between type of noun retrieval impairment and most effective treatment across subjects. Of three subjects with primarily phonologic stage word retrieval impairments, one improved more for phonologic than semantic treatment, and two improved as much for phonologic as for semantic treatment. A fourth subject with semantically based word retrieval impairment showed no improvement with either semantic or phonologic treatment.

Fink, Martin, Schwartz, Saffran, and Myers (1992) contrasted two treatments for verb retrieval impairment in one subject. However, both treatment procedures emphasised phonologic aspects of verb retrieval. The contrasting effects of semantic versus phonologic treatment for verb retrieval impairment have not been examined in the same individuals. This question is of considerable interest because semantic treatment, in which information relevant to the verb argument structure may be activated (Mitchum & Berndt, 2001), may have greater consequences for sentence production abilities than phonologic treatment, in which the sound structure of words is emphasised. The purpose of the current study was to examine the verb retrieval impairment in our subject, WR, who had a nonfluent form of aphasia. We report a single-subject investigation of the effects of contrasting verb retrieval treatments on WR's picture-naming and sentence-production abilities.

BACKGROUND INFORMATION

Subject

WR was a 54-year-old right-handed woman with a seventh-grade education (discontinued schooling at 13 years of age) who worked as a hairdresser. She suffered a left hemisphere cerebrovascular accident (CVA) that resulted in a right hemiparesis and nonfluent aphasia. A CT scan performed at the time of the CVA revealed a left dorsolateral frontal lesion encompassing a portion of Broca's area, the anterior insular region, and some subcortical white matter. In standardised aphasia testing with the Western Aphasia Battery (WAB) (Kertesz, 1982) 3 months post stroke, WR demonstrated transcortical motor aphasia, as her repetition abilities were noticeably better than her nonfluent spontaneous verbal output (Table 1). As has been reported in some individuals with transcortical motor aphasia, WR had relatively better performance in naming subtests than in fluency subtests. In the WAB picture description, WR labelled 15 noun elements

TABLE 1
Results of WR's standardised aphasia testing

	Pre-testing	Post-treatment follow-up
Western Aphasia Battery		
Aphasia Quotient	80.0/100	81.2/100
Information Content	8/10	8/10
Fluency	5/10	5/10
Comprehension	9.6/10	10/10
Repetition	9.1/10	9.5/10
Naming	8.3/10	8.6/10
Boston Naming Test	44/60	–
Action Naming Test	37/62	48/62

and, with repeated reminders to tell a story about the picture, produced four simple active progressive verb+ing sentences. Results of the Boston Naming Test (Kaplan, Goodglass, & Weintraub, 1983) indicated that picture naming for nouns was minimally affected for her level of education (44/60 correct), whereas picture naming for verbs on the Action Naming Test (Obler & Albert, 1986) was somewhat reduced (37/62 correct). On the Battery of Adult Reading Function (Rothi, Coslett, & Heilman, 1984), WR experienced difficulty in reading aloud regular words (18/30 correct), exception words (18/30 words correct), and especially nonwords (1/30 correct). All verbal responses were intelligible with only mild evidence of apraxia of speech.

Experimental testing

WRs most notable language problem was nonfluent sentence production. However, we initiated her experimental testing with a focus on verb retrieval difficulties, which potentially played a role in her nonfluent production. To evaluate word retrieval abilities further, WR was administered a noun/verb battery developed using stimuli provided by Zingeser and Berndt (1990). Their list includes 30 verbs and two sets of 30 nouns matched to the cumulative and base frequencies, respectively, of the verb set. The battery included four lexical tasks, the first two developed by Zingeser and Berndt, and the latter two devised by Williamson, Raymer, Adair, and Heilman (1995). Tasks were administered in counterbalanced blocks across sessions.

(1)   Picture naming: WR viewed each of the 90 black and white line drawings of the noun and verb stimuli and provided a one word label for the object or action depicted in each picture.

(2)   Sentence completion: The examiner read aloud a phrase as WR also read along. She then completed each of the 90 sentences with an appropriate noun or verb.

(3)   Crossmodal picture-to-word matching: WR pointed to one of three words that corresponded to the target picture (e.g., write). In the related condition, both distractor words were semantic coordinates of the 90 targets (e.g., read, draw), and in the unrelated condition, both distractor words were unrelated to the 90 targets (e.g., ask, take).

(4)   Picture–picture associate matching: WR pointed to one of two pictures that was most closely related to a target picture (e.g., baking a pie). The distractor pictures were semantic coordinates of the 90 correct pictures in one condition (e.g., correct—grilling a steak; distractor—peeling a potato) and were unrelated in a second condition (e.g., correct—peeling a potato; distractor—leaking water). For half of the picture associate pairs, in the unrelated condition, the distractor picture from the related condition became the correct answer when a completely unrelated foil picture replaced the other associate picture.

WR's performance on the noun/verb battery was compared to the performance of 12 normative subjects, similar in age and education, who were examined with the same battery. A score that was greater than two standard deviations below the normative mean score was considered impaired.

WR's results on the noun/verb battery are displayed in Table 2. In the picture naming and sentence completion tasks, WR had a mild impairment compared to normal levels for both nouns and verbs. Although performance in the two naming tasks was poorer for verbs than for nouns, this difference was not significant ($\chi^2 = 2.88$, n.s.). The 14 errors in

TABLE 2
Florida Noun/Verb Battery

	Nouns		Verbs	
	WR	Normative	WR	Normative
		Mean/SD		Mean/SD
Oral Picture Naming	52/60*	58.4 ± 0.88	22/30*	28.58 ± 1.31
Sentence Completion	52/60*	57.2 ± 1.41	24/30	29.5 ± 0.80
Picture–Picture Associate Match				
Related	45/60*	50.7 ± 1.65	21/30*	25.0 ± 1.35
Unrelated	57/60*	59.3 ± 0.49	29/30	29.8 ± 0.62
Crossmodal Picture–Word Match				
Related	56/60*	59.3 ± 0.63	28/30*	30.0
Unrelated	60/60	60	30/30	30.0

Number of items correct for WR and group of normative subjects (mean and standard deviation) on the Florida Noun/Verb Battery, a set of lexical tasks for noun and verb comprehension and retrieval.

*Denotes greater than 2 standard deviations below normal mean scores.

verb naming for pictures and sentence completion included 8 semantically related verbs, 4 semantically related nouns, 1 neologism, and 1 no-response. The 16 errors in noun naming for pictures and sentence completion included 12 semantically related nouns, 3 no-responses, and 1 phonemic paraphasia.

To determine whether the basis for WR's naming impairment related to semantic or phonologic aspects of lexical processing, performance was examined for the two matching tasks which rely on semantic processing for correct responses. Impairment on the matching tasks would suggest that semantic dysfunction contributed to her word retrieval difficulties. WR's performance in crossmodal matching and picture associate matching for both nouns and verbs was slightly below levels observed with the normative subjects in the related condition in which semantic processing is particularly stressed. There was no difference between nouns and verbs in the matching tasks.

These findings of mildly impaired performance in all naming and comprehension tasks suggest that a semantic dysfunction undermined WR's lexical processing abilities for both nouns and verbs. Because her verb impairment may have contributed to her significantly nonfluent verbal output, we undertook this verb retrieval treatment investigation with WR's consent. Our intention was to examine the effects of verb naming treatment for sentence production abilities.

TREATMENT EXPERIMENT DESIGN

Probe tasks and stimuli

Verb picture naming: WR named 222 black and white line drawings of various actions that had been piloted with 10 people who had no history of neurologic illness. A correct response in verb picture naming was the target verb, a synonym verb, or a simple phonemic error for the target verb. Because WR occasionally produced nominalisation errors (e.g., "matrimony" for marrying), we coded as errors any response in which the verb/noun distinction was ambiguous (e.g., "screw" for screwing). We reminded her across test sessions to tell us "what was happening" or "what the person is doing" to encourage her to respond with the progressive "ing" form of the verb, to help us disambiguate her noun and verb responses.

Analysis of errors in two baseline administrations of the 222 pictures indicated that WR made 44–45% errors in verb naming. Of her 194 errors, 50.5% (98) were related nouns (e.g., "oven" for cook; "party" for celebrate), 22.7% (44) were related verbs (e.g., "swimming" for floating; "erase" for polishing), 8.8% (17) were nominalisations ("a guard" for guarding; "eraser" for erasing), 3.1% (6) were ambiguous ("screw" for screwing), 9.8% (19) were no-responses, and 5.2% (10) were others such as unrelated words (e.g., "warrior" for tying) or related phrases (e.g., "How do you do?" for greeting).

On the basis of WR's baseline performance, we selected as experimental stimuli 60 verbs that WR had consistent difficulty in naming across two baseline administrations: 20 in the phonologic treatment set, 20 in the semantic treatment set, and 20 in the control set that later became the rehearsal treatment set. WR named these 60 verbs in a third baseline administration. We added 10 new control verbs later in the experiment when WR initiated rehearsal treatment. Our primary means of matching treatment sets was on the basis of WR's level of baseline naming performance (below 20% accuracy across sets). Post hoc analyses indicated that mean cumulative verb frequencies (Francis & Kucera, 1982) in the phonologic and semantic sets (142.2 and 180.1, respectively) were considerably higher than the frequencies in the rehearsal training and control sets (38.5 and 6.4, respectively). Argument structure complexities of the training verbs, which potentially could influence verb retrieval and sentence production, were comparable across sets (Table 3).

Sentence production: To assess generalisation of verb naming treatment to a task representing changes in her verbal nonfluency, we observed WR's performance for sentence production for the same sets of 60 verb pictures used in naming training. To be coded as correct, WR had to produce any sentence that included an appropriate verb embedded in a grammatically and semantically correct context for the given picture. Among the responses coded as errors in baseline sentence production were failures to include an appropriate verb in a sentence response (e.g., guarding: "It's a guard and he's *taking care* of the castle"; writing: "She is *getting up* her lessons"), absence of a required argument (e.g., picking: "Picking apples"; decorating: "Decorating a cake"), or labelling objects in the picture (gossiping: "A secret"; marrying: "He is matrimony"; celebrating: "It's a party").

Oral word reading: To control for effects of spontaneous recovery and repeated measures, we included a probe oral word reading task that we anticipated would not improve with our verb treatment, but that was related to the process of word retrieval. We identified 20 abstract nouns that WR was consistently unable to read aloud

TABLE 3
Argument structure complexity of training verbs

	Semantic n = 20	Phonologic n = 20	Rehearsal n = 20	Control n = 10
3 place obligatory	1	–	–	–
2 place obligatory	8	12	10	6
2 place optional	10	8	7	4
1 place (intransitive)	1	–	3	–

correctly in baseline administrations. A word was coded as correct if the target was pronounced exactly as written. Errors in word reading during baseline sessions were mostly visually similar words (e.g., "exit" for edit; "tractor" for tragic) and occasional no-responses.

Reliability

Inter-rater reliability of scoring on the probe measures was completed for 30% of experimental sessions. The examiners surpassed 90% agreement across the experimental tasks over the course of the experiment.

Treatment design

The treatment protocol consisted of a single-subject crossover treatment design with multiple baselines across behaviours (McReynolds & Kearns, 1983). During the baseline phase, the probe tasks were administered for three consecutive sessions to verify the presence of stable baselines. During treatment phases, each session was initiated with daily probe tasks to assess acquisition for the trained verb naming set, generalised sentence production for trained verbs, generalised verb naming and sentence production for untrained verbs, and maintenance of performance in the control oral reading task. In each daily probe, WR named all 20 training verbs and provided responses for half of the untrained naming, sentence production, and oral reading stimuli such that every two sessions she responded to all untrained stimuli and tasks.

Following daily probe measures, WR participated in a treatment for one set of verb picture stimuli. The treatment phase ended when she reached the criterion of 90% correct in two sessions for the trained set, or until she completed a maximum of 10 treatment sessions. WR participated in two to three 1-hour sessions per week over the course of 4 months with a 6-week holiday break between treatment phases 2 and 3.

The verb retrieval treatments were patterned after treatments reported in noun retrieval treatment studies (e.g., Ennis, 1999; Howard et al., 1985). In treatment phase 1, WR received a phonologic treatment for one set of verbs. Following a 1-week break, WR initiated treatment phase 2 in which she underwent semantic treatment for a second set of verbs. In both the phonologic and semantic treatment protocols, the examiner presented a picture for WR to name aloud. The examiner then gave feedback as to response accuracy and proceeded directly into a series of two yes/no questions sequenced to help WR develop a word retrieval strategy consistent with the typical word retrieval process. The questions were counterbalanced across sessions such that 50% of the answers were "yes" and 50% of the answers were "no". In phonologic treatment, the two questions encouraged WR to develop information about the *sound* of the target word (e.g., pay). (1) Initial phoneme question: Does "pay" start with "p"? (2) Rhyming word question: Does "pay" sound like "way"? In semantic treatment, the two questions helped her to develop information about the *meaning* of the target word (e.g., bake). (1) Coordinate verb question: Is this similar to "grilling"? (2) Associated noun question: Does this have to do with pie? After the questions, the treatment protocol ended with a rehearsal phase in which WR repeated the word three times, rehearsed silently, reattempted naming, and then repeated the word again three times.

Following phonologic and semantic treatment phases, we were concerned that changes observed may have related largely to the common rehearsal phase included in the final steps of each treatment protocol, and less to the questions that were part of the treatment protocol. Therefore, after a 6-week holiday break, we added a third rehearsal treatment phase in which we evaluated WR's improvements for the set of control verbs using only the four rehearsal steps of treatment. No questions were included. At this point we added a new set of untrained control verbs for naming.

TREATMENT RESULTS

Verb picture naming

Figure 1 depicts WR's naming performance for verb picture sets. Performance was low and stable during baseline observations (5–20% correct). When phonologic treatment was applied to the phonologic set, verb naming performance rose from an average of 8.33% correct in three baseline sessions to a 90% correct criterion level after six treatment sessions. The improvement from the final baseline performance (15%) to the final phonologic treatment probe (95%) was significant (McNemar's test: $\chi^2 = 14.06$, $p < .001$). In contrast, naming of the untrained semantic and rehearsal verb sets remained at baseline levels, never surpassing 25% correct during phonologic training.

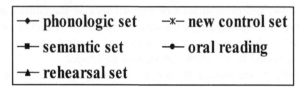

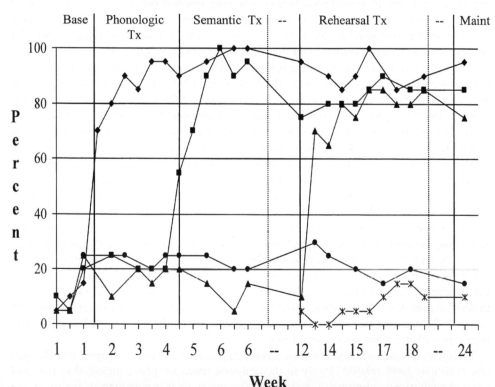

Figure 1. WR's accuracy for verb naming and control oral reading tasks.

WR subsequently received the semantic treatment for the second verb picture set. She again demonstrated swift improvement in verb naming accuracy from an average 17.5% correct across the extended untrained baseline sessions to a 100% criterion level after four treatment sessions. Again there was significant improvement when comparing the final baseline probe (20%) to the final treatment probe (95%) (McNemar's test: χ^2 = 13.07, $p < .001$). Performance for the untrained rehearsal set remained at baseline levels of less than 20% correct during semantic training.

Finally, we instituted a new set of control stimuli and applied the rehearsal treatment to the third verb picture set which had averaged 12.2% correct across prior extended baseline phases of the experiment. WR never reached criterion with rehearsal training over the course of 10 sessions, reaching a maximum of 85% naming accuracy. This was a significant improvement compared to the final baseline probe (15%) (McNemar's test: χ^2 = 16.13, $p < .025$). Performance for the new control picture naming set never surpassed 15% correct during rehearsal training.

In a final maintenance probe 1 month following completion of the experiment, WR demonstrated accurate verb naming for 95% of the phonologic training pictures, 85% of the semantic training pictures, 75% of the rehearsal training pictures, and only 15% of the control untrained pictures. That is, accuracy for all three trained sets was maintained significantly greater than baseline naming levels (McNemar's test: phonologic set, χ^2 = 14.07, $p < .001$; semantic set, χ^2 = 7.69, $p < .01$; rehearsal set, χ^2 = 4.90, $p < .05$).

A number of metrics can be implemented to compare the effectiveness of the three different treatments for verb naming. In the number of sessions to meet criterion, semantic treatment (4 training sessions) and phonologic treatment (6 training sessions) both surpassed results of rehearsal treatment which was terminated after 10 training sessions and criterion was not met. To compare the naming response accuracy noted in the three treatment protocols, we analysed results with respect to the number of correct responses attained in the final training probe in each respective treatment phase (phonologic training set: 19/20; semantic training set: 19/20; rehearsal training set: 17/20). There was no difference across treatments in the naming results for trained verbs (χ^2 = 1.72, df = 2, n.s.). In a follow-up maintenance probe, we compared accuracy of naming responses for the three sets of training verbs (phonologic: 19/20; semantic 17/20; rehearsal 15/20) and again found no significant difference among treatments in comparisons of naming response accuracy (χ^2 = 3.14, df = 2, n.s.).

Sentence production

Figure 2 depicts WR's performance in sentence production for the three verb sets. Following a low baseline performance, WR demonstrated significant improvements in production of grammatically and semantically correct sentences incorporating target verbs as treatment was applied, first for the phonologic verb picture set (final probe 75% correct) (McNemar's test: χ^2 = 8.10, $p < .01$), then for the semantic verb picture set (final probe 70% correct) (McNemar's test: χ^2 = 4.17, $p < .05$), and then for the rehearsal verb picture set (final probe 55% correct) (McNemar's test: χ^2 = 6.13, $p < .05$). Most correctly formed sentences included present progressive forms of the trained verbs. As treatment progressed in each phase, errors in sentence production stemmed less from verb retrieval failures than from mis-selecting or omitting noun/pronoun arguments depicted in the given picture (e.g., "He is polishing the *furniture*." [silver is depicted]; "*He* [she] is decorating a cake."; "Paddling the boat."). At the maintenance probe 1 month following

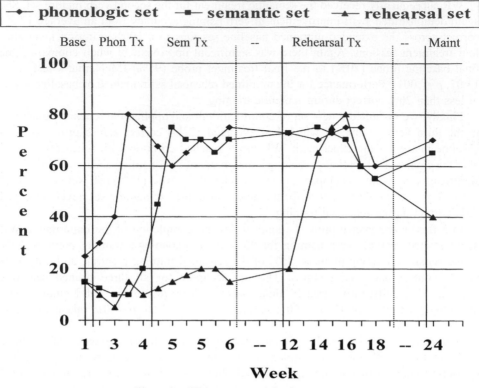

Figure 2. WR's sentence production accuracy.

completion of training, WR's sentence production was accurate for 70% of phonologic training pictures, 65% of semantic training pictures, and only 40% of rehearsal training pictures. These levels of sentence production accuracy were maintained significantly above baseline levels for phonologic and semantic treatment sets (McNemar's test: phonologic set, $\chi^2 = 4.05$, $p < .05$; semantic set, $\chi^2 = 4.17$, $p < .05$; rehearsal set, $\chi^2 = 3.20$, n.s.).

To compare the sentence production accuracy across the three treatment protocols, we analysed results with respect to the numbers of correct sentences attained in the final probe of each treatment phase (phonologic training set: 15/20; semantic training set: 15/20; rehearsal training set: 11/20). Although results for verbs trained with phonologic and semantic treatment were greater than for verbs trained in rehearsal treatment, these differences were not significant ($\chi^2 = 2.47$, df = 2, n.s.). In a follow-up maintenance probe, there was no significant difference among treatments in sentence production accuracy (phonologic: 14/20; semantic 13/20; rehearsal 8/20), although performance for semantic and phonologic verbs was greater than for rehearsal training verbs ($\chi^2 = 2.66$, df = 2, n.s.).

Oral reading

Performance for the control oral reading task is displayed in Figure 1. WR demonstrated low levels of oral word reading performance, ranging 15 to 30% accuracy across all phases of the experiment. No changes were evident from initial baseline to final probe measures (McNemar's test: $\chi^2 = 1.33$, n.s.).

Follow-up standardised testing

Results of standardized testing administered at the completion of the treatment experiment are displayed in Table 1. On the Western Aphasia Battery, increases were evident in naming, repetition, and comprehension subtests. WR also demonstrated significantly improved naming performance on the Action Naming Test from pre-treatment to post-treatment ((McNemar's test: $\chi^2 = 5.50$, $p < .02$). Of the four verb training stimuli that also appear on the ANT, WR correctly named three of four verbs on both test administrations. In contrast to the pretest WAB picture description in which WR labelled most items and failed to provide complete sentences, in post-testing she labeled three items and used six present progressive sentences to describe actions depicted in the picture. One of those sentences included a verb (sailing) that was among the training stimuli. Overall at the completion of the experiment, WR's verbal production in spontaneous conversation and picture description measures remained largely nonfluent, grammatically simplified, and limited to less than 30 words per minute.

DISCUSSION

Following a left hemisphere stroke, WR developed a nonfluent aphasia and mild word retrieval difficulties, including for the category of verbs. Because our experimental testing indicated that mild difficulties were evident in both retrieval and comprehension of verbs, we proposed that her verb impairment arose at a semantic stage in lexical processing. We considered the possibility that verb retrieval difficulty potentially contributed to her sentence production impairment and we instituted verb naming treatment to address this possibility. Subsequent to three distinct treatments for her verb naming impairment, WR demonstrated significant increases in naming performance. As naming performance improved for each trained verb set, WR also improved in her production of grammatically correct sentences using the trained verbs. These findings warrant discussion along a number of avenues: extraneous factors influencing treatment findings, a comparison of treatment effectiveness, the implications of naming training for sentence production, and the relationship of treatment effectiveness to type of lexical impairment.

Effects of extraneous factors

Prior to providing interpretations of the treatment results demonstrated in this study, it would be prudent to consider whether other extraneous factors such as spontaneous recovery or repeated exposure to the experimental stimuli contributed to WR's verb naming and sentence production improvements. These possibilities are less likely for a number of reasons. If spontaneous recovery or repeated exposure led to improvements in verb naming and sentence production abilities, it is likely that we would also have observed unexpected improvements in her control oral word reading task. However, WR demonstrated no improvement in oral reading despite repeated attempts to read those words over the three treatment phases. Also, it was evident in each phase of the study that improvements for verb naming occurred only when treatment was applied for that training verb set. Oral word reading and verb naming sets in extended baseline did not benefit from the treatment and did not seem to be affected by confounding effects of spontaneous recovery or repeated exposure. Therefore WR's treatment effects for naming and sentence production appear to be related largely to participation in the treatments.

Contrasting treatment effects

We trained verb naming using three distinct treatment protocols that we termed phonologic, semantic, and rehearsal training. All three treatments, applied sequentially, led to significant improvements in verb naming and sentence production with trained verbs and no generalisation to untrained verbs. The question remains whether one treatment protocol was ultimately more effective than the others. WR's verb naming performance for the phonologic and semantic treatments quickly reached criterion levels in four to six sessions, as compared to rehearsal treatments, which did not reach criterion after ten treatment sessions. A second measure of treatment effectiveness, the level of performance attained in the final session of each treatment phase, indicated that phonologic and semantic treatments were not significantly more effective than rehearsal treatment for improving verb naming and sentence production. A final comparison among treatments focused on the level of performance maintained at the end of the experimental phases. These results indicated that WR maintained levels of performance significantly above baseline levels in verb naming for all three types of treatment, and in sentence production for only the semantic and phonologic treatment. Therefore, there is minimal evidence of differences among the three treatments, as all three treatments led to significant gains in naming and sentence production abilities.

A confounding issue that may have influenced the comparison among the three treatments is order of treatment administration. Phonologic treatment, which was administered first, may have been effective because WR's recovery potential early in the experiment surpassed her potential in later phases of recovery when she received semantic and rehearsal treatments. If rehearsal treatment had occurred first, for example, perhaps greater and swifter improvement would have been noted for those verbs. This possibility cannot be ruled out until the contrasting treatments are replicated in counterbalanced orders in other similar participants with aphasia.

Another factor that may have influenced results across the three treatments relates to the psycholinguistic characteristics of the different sets of verbs used across treatment phases. The experimental verb sets were equated as to baseline level of difficulty for WR at the onset of the experiment. However, the word frequencies of verbs used in semantic and phonologic treatment were notably higher than those of the rehearsal treatment verbs. Although word frequency reportedly has less influence on verb retrieval than other lexical factors (Kemmerer & Tranel, 2000), it is possible that those less frequent verbs are used infrequently in daily life conversations and may account for some of the decline in WR's performance for the rehearsal verbs in the maintenance phase of the study. A more potent factor on verb retrieval is grammatical argument structure complexity (Kim & Thompson, 2000; Thompson et al., 1997), which was more closely balanced among the stimulus sets. Each set had similar number of obligatory and optional 2-place verbs, and only one 3-place verb (give) was included in the experimental stimuli. Effects of these and other lexical factors cannot be entirely ruled out in shaping the outcomes of the three different treatment protocols. Despite any lexical factors that may have impeded treatment effects, WR improved her verb naming and sentence production abilities for all sets of verbs.

Naming treatment and sentence production

To assess whether improvements in verb retrieval had any consequences for verbal fluency, we observed performance in sentence production for the verbs incorporated in the treatments. As WR improved her verb naming abilities in three different treatment protocols, she also improved her production of correct, grammatical sentences. Sentence production never reached criterion levels in any treatment. Although WR increased her retrieval of the target verbs in her sentence attempts, she continued to make errors related to the arguments and grammatical elements surrounding the correctly retrieved verbs.

Mitchum and Berndt (2001) reviewed studies reporting the effects of verb retrieval treatments on sentence production abilities and noted that verb retrieval treatments involving repeated practice, somewhat like WR's rehearsal treatment, often have not led to improved sentence production abilities. They proposed that these types of treatments neglect the semantic and thematic characteristics of the verbs that are more fully addressed in semantic treatments that involve verb generation in relation to noun information. WR's results for rehearsal training are contrary to expectations from this proposal as she improved sentence production not only for semantic treatment, but also for phonologic and rehearsal treatments, unlike other patients undergoing similar treatments.

Although WR reached criterion levels in verb naming, she did not reach criterion in sentence production across treatment sets. To rectify this observation we may propose that WR had multiple impairments underlying her failure to produce fluent, grammatical sentences. Only one of these impairments related to failure to retrieve the verb. As the verb retrieval impairment was addressed, sentence production abilities improved, but only to a point. Once the verb was retrieved, other impairments became evident as she attempted to construct the full sentence and failed to include all of the appropriate arguments and grammatical constituents necessary for a variety of well-formed sentences. These impairments would need to be targeted with alternative types of sentence production treatments such as mapping therapy or direct training of sentence forms (see Mitchum & Berndt, 2001).

As has been reported in a number of earlier studies, verb naming impairments are amenable to naming treatments that incorporate phonologic and semantic distinctions. What distinguishes the current study is its direct comparison of phonologic, semantic, and rehearsal treatments for verb naming in the same individual. In this case, WR, who had a verb naming impairment that presumably related to semantic dysfunction, benefited from all treatments. Therefore, there was no clear correspondence between the type of verb retrieval impairment, presumably semantic, and type of treatment that was effective— semantic, phonologic, and rehearsal.

How were treatments exerting their effects?

It is premature to make any strong claims on the basis of the findings of this single participant until the results are replicated. However, we might provide some speculations as to why all three treatments had positive effects on WR's verb retrieval and sentence production abilities. First, WR was somewhat unique among individuals with nonfluent aphasia as she had only minimal difficulty with motor speech programming. Therefore she did not have post-lexical impairments to impede her verb retrieval abilities in any of the treatments and was able to reach her potential in lexical treatment. But more to the point as to why WR's semantically based verb naming dysfunction improved with all three treatments is a consideration of the lexical processes incited during the course of each treatment protocol. When one sees a picture to name, activation will cascade through the lexical system engaging visual, semantic, and phonologic information relevant to the picture (Nickels, 2001). When WR simply practised repeating the name of the picture (rehearsal training) or answered questions about the sound structure of the target words (phonologic training), we were expecting to target primarily phonologic aspects of lexical processing. We anticipated that those treatments would not be as effective in influencing her semantically based verb impairment. However, because she practised producing verb names in the context of a picture, it is likely that semantic processing was indeed also activated. Because WR had a rather mild semantic dysfunction underlying her verb retrieval impairment, perhaps the levels of semantic activation resulting from rehearsal, phonologic, and semantic treatments were all sufficient to change semantic activation levels for the trained words. These semantic changes were adequate to improve the potential for accurate verb retrieval in future attempts, whether in naming or in sentence production.

The presence of the picture stimulus during each treatment protocol may be a key factor that influenced WR's treatment outcomes (Nickels & Best, 1996). Earlier studies reporting that certain phonologic treatments were less effective than other semantic or phonologic treatments sometimes involved treatment tasks (word repetition, oral word reading, rhyme judgements) that were performed with the target pictures absent (e.g., Howard et al., 1985; Miceli, Amitrano, Capasso, & Caramazza, 1996). For example, Fink and colleagues (1992) found verb retrieval abilities improved more for direct verb training practice in the context of a verb picture than for verb priming practice involving repetition of sentences containing training verbs in the absence of a picture. That is, without the picture present, the opportunity for semantic activation during training was fairly limited and effects on subsequent naming assessments were also less evident. The presence of the picture during word retrieval training activities appears to be an important step in optimising phonologic treatment effects.

Summary

The results of this investigation of treatment for verb naming impairment in one subject indicated that phonologic, semantic, and rehearsal treatments induced significant improvements in verb naming abilities. These improvements were also manifested in increased ability to use sentences incorporating the verb names. No clear differences in treatment effectiveness were evident across the three treatment protocols. Although these findings await systematic replication in additional subjects, it appears that different semantic, phonologic, and rehearsal treatments can be equally effective in improving verb naming abilities in some individuals as long as training takes place in the context of pictured targets.

REFERENCES

Berndt, R.S., Mitchum, C.C., Haendiges, A.N., & Sandson, J. (1997). Verb retrieval in aphasia. 1. Characterizing single word impairments. *Brain and Language, 56,* 68–106.

Breedin, S.D., Saffran, E.M., & Schwartz, M.F. (1998). Semantic factors in verb retrieval: An effect of complexity. *Brain and Language, 63,* 1–31.

Caramazza, A., & Hillis, A.E. (1991). Lexical organization of nouns and verbs in the brain. *Nature, 349,* 788–790.

Damasio, A.R., & Tranel, D. (1993). Nouns and verbs are retrieved with differently distributed neural systems. *Proceedings of the National Academy of Sciences, 90,* 4957–4960.

Ennis, M.R. (1999). *Semantic versus phonological aphasia treatments for anomia: A within-subject experimental design.* Unpublished doctoral dissertation, University of Florida.

Fink, R.B., Martin, N., Schwartz, M.F., Saffran, E.M., & Myers, J.L. (1992). Facilitation of verb retrieval skills in aphasia: A comparison of two approaches. In M.L. Lemme (Ed.), *Clinical aphasiology, Vol. 21* (pp. 263–275). Austin, TX: Pro-Ed.

Fink, R.B., Schwartz, M.F., Sobel, P.R., & Myers, J.L. (1997). Effects of multilevel training on verb retrieval: Is more always better? *Brain and Language, 60,* 41–44.

Francis, W.N., & Kucera, H. (1982). *Frequency analysis of English usage: Lexicon and grammar*. Boston: Houghton Mifflin.

Goodglass, H., & Kaplan, E. (1983). *Boston Diagnostic Aphasia Examination*. Philadelphia: Lea & Febiger.

Hillis, A.E. (1989, November). *Treatment of naming verbs: An information processing approach?* Paper presented at the Annual Convention of the American Speech, Language, Hearing Association, St. Louis, Missouri.

Hillis, A.E. (1993). The role of models of language processing in rehabilitation of language impairments. *Aphasiology, 7*, 5–26.

Hillis, A.E. (2001). The organization of the lexical system. In B. Rapp (Ed.), *The handbook of cognitive neuropsychology* (pp. 185–210). New York: Psychology Press.

Howard, D., Patterson, K., Franklin, S., Orchard-Lisle, V., & Morton, J. (1985). Treatment of word retrieval deficits in aphasia. *Brain, 108*, 817–829.

Kaplan, E., Goodglass, H., & Weintraub, S. (1983). *The Boston Naming Test*. Philadelphia: Lea & Febiger.

Kemmerer, D., & Tranel, D. (2000). Verb retrieval in brain-damaged subjects: 1. Analysis of stimulus, lexical, and conceptual factors. *Brain and Language, 73*, 347–392.

Kertesz, A. (1982). *Western Aphasia Battery*. Orlando: Grune & Stratton.

Kim, M., & Thompson, C.K. (2000). Patterns of comprehension and production of nouns and verbs in agrammatism: Implications for lexical organization. *Brain and Language, 74*, 1–25.

Marshall, J. (1999). Doing something about a verb impairment: Two therapy approaches. In S. Byng & K. Swinburn (Eds.), *The aphasia therapy file* (pp. 111–130). Hove, UK: Psychology Press.

Marshall, J., Pring, T., & Chiat, S. (1998). Verb retrieval and sentence production in aphasia. *Brain and Language, 63*, 159–183.

McReynolds, L.V., & Kearns, K.P. (1983). *Single-subject experimental designs in communicative disorders*. Baltimore: University Park Press.

Miceli, G., Amitrano, A., Capasso, R., & Caramazza, A. (1996). The treatment of anomia resulting from output lexical damage: Analysis of two cases. *Brain and Language, 52*, 150–174.

Miceli, G., Silveri, C., Villa, G., & Caramazza, A. (1984). On the basis for agrammatics' difficulty in producing main verbs. *Cortex, 20*, 207–220.

Mitchum, C.C., & Berndt, R.S. (1994). Verb retrieval and sentence construction: Effects of targeted intervention. In G.W. Humphreys & J.M. Riddoch (Eds.), *Cognitive neuropsychology and cognitive rehabilitation* (pp. 317–348). Hove, UK: Lawrence Erlbaum Associates Ltd.

Mitchum, C.C., & Berndt, R.S. (2001). Cognitive neuropsychological approaches to diagnosing and treating language disorders: Production and comprehension of sentences. In R. Chapey (Ed.), *Language intervention strategies in aphasia and related neurogenic communication disorders* (4th ed., pp. 551–571), Baltimore, MD: Williams & Wilkins.

Nickels, L. (2001). Spoken word production. In B. Rapp (Ed.), *The handbook of cognitive neuropsychology* (pp. 291–320). New York: Psychology Press.

Nickels, L., & Best, W. (1996). Therapy for naming disorders (Part I): Principles, puzzles, and progress. *Aphasiology, 10*, 21–47.

Obler, L.K., & Albert, M.L. (1986). *Action Naming Test*. Unpublished test.

Raymer, A.M., & Rothi, L.J.G. (2000). Semantic system. In S. Nadeau, L.J.G. Rothi, & B. Crosson (Eds.), *Aphasia and language: Theory to practice* (pp. 108–132). New York: Guilford Publications.

Raymer, A.M., & Rothi, L.J.G. (2001). Cognitive approaches to impairments of word comprehension and production. In R. Chapey (Ed.), *Language intervention strategies in aphasia and related neurogenic communication disorders (4th Edn.)* (pp. 524–550). Baltimore, MD: Williams & Wilkins.

Reichmann-Novak, S., & Rochon, E. (1997). Treatment to improve sentence production: A case study. *Brain and Language, 60*, 102–105.

Rothi, L.J.G., Coslett, H.B., & Heilman, K.M. (1984). *Battery of adult reading function, experimental edition*. Unpublished test.

Thompson, C.K., Lange, K.L., Schneider, S.L., & Shapiro, L.P. (1997). Agrammatic and non-brain-damaged subjects' verb and verb argument structure production. *Aphasiology, 11*, 473–490.

Williamson, D.J.G., Raymer, A.M., Adair, J.C., & Heilman, K.M. (1995). *Florida Noun–Verb Battery*. Unpublished test.

Zingeser L.B., & Berndt, R.S. (1990). Retrieval of nouns and verbs in agrammatism and anomia. *Brain and Language, 39*, 14–32.

APHASIOLOGY, 2002, *16* (10/11), 1047–1060

Improving word finding: Practice makes (closer to) perfect?

Lyndsey Nickels

Macquarie University, Sydney

Background: One application of a task, such as word-picture matching or repetition, has been demonstrated to affect subsequent picture naming ('facilitation' or 'priming') in both aphasic and non-aphasic subjects. As aphasia assessment frequently involves repeated use of the same stimuli in different tasks, it is suggested that some aphasic individuals may have improved performance in picture naming as a result of assessment.

Aims: The aim of this paper is to demonstrate that there can be improvements in picture naming as a result of repeated presentation of stimuli and promote discussion regarding the mechanisms that may have caused such effects and their corresponding implications for treatment.

Methods & Procedures: This paper describes a single case study of JAW, a man with aphasia. JAW's picture naming had been observed to improve over time while other tasks remained stable. An investigation was performed to identify the source of this improvement. Three treatment tasks were used, attempting to name the picture, reading aloud and delayed copying of the picture names.

Outcomes and Results: All three tasks significantly improved subsequent picture naming of the treated items despite the fact that no feedback or error correction was provided. It is argued that the source of this improvement is from priming of retrieval of the phonological form. In the 'attempted naming' condition, this priming occurred every time a picture name was successfully produced. As JAW was not perfectly consistent, on each attempt at naming some additional items were primed. Thus, over time an increasing proportion of stimulus items were primed and were hence more likely to be successfully produced.

Conclusions: This study demonstrated that for at least one aphasic man, JAW, practice makes (closer to) perfect, even without correction. Not only was there significant improvement from tasks that provided the word form (reading aloud and delayed copying) as has been shown in the past, but also there was the novel finding that simply attempting to name a picture can improve subsequent word retrieval. It is argued that this novel finding could be applicable to other aphasic individuals and has functional significance.

In recent years there has been a relatively large body of research into rehabilitation of the word-finding difficulties that are so prevalent in aphasia (e.g., Hillis & Caramazza, 1994; Howard, Patterson, Franklin, Orchard-Lisle, & Morton, 1985a; Marshall, Pound, White-Thomson, & Pring, 1990; Nickels & Best, 1996a,b; Raymer, Thompson, Jacobs, & Le Grand, 1993). A number of specific tasks have been demonstrated to be effective in

Address correspondence to: Dr Lyndsey Nickels, Macquarie Centre for Cognitive Science (MACCS), Macquarie University, Sydney, NSW 2109, Australia. Email: lyndsey@maccs.mq.edu.au

Thanks to JAW and his wife for welcoming me into their home and participating so enthusiastically in my research. Thanks to Chris Code for acting as editor for this paper, Carolyn Bruce, Matti Laine, and David Howard for helpful comments on an earlier version, and David Howard for inspiring the title. An earlier version was presented at the Aphasia Rehabilitation Workshop, Milan, May 1997. A Wellcome Trust Advanced Training Fellowship and an Australian Research Council QEII Fellowship funded this research.

http://www.tandf.co.uk/journals/pp/02687038.html   DOI:10.1080/02687040143000618

improving subsequent picture naming for particular people with aphasia, including word-picture matching (e.g., Marshall et al., 1990) and reading aloud (e.g., Hillis & Caramazza, 1994)[1].

This paper investigates a related topic—whether attempting to name a picture can in itself improve word-retrieval. The impetus behind the investigation was the observation that over a 3-month period, during the course of assessment, JAW, a man with aphasia, showed marked improvement in picture naming that was unlikely to be the result of spontaneous recovery.

Current aphasia assessment, particularly within the cognitive neuropsychological approach, frequently involves repeated use of the same stimuli in different tasks. For example, in Psycholinguistic Assessments of Language Processing in Aphasia (PALPA, Kay, Lesser & Coltheart, 1992), subtest 53 requires spoken and written picture naming, reading, repetition and writing to dictation of the same items. As noted above, when used as therapy techniques some of these tasks improve subsequent picture naming in aphasia. Similarly one application of a task, such as word-picture matching or repetition, has also been demonstrated to affect subsequent picture naming ('facilitation' or 'priming'). For aphasic subjects, greater accuracy is observed (e.g., Howard, Patterson, Franklin, Orchard-Lisle, & Morton, 1985b; Best, Herbert, Hickin, Osborne, & Howard, 2002) and for non-aphasic subjects, faster responses (e.g., La Heij, Puerta-Melguizo, Oostrum, & Starreveld, 1999). It would not be surprising, therefore, if in fact some aphasic individuals improved performance as a result of assessment. Thus, the aim of this paper is to demonstrate that there really can be improvements as a result of repeated presentation of tasks that are used in assessment and promote discussion regarding the mechanisms that may have caused such effects and their corresponding implications for treatment.

CASE HISTORY

JAW was a 60-year-old carpenter with a history of hypertension, who had been working until his CVA in October 1992. A CT scan revealed a left middle cerebral artery infarct but no other focal lesions. There was evident low attenuation in the left cerebral cortex bounded medially by the posterior horn of the lateral ventricle.

Speech and Language Therapy notes report that initially JAW had "empty speech with some jargon and no functional comprehension". He was unable to name pictures and objects. All the testing reported here was carried out in 1994, over a year after his stroke. By this time he had moderate auditory comprehension difficulties. His spontaneous speech was fluent but anomic, with errors being omissions, semantic errors, and phonologically related real word errors. Naming was still extremely impaired.

AUDITORY PROCESSING

Auditory comprehension was poor, which was determined to be due to an impairment in pre-lexical auditory processing. Despite a normal Pure Tone Audiogram, JAW performed relatively poorly on a nonword minimal pairs test (Howard, unpublished; 81% correct). Speech-reading had no effect on his performance. Auditory lexical decision was correspondingly severely impaired (Howard & Franklin, unpublished; 67% correct).

---

[1] Unfortunately, it still remains unclear how these tasks are effecting the improvement in picture naming for many individuals. For further discussion of the relationship between impairment and the efficacy of a particular therapy task, see Best and Nickels (2000).

Auditory comprehension was characterised by large numbers of phonological errors. For example on a test of word–picture matching with phonological distractors (Target: fan; Distractors: van/man; Kay et al., 1992) he scored only 65% correct.

SEMANTIC PROCESSING

Due to his (relatively) peripheral auditory processing deficits, we will primarily consider JAW's performance on tests of semantic processing involving written and picture presentation (Table 1). JAW performed within normal limits on Pyramids and Palm trees (Howard & Patterson, 1992) both with a picture stimulus (three-picture version) and with a written word stimulus (written word–picture version). Similarly on a written word–picture matching test with semantic and visual distractors (from PALPA, Kay et al., 1992) JAW performed well within normal limits. However on more difficult tests including abstract words he performed more poorly (abstract synonym judgements; word–picture matching with abstract words). This suggests that he had a deficit in semantic processing for low-imageability or abstract words. Nevertheless it seems that semantic processing was good for high-imageability (pictureable) items.

NAMING

Spoken naming

JAW's naming was studied initially using 130 black and white line drawings. This set varied frequency and length orthogonally (Nickels & Howard, 1994). Scoring was on the basis of initial response with no time limit. As Table 2 shows, JAW's spoken naming was poor with a marked effect of frequency on success: χ^2 (1) = 4.81, $p < .05$. There was a consistent but nonsignificant trend for an effect of word length in syllables (Jonckheere Trend Test [JTT], $z = 1.54$, $p = .06$). He produced large numbers of real words both phonologically related (16% of responses) and unrelated (29% of responses) to the targets.[2] There were also smaller numbers of nonword responses, once again both

TABLE 1
Comprehension assessments

Task	n	Proportion correct
PYRAMIDS & PALM TREES[1] 3 pictures	52	.94
PYRAMIDS & PALM TREES[1] Written Word, 2 pictures	52	.94
WRITTEN WORD–PICTURE MATCHING PALPA[2] 48	40	.98
WRITTEN SYNONYM JUDGEMENTS[3] High imageability	38	.97
WRITTEN SYNONYM JUDGEMENTS[3] Low imageability	38	.66*
DIFFICULT WORD–PICTURE MATCHING[4] Concrete	30	.93
DIFFICULT WORD–PICTURE MATCHING[4] Abstract	30	.57*

[1] Howard and Patterson (1992)
[2] Kay et al. (1992)
[3] Coltheart (unpublished)
[4] Shallice and McGill (unpublished)
* Performance outside the range of control subjects.

---

[2] The criterion for an error to be classified as phonologically related was for the error to contain at least 50% of the phonemes of the target or vice versa.

TABLE 2
Proportion correct in spoken naming of Nickels and Howard (1994) picture set

	1 syllable (n = 25)	2 syllable (n = 25)	3 syllable (n = 15)	Mean
High frequency	.36	.28	.13	.26
Low frequency	.16	.12	.07	.12
Mean	.26	.20	.10	.19

phonologically related (5% of responses) and unrelated (8% of responses) to the targets. He produced relatively few semantic errors (10% of responses which is well within the control mean for this set; Nickels & Howard, 1994).

Given his good performance on comprehension tasks involving access to semantics for pictureable items, and his relative lack of semantic errors in picture naming, it seems unlikely that a semantic impairment underlies his poor spoken naming performance. Instead it is more likely he has impaired phonological processing.[3]

Written naming

JAW's written naming was also poor (18% correct on the same stimuli as spoken naming). Once again he showed effects of frequency and word length on accuracy. However, he showed a different error pattern to spoken naming, with the majority of errors being nonwords orthographically related to the targets (31% of responses) with relatively few related word responses (4%) or the unrelated responses that characterise his spoken naming (responses orthographically unrelated to the targets: words 4%; nonwords 3%). Semantic errors were once again within the limits of control subjects (8%). Given this error pattern, JAW's impairment in written naming can most plausibly be attributed to impaired orthographic processing (possibly an orthographic buffer impairment). However, it is also likely that there is a close relationship between written and spoken naming—it is difficult (if not impossible) to get JAW to perform this task silently, and a proportion (albeit a small proportion—8%) of errors are phonologically plausible (erroneous) spellings (e.g., saddle → sadele; tongue → tung).

REPETITION

JAW was unable to repeat nonwords (see Table 3), although some of his errors (28%) were phonologically related to their targets. Real word repetition was also poor and no better than naming of the same items. As in naming, errors were primarily unrelated to their targets but with a higher proportion of nonword responses in this task (19% unrelated words, 23% unrelated nonwords). Phonologically related errors were also common (18% phonologically related words; 12% phonologically related nonwords). His auditory processing deficit was a large contributory factor to his difficulty in repetition (in addition to his spoken word production impairment).

---

[3] The functional localisation of JAW's naming impairment is not straightforward, and relates directly to controversies regarding the origin of formal paraphasias in naming (see e.g., Best, 1996; Martin, Dell, Saffran, & Schwartz, 1994). Detailed argument is not appropriate here, and is discussed in detail in Nickels (2000, 2002).

TABLE 3
Repetition and reading of the Nickels and Howard set, and matched nonwords

	1 syllable (n = 25)	2 syllable (n = 25)	3 syllable (n = 15)	Mean
Word repetition				
High frequency	.24	.28	.13	.22
Low frequency	.28	.12	.13	.18
Mean	.26	.20	.13	.20
Word reading				
High frequency	.88	.68	.67	.74
Low frequency	.72	.48	.27	.49
Mean	.80	.58	.47	.62
Nonword repetition	0	0	0	0
Nonword reading	.44	.32	.07	.31

READING

JAW had some ability to read aloud nonwords but showed a marked length effect (JTT, $z = 2.19$, $p = .01$). Word reading was markedly better than both repetition and naming of the same items. He showed significant effects of length and frequency on his reading aloud: Length; JTT, $z = 3.05$, $p < .01$: Frequency: $\chi^2 (1) = 7.50$, $p < .01$. Further testing also showed effects of imageability and regularity on reading aloud. Errors were usually nonwords that were phonologically/visually related to their targets, with some regularisation errors on irregular words. The combination of imageability and regularity effects on reading aloud of words makes it likely that he uses a combination of sublexical and lexical-semantic routes to reading.

CHANGE OVER TIME

As a research subject, JAW's picture naming was assessed, using the same materials, three times in 4 months. His repetition and reading of these items was assessed twice in the same period. As mentioned earlier, it was clear that over the course of testing his spoken naming improved (January 1994, 19% correct; February 1994, 24%; April 1994, 31%). However, his repetition, and reading of the same items showed no change (Repetition: January 20%, April 16%; Reading: January 62%, April 60%). This implies that the improvement in naming was not due to general recovery but rather was specific to (spoken) naming.[4]

Why should this have occurred? During the assessment period JAW had been exposed to the same stimuli on several different occasions in different tasks—repetition, reading, naming. However, he had on no occasion received (external) feedback on his performance or corrections for any stimulus item. Thus, it was not the case that these tasks were in any traditional sense being used as therapy. However, could it be that the assessment itself had been helpful, and if so how? There are two main possibilities: first that there are "practice" effects in picture naming—in other words, that the more you do a task the better you become (without specifying the nature of the mechanism underlying this effect). Second, there is the possibility that doing other tasks that utilise the same stimuli but with different processing demands (e.g., repetition and reading) are beneficial to producing the same stimuli at a later point in the picture naming task.

---

[4] Written naming was only assessed once during this period.

In order to distinguish between these possibilities, JAW agreed to participate in a study to examine in more detail the hypothesised "therapeutic effects of assessment" with the aim of establishing whether these effects were replicable, and what might have been their source.

Two specific questions were addressed:

(1)   Do repeated attempts at naming a picture facilitate subsequent naming?
(2)   Is there a facilitative effect from other (assessment) tasks on subsequent naming?

METHOD

A new set of 102 pictures was used that JAW had not seen before. Two pre-therapy picture naming baselines were taken 1 week apart (see Table 4). Any items where a correct response was produced within a 20-second time limit, were counted as correct for the purposes of this study (both pre and post "treatment"). JAW was also asked to write the names of the pictures (once), immediately prior to the onset of therapy. JAW's responses on these picture-naming tasks were consistent with the pattern reported earlier.

The set of picture stimuli was divided into three subsets each containing equal numbers of items that had been named correctly in the (spoken naming) baseline and approximately matched for word length and frequency (Appendix 1). No systematic control was made for semantic relationship between the sets (all sets contained a diverse range of stimuli, as are characteristic of stimuli of this type).

JAW was then given three periods of "treatment", one on each set of pictures. Each period of "treatment" was brief—he performed the treatment task daily for 6 days, followed by a reassessment on the seventh day. One week later (after a week with no treatment) he was reassessed on written naming and then the next period of treatment would be started. All the treatment tasks were carried out by JAW on his own, at home, with no (external) feedback regarding his performance on the task, and no intervention from his wife.

Three different treatment tasks were used, each on a different subset of pictures (or picture names).

TABLE 4
Investigation of effects of different tasks on picture naming

Number correct	Week number									
	1	2	3	4	5	6	7	8	9	10
Spoken naming										
Naming set (n = 34)	9	9	→	15*		17		15		17
Reading set (n = 34)	9	10		10		→ 22*		16		17
Copying set (n = 34)	9	10		11		9		→ 18*		16
Written naming										
Naming set (n = 34)			6 →		**9**		6		8	
Reading set (n = 34)			9		8 →		13*		12	
Copying set (n = 34)			8		9		5 →		**14***	

——→ represents treatment of that set with the task suggested by its name (i.e., naming set treated using "attempted naming"; reading set with reading aloud; copying set with delayed copying.

First assessment of a set in each modality after treatment is printed in **bold**.

* Wilcoxon *p* < .05

- Attempted naming: In order to examine whether repeated presentation of the pictures for naming could be beneficial, JAW was required to attempt to name the pictures. No feedback or correction was given and he was instructed not to dwell on a picture too long but to move on if he was unable to name it.
- Reading aloud: This task was used to investigate whether other assessment tasks may have played a role in the observed improvement in naming. JAW was given a set of words written individually on cards and told to try to read them aloud, but to move on if he was unable to read a word. The words corresponded to the picture names but the pictures were not present. As before, no feedback or correction was given.
- Delayed copying: This task was chosen as a control task which involved neither presentation of the picture nor oral production of the target. JAW was required to look at the written picture name, then turn the paper over and write the word on the reverse. He was instructed to perform this task silently.

RESULTS

As shown in Table 4 and Figure 1, all three tasks were found to significantly improve spoken naming. However the improvement was specific to those items that had been treated in each case. These effects were robust over time. In contrast, there was no significant or sustained change in his written naming as a result of the attempted naming therapy (see Table 4). However, there were significant *and* sustained effects on written naming from reading aloud, and significant effects from delayed copying (sustained performance was not studied).

To ensure that the tasks were carried out as had been intended, on the first day of the treatment JAW was observed doing the task (but without intervention) to ensure that he was able to carry it out correctly without further instruction. Without exception JAW carried out the task correctly without the need for further instruction. At the end of the week, both JAW and his wife were questioned about the task and how it was performed—once again there was no evidence that he had not performed the task as requested.

DISCUSSION

This small-scale study used tasks that are commonly used in assessment: picture naming, reading aloud, and delayed copying. For JAW all three tasks resulted in improved picture naming. This improvement occurred despite the fact that no feedback or correction was provided.

Critical factors

Are there any elements of the tasks that are crucial to the improvement in naming? In other words, is there one common factor present in all three tasks which can explain the improvement in picture naming?

Presence of a picture?   One possible explanation for JAW's improved naming could be simply that he became more familiar with the pictures and better able to recognise them. This is what might be traditionally be thought of as a practice effect (where the improvement does not reflect any "true" improvement but rather reflects familiarity with the task constraints and materials).

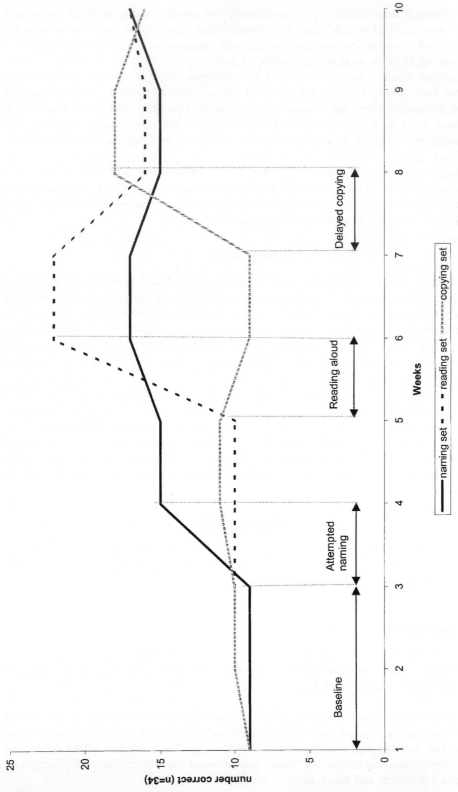

Figure 1. Effects of different tasks on spoken naming performance.

This explanation seems unlikely, as reading aloud and delayed copying, which did not involve presentation of the picture, were equally effective. In other words, for JAW the improvement in naming cannot be attributed to a "practice effect", as it is not necessary to have a picture present to improve naming (nor to "practice" the naming task itself).

Oral production?   It has been suggested (Miceli, Amitrano, Capasso, & Caramazza, 1996; Nickels & Best, 1996b) that oral production of the stimulus can be important for the success of therapy. Many of the case studies that have shown a treatment to be effective have necessitated production of the stimulus (usually in addition to a semantic task, e.g., Marshall et al., 1990; Nickels & Best, 1996b).

However, JAW showed improvement even on a task when no oral production was allowed (delayed copying). There is of course the possibility that overt production isn't the critical factor—perhaps activation of the phonological representation could be enough. Certainly JAW may still have been activating a phonological representation in delayed copying (but without overt production; Monsell (1987) discusses the possibility that in writing, phonology is automatically activated). However, he also showed improvement in the attempted naming condition where activation of the phonological representation will not always have been possible (see later for further discussion of this issue).

Presence of the word form?   Le Dorze, Boulay, Gaudreau, and Brassard (1994) argue that inclusion of word forms in semantic tasks could be crucial for improving naming. Their aphasic subject (who probably had a semantic disorder) failed to benefit from therapy where the semantic tasks (e.g., picture selection) only used a definition (e.g., the mollusc with long legs) but showed improvement when the same tasks were performed including the picture name (e.g., octopus). Provision of the word form is clearly not necessary for JAW to improve, as demonstrated by the attempted naming condition, where only the picture is provided and the only phonology that is available is that generated by JAW himself.

Thus, no single element common to all of these tasks is crucial to effect improvement in JAW's naming. What then could be the precise mechanism by which the therapy tasks are effective for JAW? Of course, there need not be one explanation—it might be the case that each therapy task is effective in a different way. Certainly the most puzzling question raised by the results is why repeated attempts at naming the same pictures, with no feedback or correction of responses, should improve subsequent naming.

A mechanism for improvement?

Facilitation of semantic processing?   Semantic activation is likely to occur in all three tasks. JAW performed within normal limits on semantic tasks involving both pictures and written stimuli (at least for concrete words). Thus, even when given a written word in therapy (for reading aloud or delayed copying) he may automatically access the semantic representation, just as happens when presented with a picture. As he has little apparent impairment to semantic processing, one also might not expect semantic priming to improve naming. However, it is still possible that additional activation at the semantic level could lead to improved lexical retrieval (from additional activation at the lexical level as a result of increased semantic activation).

This account would predict that written naming should also improve as a result of therapy, but as we saw in Table 4 there was no significant or sustained change in his written naming as a result of the attempted naming therapy in the same way that there was in spoken naming. However, there were significant *and* sustained effects on written naming from reading aloud, and significant effects from delayed copying. This makes it unlikely that facilitation at the semantic level can account for the improvement in spoken naming as a result of attempting to name the picture.

Activation of both semantics and phonology?   Marshall et al. (1990) described the improvement in their aphasic subjects' naming, following a word-to-picture matching task, as resulting from a strengthening of the links between semantics and phonology. This can be thought of as increasing the appropriate weights on the connections between the semantic and phonological levels, given the simultaneous access of phonological form and semantic representation (Howard, 2000). This seems an appropriate explanation for reading aloud and delayed copying where the form of the word is provided (given that JAW shows evidence of both semantic access from print and some ability to derive phonology from print using sublexical processes) but not for the attempted naming task where no phonological form is given. Under this account, without an appropriate target, learning (changing of weights) cannot occur.

A result of inconsistency?   JAW is not perfectly consistent—there are some words that he will name on one occasion but not on the next.[5] For example, in the two pre-therapy baselines 12% of items were named correctly on only one of the two attempts (81% of items he named correctly on the first attempt were named correctly on the second, and 9% of the items he failed to name were named successfully). Perhaps it is only the words that he successfully retrieves on at least one occasion during therapy that improve. Certainly, there is a tendency to have more success with items that were previously inconsistent (75% (3/4) that were inconsistent at baseline were successfully named post-therapy, as opposed to 26% (6/23) that were incorrect twice at baseline; Fisher Exact Test, $p = .0933$; 2-tailed).

Thus, we may hypothesise that when JAW successfully retrieves an item, this increases the activation of that item at the lexical level. This change in the "resting level" of activation will persist and hence make it more likely that he will successfully retrieve that item on a subsequent attempt at naming. Because of the inherent variability in his success, over time more and more items will have increased resting levels of activation and hence his naming performance will improve (cf. Howard, 2000).[6] Alternatively, we could conceptualise the change as one of increased weights (strengthened connections) in the mapping between semantics and phonology. These accounts are conceptually very similar and it is beyond the scope of this paper to attempt to discriminate between them.

This facilitation of subsequent word production by an earlier production of (or exposure to) that word is well documented in terms of response latencies in

---

[5] As JAW shows effects of frequency and length on performance, there will always be a degree of consistency as it will always be the case that a high-frequency, short word is more likely to be produced correctly and a low-frequency, long item more likely to be in error.

[6] JAW is inconsistent in the errors he produces to particular stimuli. At pretest, of the stimuli that were treated using attempted naming, 16/17 of the items he named incorrectly on more than one occasion produced different error responses (excluding items where two no-responses were produced). Thus it is unlikely that there is also reinforcement of specific error responses.

experiments with non-aphasic subjects (e.g., Cave, 1997; Ferrand, Grainger, & Segui, 1994; Ferrand, Humphreys, & Segui, 1998; Griffin & Bock, 1998; La Heij et al., 1999; Van Berkum, 1997; Wheeldon & Monsell, 1992). Moreover, Cave (1997) documented very long-lasting effects (up to 48 weeks) on subsequent naming latency of a *single* previous naming of the picture, supporting the idea that daily, or even weekly, repetition of the same items (as may have happened in treatment and assessment respectively) could be sufficient to produce improved performance for JAW and other aphasic individuals.

As frequency predicts JAW's naming success, one might predict that there would be a frequency effect for the improvement in naming. Intuitively perhaps one might expect the higher-frequency items to be more likely to improve than the lower-frequency items. Although the number of items is small for statistical analysis, no significant effects of frequency were found—comparison of the treated items that were named incorrectly and correctly after therapy, of those that had been consistently incorrect before therapy: set 1 (naming): $t(21) = .804$; set 2 (reading): $t(21) = .067$; set 3 (copying): $t(17) = .519$. In fact, it is likely that our intuitions were wrong: in the (non-aphasic) priming literature, it is now well established that greater priming is observed for low-frequency items compared to high-frequency items (e.g., Forster & David, 1984; Griffin & Bock, 1998; La Heij et al., 1999; Van Berkum, 1997; Wheeldon & Monsell, 1992). Thus, for JAW one might expect that although he is more likely to retrieve a high-frequency word successfully, greater priming would occur for lower-frequency words. Thus, lower-frequency words might be more likely to be retrieved on a subsequent occasion (due to the persistence of the priming effect). The combination of these two effects would lead to no detectable effect of frequency on improvement (as was observed).

It was concluded earlier that it was unlikely a single mechanism could underpin the improvement in all three tasks. In fact, it is clear this conclusion is false. In all three tasks we argue that there is priming of the mapping from semantics to phonology.[7] What differs is that in reading aloud and writing to dictation JAW is provided with the orthographic form and can derive the phonology both via semantics and via spelling–sound correspondences (which he can do with moderate levels of success). In the case of attempted naming, the only means of phonological access is from semantics (which as we know is difficult and error-prone).

Generalisation to other aphasic individuals?

The fact that, for JAW, attempting to name a set of pictures can improve subsequent retrieval of those picture names has clear functional implications. It implies that attempting to communicate should in itself improve JAW's ability to retrieve the words he is trying to produce. Although we have no direct evidence that this is the case, JAW was insistent that over time he was "getting more words back". Do we have any grounds for believing that this phenomenon might be applicable to other aphasic individuals?

We have hypothesised that the improvement was the result of two factors: first, variability in JAW's naming success, and second, successful retrieval of a word leading

---

[7] For written naming, there will instead be priming of the mapping between semantics and orthographic form, as will occur when the orthographic form is presented for delayed copying. Given the orthographic form in reading, it is likely that the orthographic output form is accessed, just as the phonological output form is. Finally, as the conditions were not perfectly matched for pre-therapy baseline performance, without replication, it is not felt prudent to risk "overinterpretation" of the lack of a significant improvement in written naming from the "attempted naming" condition.

to long-term priming of subsequent retrieval of the same word. I shall argue that neither of these factors is unique to JAW, and we therefore might expect therapeutic effects from "attempted naming" or indeed "attempted communication" to be more widespread in the aphasic population.

Variability.   Howard, Patterson, Franklin, Moreton, and Orchard-Lisle (1984) asked 12 aphasic subjects (half "fluent" and half "nonfluent") to name 300 pictures twice. The overall proportion of correct responses was highly predictable for each subject: Every individual was significantly more likely to name a picture correctly in the second presentation (P2) if they had also named it correctly in the first presentation (P1). However, no subject was close to being completely consistent: The most consistent subject, MR, on P2 correctly named 72% of the pictures she had named correctly on P1, and 9% of those she failed; and the least consistent subject named 73% of his P1 successes and 38% of his failures. Thus, it seems that variability is a hallmark of many aphasic individuals.

Priming effects.   As discussed earlier, priming effects (of differing durations) have been widely demonstrated in aphasia—using tasks such as word–picture matching (e.g., Howard et al., 1985b), repetition (e.g., Barry & McHattie, 1991), and phonemic cueing (e.g., Best et al., 2002). Moreover, these same tasks when used repeatedly have been shown to give long-lasting benefits (e.g., Pring, White-Thomson, Pound, Marshall, & Davis, 1990). Hence it seems likely that many aphasic individuals show the effects of priming that are present in non-aphasic subjects.

Thus, it seems that the two hypothesised prerequisites for improved word retrieval as a result of "attempted naming" are likely to be available for other aphasic individuals. Indeed, there is at least one study in the literature that could exemplify the same phenomenon. Howard et al. (1995a) examined the effects of different therapy tasks on naming. Before each daily therapy session, the aphasic participants were required to name the items treated in therapy *and* a set of control items (naming controls). The naming controls were also named three times during the treatment session. Performance on both the treated items and the naming control items improved, whereas performance on a set of items that were only tested at the beginning and end of treatment (baseline controls) did not change. Howard et al. attribute the change in the "naming controls" to generalisation of the treatment effect, but the question remains why should therapy generalise to one set of items (naming controls) and not another (baseline controls)? An alternative account is that this improvement is a result of the repeated attempts at naming those pictures. This account is also more consistent with the lack of change of the "baseline controls".[8]

CONCLUSIONS

In conclusion, this study, although small in scale and preliminary in nature, has shown that for at least one aphasic man, JAW, practice makes (closer to) perfect, even without correction. Not only was there significant improvement from tasks that provided the word

---

[8] The improvement in naming of the naming controls was no longer apparent 6 weeks after the completion of therapy. I would suggest that this is consistent with a slow decay in the priming effect when the stimuli are not functionally relevant items that would receive reinforcement through continued retrieval.

form (reading aloud and delayed copying) as has been shown in the past, but also there was the novel finding that simply attempting to name a picture can improve subsequent word retrieval.

It is argued that the beneficial effects of *all* the tasks arise from the same source—a priming of word retrieval. However, for the "attempted naming" condition, it is also a result of JAW's variability in word retrieval. Thus, the beneficial effect of attempting to name a picture is a result of the cumulative effects of producing different items correctly on different occasions. This has strong functional benefits for the individual with aphasia, suggesting that for those individuals to whom it applies, the more they attempt to communicate the more they will succeed. It is argued that there are (at least) two prerequisites to benefit from attempted naming: variability and priming. This claim clearly needs to be tested in larger-scale studies with other aphasic individuals.

REFERENCES

Barry, C., & McHattie, J. (1991). *Depth of semantic processing in picture naming facilitation in aphasic patients*. Paper presented at the British Aphasiology Society Conference, Sheffield, September.

Best, W.M. (1996). When racquets are baskets but baskets are biscuits, where do the words come from? A single-case study of formal paraphasic errors in aphasia. *Cognitive Neuropsychology, 13*, 443–480.

Best, W.M., Herbert, R., Hickin, J., Osborne, F., & Howard, D. (2002). Phonological and orthographic facilitation of word-retrieval in aphasia: Immediate and delayed effects. *Aphasiology, 16*, 151–168.

Best, W.M., & Nickels, L.A. (2000). From theory to therapy in aphasia: Where are we now and where to next? *Neuropsychological Rehabilitation, 10*, 231–247.

Cave, C.B. (1997). Very long-lasting priming in picture naming. *Psychological Science, 8*, 322–325.

Ferrand, L., Grainger, J., & Segui, J. (1994). A study of masked form priming in picture and word naming. *Memory and Cognition, 22*, 431–441.

Ferrand, L., Humphreys, G., & Segui, J. (1998). Masked repetition and phonological priming in picture naming. *Perception and Psychophysics, 60*, 263–274.

Forster, K.I., & Davis, C. (1984). Repetition priming and frequency attenuation in lexical access. *Journal of Experimental Psychology: Learning, Memory and Cognition, 10*, 680–698.

Griffin, Z.M., & Bock, K. (1998). Constraint, word frequency, and the relationship between lexical processing levels in spoken word production. *Journal of Memory and Language, 38*, 313–338.

Hillis, A., & Caramazza, A. (1994). Theories of lexical processing and rehabilitation of lexical deficits. In M.J. Riddoch & G.W. Humphreys (Eds.), *Cognitive neuropsychology and cognitive rehabilitation*. Hove, UK: Lawrence Erlbaum Associates Ltd.

Howard, D. (2000). Cognitive neuropsychology and aphasia therapy: The case of word retrieval. In I. Papathanasiou (Ed.), *Acquired neurogenic communication disorders: A clinical perspective*. London: Whurr.

Howard, D., & Patterson, K.E. (1992). *Pyramids and palm trees*. Bury St. Edmunds, UK: Thames Valley Test Company.

Howard, D., Patterson, K.E., Franklin, S., Morton, J., & Orchard-Lisle, V.M. (1984). Variability and consistency in picture naming by aphasic patients. In F.C. Rose (Ed.), *Advances in neurology, 42: Progress in Aphasiology*. New York: Raven Press.

Howard, D., Patterson, K.E., Franklin, S., Orchard-Lisle, V., & Morton, J. (1985a). The treatment of word retrieval deficits in aphasia: A comparison of two therapy methods. *Brain, 108*, 817–829.

Howard, D., Patterson, K.E., Franklin, S., Orchard-Lisle, V., & Morton, J. (1985b). The facilitation of picture naming in aphasia. *Cognitive Neuropsychology, 2*, 49–80.

Kay, J., Lesser, R., & Coltheart, M. (1992). *Psycholinguistic Assessment of Language Processing in Aphasia*. Hove, UK: Lawrence Erlbaum Associates Ltd.

La Heij, W., Puerta-Melguizo, M.C., Van Oostrum, M., & Starreveld, P. (1999). Picture naming: Identical priming and word frequency interact. *Acta Psychologica, 102*, 77–95.

Le Dorze, G., Boulay, N., Gaudreau, J., & Brassard, C. (1994). The contrasting effects of semantic versus a formal-semantic technique for the facilitation of naming in a case of anomia. *Aphasiology, 8*, 127–141.

Marshall, J., Pound, C., White-Thomson, M., & Pring, T. (1990). The use of picture/word matching tasks to assist word retrieval in aphasic patients. *Aphasiology, 4*, 167–184.

Martin, N., Dell, G.S., Saffran, E.M., & Schwartz, M.F. (1994). Origins of paraphasias in deep dysphasia:

Testing the consequences of a decay impairment to an interactive spreading activation model of lexical retrieval. *Brain and Language*, *47*, 609–660.

Miceli, G., Amitrano, A., Capasso, R., & Caramazza, A. (1996). The remediation of anomia resulting from output lexical damage: Analysis of two cases. *Brain and Language*, *52*, 150–174.

Monsell, S. (1987). On the relation between lexical input and output pathways for speech. In A. Allport, D. MacKay, W. Prinz & E. Scheerer (Eds.), *Language perception and production: relationships between listening, speaking, reading and writing*. London: Academic Press.

Nickels, L.A. (2000). Phonological errors in aphasia—when real words predominate. In A. Ferguson (Ed.), *Proceedings of the Aphasia Symposium of Australia, Melbourne, October 1999*.

Nickels, L.A. (2002). *Real word errors in aphasic naming: Formal paraphasias?* Manuscript in preparation.

Nickels, L.A., & Best, W. (1996a). Therapy for naming deficits (part I): Principles, puzzles and progress. *Aphasiology*, *10*, 21–47.

Nickels, L.A., & Best, W. (1996b). Therapy for naming deficits (part II): Specifics, surprises and suggestions. *Aphasiology*, *10*, 109–136.

Nickels, L.A., & Howard, D. (1994). A frequent occurrence? Factors affecting the production of semantic errors in aphasic naming. *Cognitive Neuropsychology*, *11*, 289–320.

Pring, T., White-Thomson, M., Pound, C., Marshall, J., & Davis, A. (1990). Picture/word matching tasks and word retrieval; Some follow-up data and second thoughts. *Aphasiology*, *4*, 479–483.

Raymer, A.M., Thompson, C.K., Jacobs, B., & Le Grand, H.R. (1993). Phonological treatment of naming deficits in aphasia: Model-based generalisation analysis. *Aphasiology*, *7*, 27–53.

Van Berkum, J.J.A. (1997). Syntactic processes in speech production: The retrieval of grammatical gender. *Cognition*, *64*, 115–152.

Wheeldon, L.R., & Monsell, S. (1992). The locus of repetition priming in spoken word production. *Quarterly Journal of Experimental Psychology*, *44A*, 723–761.

APPENDIX 1: MATCHING DATA FOR TREATMENT SETS

Treatment set	Mean no. of syllables (Standard deviation)	Mean log frequency (Standard deviation)
Naming set (n = 34)	1.85 (.80)	1.13 (.71)
Reading set (n = 34)	1.82 (.80)	1.10 (.72)
Copying set (n = 34)	1.85 (.82)	1.07 (.61)

APHASIOLOGY, 2002, 16 (10/11), 1061–1086

A computer-implemented protocol for treatment of naming disorders: Evaluation of clinician-guided and partially self-guided instruction

Ruth B. Fink, Adelyn Brecher and Myrna F. Schwartz

Moss Rehabilitation Research Institute, Philadelphia, USA

Randall R. Robey

University of Virginia, USA

Background: Computer-based rehabilitation programs are now available for patients' use at home and in the clinical setting, yet we have meagre outcome data associated with their usefulness under self- and/or clinician-guided conditions.

Aims: We assess the benefits of a computer-delivered, hierarchical phonological cueing protocol (cued naming) under two conditions of instruction, (1) with full clinician guidance or (2) in partial independence.

Methods & procedures: We employed a single-subject experimental design, which was replicated over six chronic aphasic subjects, three in each instruction condition. Subjects with deficits identified as primarily phonological in nature were administered a phonological treatment, utilising a computerised therapy program (MossTalk Words), under one of the two conditions.

Outcomes & Results: Training-specific acquisition and maintenance was demonstrated in both conditions. Limited and variable generalisation patterns were noted.

Conclusions: Chronic aphasic individuals with moderate-to-severe phonologically based naming impairment can benefit from a computerised cued-naming protocol and independent work on the computer can be an effective adjunct to clinician-guided therapy.

Computers have been used in aphasia therapy for a number of years and are now becoming more widely available for patients' use at home and in the clinic. Furthermore, the technology has improved to the point where computers can be programmed to deliver a wide variety of cues and corrective feedback in both speech and writing. With shrinking funding from health insurance companies and shorter lengths of treatment, patients are being encouraged to practise more independently, often with the use of computer software. Although reviews of computer-based rehabilitation have been less than enthusiastic (Bluestone, 1998; Robertson, 1990), there are convincing recent reports of positive outcomes associated with self- and/or clinician-guided aphasia therapy

Address correspondence to: Ruth B. Fink, Moss Rehabilitation Research Institute, Korman 213, 1200 West Tabor Rd, Philadelphia, PA 19141, USA. Email: fink@shrsys.hslc.org

This study was supported by a grant from the NIH National Institute on Deafness and Other Communication Disorders (#ROIDC00191), and by a grant award by the Peer Review Committee of the Moss Rehabilitation Research Institute. The authors wish to thank Rachel Goldmann, for her assistance in data collection, and Lyndsey Nickels, David Howard, and an anonymous reviewer for helpful suggestions on an earlier draft.

http://www.tandf.co.uk/journals/pp/02687038.html   DOI:10.1080/02687030244000400

administered via computers (e.g., Aftonomous, Steele, & Wertz, 1997; Katz & Wertz, 1997; Linebarger, Schwartz, & Kohn, 2001).

The present study involves a computerised therapy system called MossTalk Words (Fink, Brecher, Montgomery, & Schwartz, 2001) which was designed to be used in the clinical setting, as well as by patients working independently. The central aim of the study was to standardise and implement a popular clinical intervention—cued naming—and evaluate its effectiveness when the mode of instruction was either entirely clinician-guided, or when patients worked independently for two-thirds of the sessions.

THE CUEING APPROACH

Word-finding deficit is a hallmark of aphasia and so too is the responsiveness of this deficit to therapeutic intervention (for review see Nickels & Best, 1996a,b). Following the seminal studies of Howard, Patterson, Franklin, Orchard-Lisle, and Morton (1985a,b), researchers have distinguished between semantic approaches, which aim to strengthen word meaning, and phonologic approaches, which aim to improve phonological production. Either approach can involve delivery of "cues" designed to elicit the spoken word. An example of a phonological cue is the presentation of a word's initial sound; an example of a semantic cue is presentation of its definition.

In clinical practice, speech pathologists routinely use a variety of cueing techniques (semantic and phonologic) to improve word retrieval. It is common for therapists to informally define a hierarchy of cue effectiveness for individual patients and incorporate it into a general stimulation programme. This informal approach contrasts with the systematic delivery of cues which has been the focus of a small number of treatment studies. Such studies have generally demonstrated good acquisition of the trained vocabulary but conflicting results with respect to generalisation and maintenance of treatment effects (e.g., Linebaugh & Lehner, 1977; Raymer, Thompson, Jacobs, & LeGrand, 1993; Thompson & Kearns, 1981; Thompson, Raymer, & LeGrand, 1991).

The present study was influenced by these systematic cueing studies. From Linebaugh and Lehner (1977), we took the idea of individuating the cueing hierarchy and moving up and down the hierarchy on each trial. In a departure from Linebaugh, and Lehner, but similar to Thompson and Kearns (1981), Thompson et al. (1991), and Raymer et al. (1993), our hierarchy of cues was largely of the phonological type. However, we eschewed rhyming cues because of the limits this placed on stimulus selection. The most innovative aspect of our approach is the computerised implementation of the cueing protocol and the assessment of acquisition, maintenance, and generalisation under two modes of instruction: clinician-guided (CG) and partially self-guided (PSG).

VARIETIES OF NAMING DEFICIT

The application of psycholinguistic models to aphasia diagnosis has brought about refinement in the functional characterisation of word retrieval deficits, leading to the recognition of at least three subtypes: (a) *central semantic deficit*—diagnosed by semantic errors in word comprehension, oral reading, and picture naming; (b) *phonological retrieval deficit* (inability to access output phonology from semantics)—good comprehension, with semantic errors (and null responses) in picture naming; (c) *phonological encoding deficit*—good comprehension, with phonological errors in naming, reading, and repetition tasks. These subtypes are rarely pure. Patients who would qualify as being of type c on the basis of their good comprehension and phonological error production also may generate semantic errors in naming. Such patients presumably have a combination of retrieval and encoding problems. Moreover, while the ideal type-c patient produces phonological errors at comparable rates on all single word production tasks, it is common to find patients who perform markedly better on oral reading or repetition; this presumably is due to the support to production afforded by hearing the word spoken aloud or having some capacity to translate from print to sound. Finally, as aphasic comprehension is rarely intact when tested with sensitive measures, whether or not a patient qualifies as having a central semantic deficit often amounts to a judgement call based on relative degree of deficit.

These caveats aside, patients with central semantic deficits are thought to be poor candidates for phonological treatment techniques, as the locus of their deficit is by hypothesis outside the phonological system (see Hillis, 1991, and Nettleton & Lesser, 1991, for evidence that such patients benefit from semantically based protocols.) On the other hand, evidence suggests that the benefits of the phonological techniques are not limited to patients with pure deficits in phonological access or encoding (Greenwald, Raymer, Richardson, & Rothi, 1995; Hillis & Caramazza, 1994).

The patients in this study represent sub-types b and c in the classification given earlier, in more or less pure form. Naming subtype was not a controlled variable in this study. In the discussion, we speculate on how it might have contributed to the observed variation in acquisition profiles.

METHOD

Subjects

Six chronic aphasic individuals with moderate to severe naming impairments were included in this study. Five were male, one was female, ranging in age from 54–64 years. All subjects were native speakers of English, had experienced a single left hemisphere CVA, and were between 2.3 and 7.5 years post-onset. None was currently receiving speech-language therapy. In addition all subjects demonstrated adequate auditory and visual acuity for computer-delivered stimuli. That is, they passed a hearing screen at 40dB HL at 1000 and 2000 Hz and successfully navigated through a non-verbal computer game. Subject demographics are shown in Table 1.

Patients were screened with multiple language measures as follows:
Input measures
(1) Lexical Comprehension sub-tests of the Philadelphia Comprehension Battery (PCB) (Saffran, Schwartz, Linebarger, Martin, & Bochetto, 1988). This spoken word to picture matching task is designed to assess lexical-semantic knowledge. In Part 1, (within category) each target word is presented with three semantically related foils, for a total of 16 trials. In Part 2 (across category) these items (plus 12 additional items) are presented with three semantically unrelated foils, one of which is either perceptually or phonologically related.
(2) Philadelphia Naming Verification Test (PNVT). This spoken word-to-picture name verification test uses 162 of the 175 pictured items from the Philadelphia Naming Test (see next). These items are administered three times for a total of 486 trials. Randomly, over the course of the three administrations, the subject sees the picture and hears via tape recorder either the picture's correct spoken name (162 match trials) or one of four foils: a semantically related word (non-match trial: 81 close and 81 remotely related) or a phonologically related non-word (non-match trial: 81 close and 81 remotely related). The subject must indicate whether what is heard is or is not a match to the picture.

TABLE 1
Demographic information and language classification

	Clinician-guided			Partially self-guided		
	GM	AS	BM	EL	EG	RH
Age (rounded year)	54	64	60	59	63	63
Gender	M	M	M	F	M	M
Handedness	R	R	L	R	R	L
Time post-onset (months)	92	40	28	34	40	61
Education (years)	16	16	12	12	12	16
Occupation	minister	office manager	govt. inspector	health aide	graphic artist	accountant
Prior language therapy (months)	12	9	9	5	8	11
Aphasia subtype	Conduction	Broca	Anomic	Conduction	Conduction	Anomic
BDAE severity level	4	2	2	3	2	2

Output measures

(1) Philadelphia Naming Test (PNT), a 175-item picture-naming test (for details see Roach, Schwartz, Martin, Grewal, & Brecher, 1996).

(2) Philadelphia Repetition Test (PRT), a repetition version of the PNT (Dell, Schwartz, Martin, Saffran, & Gagnon, 1997).

(3) Philadelphia Oral Reading Test (PORT), an oral reading version of the 175 targets from the PNT.

Performance on these measures was used to: (1) characterise the subjects' deficits; and (2) exclude individuals with an unambiguous central semantic deficit. Results of this testing are shown in Table 2. The individual subjects, grouped by treatment condition, are described next.

Details of subjects

Clinician-Guided Group (CG)

Pt. GM.   As Table 2 shows, GM's performance in the two comprehension tasks was strong (100% and 95%). Spoken picture naming was moderately impaired (64% correct) with somewhat better performance on single word repetition (77%) and superior performance on oral reading (96%). Most of his errors in naming, repetition, and reading were phonological. In his attempts at word retrieval, GM frequently produced multiple attempts that mentioned all or most of the target phonemes in different combination (so-called *conduite d'approche*). He was invariably cognisant of his errors and recognised when he was finally successful. His pattern of good performance on semantic tasks and primarily phonological errors in naming and repetition suggests that GM's primary locus of impairment is at the level of phonological encoding. Single word oral reading is less affected, presumably because of support he derives from the printed word.[1]

---

[1] Additional testing with the PALPA: Psycholinguistic Assessments of Language Processing in Aphasia (Kay, Lesser, & Coltheart, 1992) had shown that GM's reading was affected both by lexical factors (imageability and frequency) and by orthographic regularity (higher scores on regular than irregular words). His nonword reading was poor, but he did succeed in reading some short nonwords. This, coupled with the regularity effect, suggests that GM had some capacity to derive phonology directly from print, which could have contributed to his reading success and helped minimise phonological errors.

TABLE 2
Percent correct and error breakdown on five lexical tasks

	Clinician-guided			Self-guided		
	GM	AS	BM	EL	EG	RH
PCB Lexical Comprehension[a]						
within category (n = 16)	100	100	81	100	100	94
across category (n = 28)	100	100	96	100	100	100
PNVT–spoken word → picture name verification						
% correct (n = 486)	94.6	96.3	89.6	94.2	98	96.3
% phonological errors	3.6	0.4	4.3	0	0.4	0.8
% semantic errors	1	2.6	5.9	2	1.4	1.6
% errors on a correct match	1	0.6	0	3.7	0.2	1
PNT–oral picture naming[b]						
% correct (n = 175)	63.8	40	35.6	77.4	17.8	69.4
% phonological errors	18.4	7.6	5.5	6.9	26.4	1.2
% semantic errors	8.6	19.8	14.7	4.6	5.2	13.3
% unrelated verbal paraphasia	1.1	7	1.8	0	5.1	2.8
% no responses	2.9	7	28.2	9.8	35	2.3
% descriptions	1.7	7	8.6	0	0.6	8.7
% perseverations	0.6	4	0	0	6	1.2
PRT–word repetition						
% correct (n = 175)	76.9	92.6	96	93.1	92.5	97.7
% phonological errors	19.7	7.4	0	6.3	6.3	2.2
% semantic errors	0	0	0	0	0	0
% unrelated verbal paraphasia	1.1	0	0	0	0	0
% no responses	1.2	0	0.6	0.6	1.1	0
% descriptions	1.2	0	0	0	0	0
% perseverations	0	0	0	0	0	0
PORT–oral word reading						
% correct (n = 175)	96	71.4	NA*	77.7	66.3	97.7
% phonological errors	4	17.1	NA*	21.1	32.6	2.3
% semantic errors	0	1.7	NA*	0	0	0
% unrelated verbal paraphasia	0	1.7	NA*	0	0	0
% no responses	0	4	NA*	1.1	1.1	0
% descriptions	0	1.1	NA*	0	0	0
% perseversations	0	1.1	NA*	0	0	0

[a] Controls mn score was 0.992 (within category) and 0.994 (across category).
[b] Controls score .97 correct or higher.
NA* = not available: unable to perform the test.

Pt. AS. Like GM, AS performed well on single word comprehension tasks. In contrast to GM, however, word repetition was strong (93%), oral reading was moderately impaired (71%), and oral picture naming severely impaired (40%). His error pattern in picture naming contained a larger proportion of semantic errors, with the remainder an equal mix of other error types. This evidence points to a deficit in accessing output phonology from semantics. However, the fact that he frequently accepted his semantic errors as correct suggests some weakness in the semantic system and/or faulty self-monitoring for meaning.

Pt. BM.   BM presented with mild weakness in semantics, as seen in both lexical comprehension and picture-name verification. Oral picture naming (36% correct) was severely depressed in contrast to repetition (96% correct). The most common oral naming errors were null responses and descriptions, followed by semantic errors. In addition, BM demonstrated profound difficulty with oral reading; after three failed attempts to get beyond practice items, he became agitated and asked to stop. Overall, his pattern suggests impaired access to phonology via semantics, with some involvement of the semantic system itself.

Partially self-guided group (PSG)

Pt. EL.   EL demonstrated strong performance on comprehension tests and also in word repetition. Oral naming and oral reading were comparable at 77% correct, but whereas most of her oral reading errors were phonological (21%), naming errors were predominately null responses, with an approximately equal number of phonological and semantic errors. Many responses were characterised by multiple phonological attempts at the target or a proclamation that the word was simply too hard to say. EL's profile suggests impaired access to phonology from semantics, and difficulty with phonological encoding.

Pt. EG.   EG also demonstrated strong performance on the comprehension tests, but his naming score was the lowest of all the patients (17.8% correct). The high frequency of null responses (35%) seemed in part a product of intact monitoring skills and propensity to avoid errors. Phonological errors made up the bulk of his overt naming errors, and the same was true in oral reading. He appears to have a deficit in phonological encoding, in which immediate word repetition is only minimally affected, presumably because of support he derives from the auditory model.

Pt. RH.   RH shows a selective impairment in picture naming relative to his good performance in comprehension, repetition, and oral reading. His most frequent type of naming error was semantic (13%), but he was generally aware that such errors missed the mark. He would sit for long periods trying to actively retrieve the picture name, but ultimately claim he "couldn't remember it" or allow the semantic alternative with a qualifier. His pattern suggests that he has difficulty accessing phonology from semantics.

In summary, all six subjects demonstrated moderate to severe naming difficulty, with primary impairments in accessing phonology from semantics or in phonological encoding, or both. None evidenced a severe semantic deficit, although BM's and RH's below ceiling lexical comprehension scores probably indicate some degree of semantic involvement.

Design and training materials

The study employed a single-subject, multiple-baseline across-behaviours design (McReynolds & Kearns, 1983), replicated over six subjects, three in each instruction condition (CG or PSG). Subjects were alternately assigned to a condition in the order they entered the study (i.e., there was no attempt to match the conditions for naming subtype or other factors). The vocabulary sets used in training were determined for each subject individually, as follows: A 339-item picture-naming test, comprising colour-printed photographs from the MossTalk software program, was administered four times.

Performance across the four administrations was used to establish a *50-item Customised Naming List* for each subject, containing words that the subject failed to name correctly on at least two of the four administrations. In general, the 50 items with the lowest proportion correct were selected for inclusion. For subjects who made consistent errors on more than 50 items, we selected higher-frequency items that were likely to be of functional significance.

In the Baseline phase, subjects attempted to name the 50 pictures without feedback. In addition, and as a control for non-specific attention/motivation effects associated with computer use, subjects engaged in a computer game that targeted nonverbal skills. This initial phase ran for as many sessions as were needed to establish a stable baseline for each individual subject. Baseline performance on the Customised Naming List was used to generate two sets of 20 items (Sets 1 and 2), of equivalent difficulty, and matched closely for frequency (Baayen, Piepenbrock, & Van Rijn, 1993) and length.[2]

In Treatment Phase 1, Set 1 was treated and Set 2 served as the control list. In Treatment Phase 2, Set 2 was treated and treatment was withdrawn for Set 1 words, which continued to be assessed for maintenance of treatment effects.

Training procedures

The Cued Naming Module of MossTalk Words delivered the picture stimuli, as well as the multiple auditory and visual cues used to facilitate picture naming. For this study we used six of the available cues—three spoken, three written. The spoken cues, ordered from least powerful (i.e., least likely to elicit the target) to most powerful, were: initial phoneme, sentence completion, and whole word (for repetition). The written cues were the same, but presented in print. We recognise that this hierarchy is somewhat arbitrary, as the power of these cues is known to vary across individuals; therefore we also developed a procedure to determine each subject's individual hierarchy.

On a given training trial, the subject attempted to name a pictured target. If unsuccessful after 20 seconds, a cue was selected which was low in power, followed by a more powerful cue, and so on up the hierarchy until the target word was produced correctly. Once correct, the subject attempted to repeat the word multiple times. (We aimed for five correct repetitions, but subjects who tended to worsen with successive repetitions were encouraged to discontinue the repetition series earlier.) The hierarchy was then reversed, such that the patient attempted to produce the target word with progressively less powerful cues (i.e., the fading cues technique) until reaching the query, "What is this?".

To determine each subject's individual hierarchy and strongest modality we tested all six cues on a weekly basis, alternating between spoken and written cues for each training item. For example, failure to name item 1 triggered an initial *spoken* phoneme cue followed by the initial *written* letter cue, then the *spoken* sentence completion, followed by the *written* sentence completion, etc., until the subject produced the word. The second failure to name (e.g., item 2) triggered first the *written* letter cue followed by the *spoken* phoneme cue, the *written* sentence completion followed by the *spoken* sentence completion etc. In the two subsequent sessions for that week, we used the modality (spoken or written) and entry point for cueing (letter, sentence completion, whole word) that was effective between 50% and 80% of the time for each patient. For

---

[2] We began with 50 items in order to end up with 40 words with low stable baseline performance, as we have found that subjects sometimes improve on particular words over repeated baseline testing.

subjects in both groups, this hierarchy was tested and modified as necessary once per week.

Clinician-Guided condition

In the CG condition, the clinician guided the patient through each of three weekly sessions (e.g., selecting the cue, contributing feedback, and encouraging self-cueing strategies).

Partially-Self-Guided condition

Patients in the PSG condition worked with clinicians only once a week, during which the modality and entry point for cueing was established and the clinician guided the patient through the session. For the remaining two sessions a week, the patient worked independently, with instructions to adhere closely to the cueing procedure established by the clinician. A research assistant monitored a portion of each independent session to record the subject's compliance with the recommended procedure.

Dependent measures

Throughout each treatment phase, uncued naming performance was assessed in session pretests for items of both Set 1 and Set 2.

Duration of treatment

Subjects received treatment three times per week. Session duration was as long as needed to complete three trials for all 20 words (typically 30–45 minutes). Treatment in each phase continued until the subject was able to generate the target words correctly without cues during session pretests. Criterion performance was 17/20 correct on three out of four consecutive sessions, or a maximum of 4 weeks (12 treatment sessions).

Post-treatment assessment

At the end of Treatment Phase 2, selected tests from the language screen were repeated. Specifically, the 339-item naming test was administered twice (three times for GM and EL), and the Philadelphia Repetition Test (PRT) and Philadelphia Oral Reading Test (PORT) were administered once. Pre–post changes on these measures were used to measure generalisation to naming, repetition, and oral reading.

Follow-up

A follow-up probe of all 40 previously trained targets was administered after an average of 4 weeks. During this period no subject received speech or language therapy; however, each subject received a packet of coloured photographs depicting 10 of their Set 1 and 10 of their Set 2 items. On each photograph the word was printed at the bottom. Subjects were instructed to practise these items for 15 minutes on as many days as possible. The practised and unpractised sets contained an equal distribution of correct and incorrect items. As stated, subjects were tested at follow-up on all 40 trained words (both the 20 practised items and the 20 others).

Scoring

Scoring was based on the final attempt. Credit was given for production of the target or an acceptable alternative (determined at outset). All other non-target responses were scored as errors, as were target attempts containing phonological errors (i.e., one or more unambiguous phoneme addition, substitution, or omission).

Reliability

Inter-rater reliability for scoring accuracy was calculated on 25% of the pretest scores for each patient. For five of the subjects, a second examiner listened to subject- and date-blinded tapes to obtain an independent score that was then compared point by point to the first examiner's scores. For the sixth subject, the second examiner scored along with the first examiner as the pretest was administered. This was done because the patient spoke very softly and there was concern that the audio tape would not be audible.

Data analysis

Inter-rater reliability was measured with the kappa statistic, to take into account the extent of agreement expected by chance. The effect of treatment on acquisition and maintenance was assessed by visual inspection of the graphical presentation of the daily pretests, and statistically, in terms of effect size, as explained next.

In a single-subject research design, the equivalent of pre–post evidence is obtained through a comparison of the baseline and withdrawal periods of an ABA design. (In our case, there is a withdrawal period only for Set 1 words, and it corresponds to the onset of treatment for Set 2 words.) The salient information is the change in the *level* of the scores from baseline to withdrawal. In contrast, the measure expressing meaningful change across the AB period (i.e., from baseline to training) is the change in *slope*.[3] We calculated the effect size (f) (Cohen, 1988) for changes in level and changes in slope, using algorithms designed specifically for serially dependent single-subject data (Kromrey & Foster-Johnson, 1996).[4] These estimators of effect size are not directly linked to a standard deviation or a standard error. Rather, they are based in regression analysis and selected for their robustness to the presence of lag-1 autocorrelation (Kromrey & Foster-Johnson, 1996; see also Faith, Allison, & Gorman, 1997).[5] Observed effect sizes were interpreted using Kromrey and Foster-Johnson's benchmarks which were fashioned after those of Cohen (1988):

---

[3] Evidence of a change in level across the AB period is complicated by early data points in the B period which are often nearly the same as the values of baseline data points; as a result the level eventually achieved in the B period is masked by lesser values observed throughout the process of effecting gradual change.

[4] Estimates of effect size were selected as quantities for analysis for two reasons. First, the research question opens a line of inquiry regarding a new treatment and so a more exploratory (e.g., descriptive) rather than confirmatory (e.g., probabilistic) analysis seemed most appropriate. Second, the only inferential tests that are unaffected by the presence of autocorrelation are ITSA (Gottman, 1981) and ITSACORR (Crosbie, 1993, 1995) ITSACORR is a variant of ITSA designed for shorter data streams (than was ITSA). However, here, as in most aphasia treatment studies, the baseline series are generally too brief for a valid application of ITSACORR (i.e., an unacceptably high Type II error rate). Therefore, the analysis consists of a descriptive quantitative analysis supplemented with visual assessments of performance graphs.

[5] Gorsuch (1983) found that trend analysis was the most robust (i.e., controlling Type I errors) and powerful (i.e., controlling Type II errors) method tested for analysing brief interrupted time series data characterised by lag-1 autocorrelation. Robey, Schultz, Crawford, and Sinner (1999) found that the predominant autocorrelative characteristic of single-subject treatment-outcome data was a lag-1 correlation.

Small effect size: 0.14–0.38
Medium effect size: 0.39–0.58
Large effect size: ≥ 0.59

To statistically evaluate the influence of Set 1 training on Set 2 words, the baseline data for Set 2 stimuli were divided into two subsets: (a) Set 2 observations made during Set 1 baseline, and (b) Set 2 observations made during Set 1 treatment. These subsets of Set 2 data were then examined for changes in slope across the Set 1 baseline–treatment crossover point. A similar examination for changes in level was conducted.

To determine whether the naming treatment generalised outside the study context, performance on the 339-item naming test before and after treatment was compared. For each study participant we computed a score for each item, which expressed the proportion of pretests on which that item was named correctly; as there were four pretests, the possible item scores were 0, .25, .50, .75, and 1.0. Next, we computed item scores for the post-tests (2 or 3, depending on the subject). Finally, we compared pretest and post-test item scores, separately for trained and untrained words, using Wilcoxon signed ranks test.

A different strategy was used to assess generalisation to word repetition and reading, as the relevant measures (PRT and PORT) were each administered only once before and after training. In these cases, we used the McNemar change test to assess the significance of improved scores on the untrained items from the post-test.

RESULTS

Reliability

Scoring reliability was high, with the mean kappa = .92; standard deviation = .036.

Acquisition and maintenance

Results are graphically depicted in multiple-baseline format in Figures 1–3 for the CG group and Figures 4–6 for the PSG group. Table 3 contains estimates of effect size for all six subjects as well as weighted averages across the three members of each group. The major findings can be summarised as follows:

(1) All subjects demonstrated measurable acquisition of Set 1 targets. The estimates of change-in-slope across the AB period (i.e., from Baseline to Treatment Phase 1) are, with one exception, large or medium effects (see Table 3).

(2) For most subjects, baseline performance on Set 2 stimuli remained low through Treatment Phase 1 and subsequently improved when these words became the targets of treatment (i.e., in Treatment Phase 2)(see Figures 1–6 and Table 3, last column). This indicates that acquisition gains were due to the treatment and not to spontaneous recovery or other non-specific factors. (However, see generalisation findings, next.)

(3) Acquisition gains for Set 1 were well maintained in the withdrawal phase (i.e., Treatment Phase 2) (see Figures 1–6). Effect sizes for change-in-level from Baseline to withdrawal were all very large.

(4) Acquisition and maintenance effects were greater on average for the patients in the CG group, compared with those in PSG. (Compare weighted averages in Table 3.)

(5) There was considerable variation across the individual subjects. Two patients met the acquisition criterion: GM, who was in the CG group, met the criterion on both

TABLE 3
Effect sizes and their interpretation

| | | Set 1 | | | | Set 2 | |
| | | Baseline vs Treatment | | Baseline vs Maintenance | | Baseline vs Treatment | |
Group	Subject	slope		level		slope	
CG	GM	0.75	(L)	4.56	(L)	1.08	(L)
	AS	0.81	(L)	2.05	(L)	0.62	(L)
	BM	0.37	(S)	1.56	(L)	0.52	(M)
Average:		0.64	(L)	2.60	(L)	0.70	(L)
PSG	EL	0.58	(M)	1.71	(L)	0.47	(M)
	EG	0.40	(M)	1.57	(L)	1.16	(L)
	RH	0.63	(L)	1.37	(L)	0.17	(S)
Average:		0.54	(M)	1.55	(L)	0.71	(L)

L = Large, M = Medium, S = Small.
Averages are weighted for sample size.

training sets; EL, who was in the PSG group, met it on Set 2. AS (CG group) and EG (PSG group) also achieved high levels of accuracy on trained targets, although they fell short of reaching criterion. The weakest performers were BM (CG group) and RH (PSG). BM's acquisition of the two training sets, although reliable in terms of effect size, did not approach the criterion level. Neither did RH's; for his Set 2 words, the effect size for change in slope from baseline to treatment was 0.17, which barely qualifies as a small effect.

Generalisation

We stated earlier that baseline performance on Set 2 stimuli generally remained low during Treatment Phase 1 and subsequently improved when these words became the targets of treatment. With respect to the change in slope for Set 2 words across the Set 1 baseline–treatment crossover, the effect size was negligible for GM and small for BM and RH. On the other hand the change in slope results for AS and EL demonstrated large effect sizes and the data for EG revealed a medium-sized effect. A similar examination for changes in level revealed only two effects: BM (small) and EL (large).

On the 339-item pre–post naming test, all subjects showed robust improvement on the vocabulary that had been trained in Sets 1 and 2 (Table 4). This indicates that the training generalised to the context of a larger test, administered off-line, with colour printouts of the digitised pictures. Two subjects, GM and AS, also showed statistically significant improvement on the vocabulary of the naming test that had never been trained.

On the PRT and PORT, scores were generally higher after training (Table 5). The opportunity to detect change on the PRT was limited by high scores on the pretest; only GM's improvement on the PRT was statistically significant. On the PORT, BM, who had demonstrated no ability to read single words on the pretest PORT, succeeded in completing the test after training and achieved a score of 56% correct. Of the remaining five patients, two made statistically significant gains on the PORT following cued naming treatment.

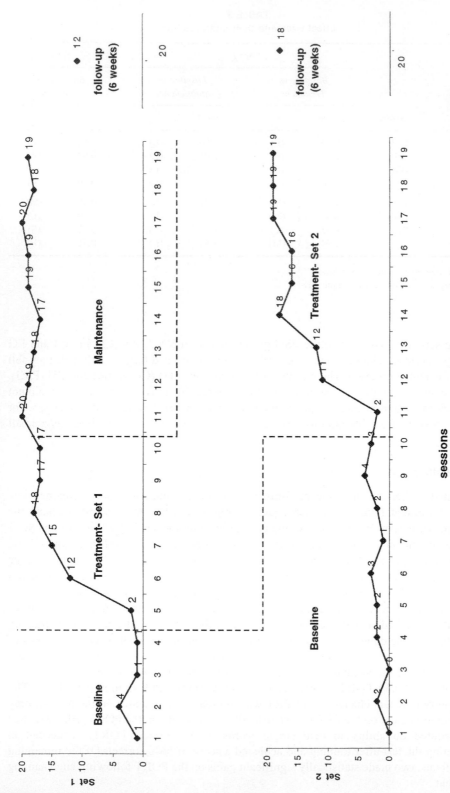

Figure 1. Results for patient GM (CG group). Numbers of correctly named targets in session pretests are shown for each baseline and treatment session and on the follow-up test. Number of items per set is 20.

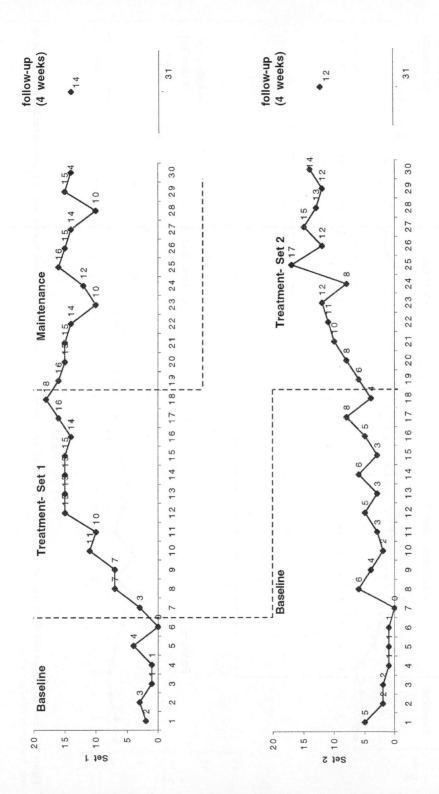

Figure 2. Results for patient AS (CG group). Numbers of correctly named targets in session pretests are shown for each baseline and treatment session and on the follow-up test. Number of items per set is 20.

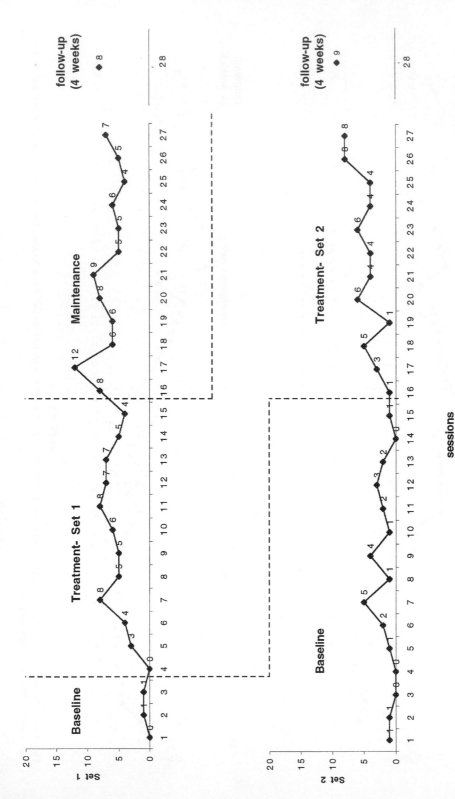

Figure 3. Results for patient BM (CG group). Numbers of correctly named targets in session pretests are shown for each baseline and treatment session and on the follow-up test. Number of items per set is 20.

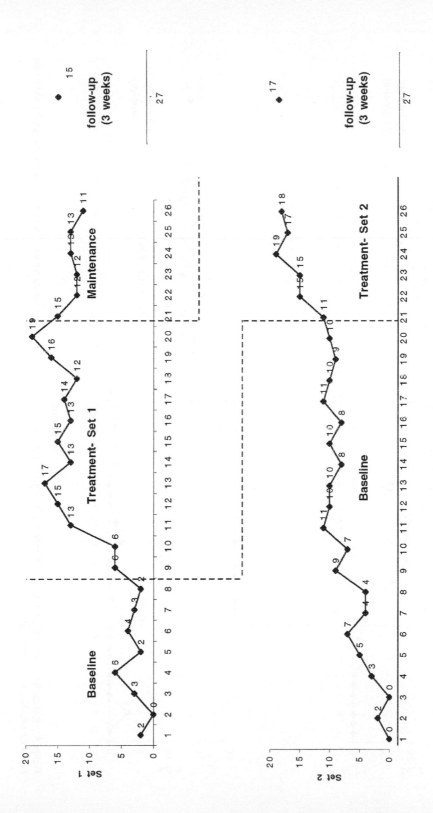

Figure 4. Results for patient EL (PSG group). Numbers of correctly named targets in session pretests are shown for each baseline and treatment session and on the follow-up test. Number of items per set is 20.

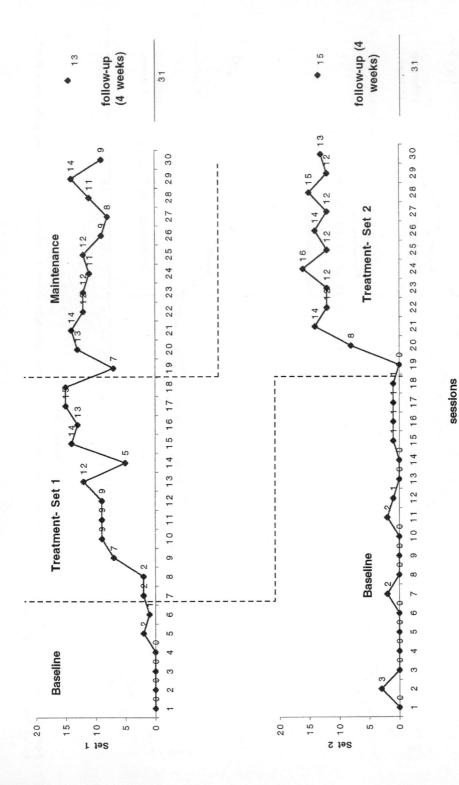

Figure 5. Results for patient EG (PSG group). Numbers of correctly named targets in session pretests are shown for each baseline and treatment session and on the follow-up test. Number of items per set is 20.

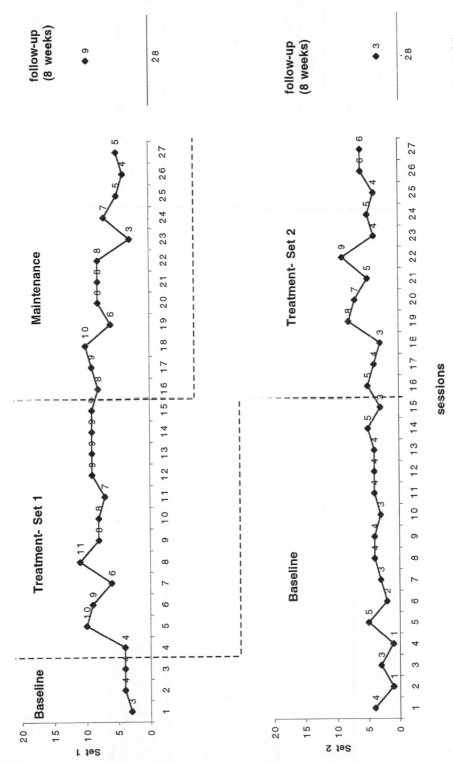

Figure 6. Results for patient RH (PSG group). Numbers of correctly named targets in session pretests are shown for each baseline and treatment session and on the follow-up test. Number of items per set is 20.

TABLE 4
Naming test

Group	Subject	Words trained					Words not trained				
		Mn. no. correct		Mean item score			Mn. no. correct		Mean item score		
		Before	After	Before	After	Wilcoxon one-tailed p	Before	After	Before	After	Wilcoxon one-tailed p
CG	GM	0.0	35.7	.00	.89	<.0001	185.3	207.0	.62	.69	<.001
	AS	0.8	27.5	.02	.69	<.0001	76.3	94.5	.26	.32	<.001
	BM	0.3	11.0	.01	.28	<.001	67.3	75.0	.23	.25	ns
PSG	EL	2.0	22.7	.05	.57	<.0001	211.3	218.7	.71	.73	ns
	EG	1.0	19.5	.03	.49	<.0001	32.3	29.0	.11	.10	ns
	RH	0.3	7.5	.01	.19	<.001	124.8	120.0	.42	.40	ns

Results for the 339-item naming test, administered four times before training and twice (AS, BM, EG, RH) or three times (GM, EL) after training. "Words trained" are the 40 words from Sets 1 and 2. "Words not trained" are the 299 remaining words, which never underwent training. The "item score" is the proportion of tests on which an item was correctly named. "Mean item score" is the average across items. Wilcoxon Signed Ranks Tests were calculated on item scores before vs after training. p-values listed as not significant were all at or above .10.

TABLE 5
Number of untrained items correct on the PRT and PORT before and after treatment

Group	Subject	No. items	PRT–word repetition			PORT–oral word reading		
			Before	After	McNemar one-tailed p	Before	After	McNemar one-tailed p
CG	GM	171	133	143	< .05	165	161	ns
	AS	162	162	163	ns	125	136	ns
	BM	163	168	170	ns	n.a.	100	–
PSG	EL	171	161	166	ns	135	152	< .01
	EG	162	149	155	ns	107	133	< .001
	RH	167	171	172	ns	171	169	ns

Follow-up

Performance on the follow-up assessment of trained items is depicted in the last panels of Figures 1–6. In virtually all cases, treatment gains were sustained during the 3–8 week interval. For four of the six patients, correct scores were evenly divided between practised and unpractised items. BM was the exception; he was correct on 13/20 practised items but only 4/20 unpractised items. For the final patient, RH, all items were unpractised, as medical complications prevented him from complying with the homework instruction.

DISCUSSION

We standardised a popular clinical intervention—hierarchical cued naming—and implemented the standardised protocol on computer. The purpose of this study was to evaluate the effectiveness of the implemented protocol under two conditions: (a) when the mode of instruction was entirely clinician-guided, and (b) when patients worked independently for two-thirds of the sessions.

Summary of findings

(1) There was strong and consistent evidence in both instruction conditions for treatment-specific acquisition of Set 1 and Set 2 words, and maintenance of gains when treatment was withdrawn (Set 1 only).

(2) On the 339-item naming test re-administered after training, every subject improved his or her scores on the subset of items that had undergone treatment. One account of this finding is that because the treated items were not selected at random but rather on the basis of the low scores they generated on the pre-test, the improvement seen at post-test simply reflects regression to the mean. However, the fact that these item scores remained low upon repeated testing in the baseline phase indicates that the pretest scores were not artifactually depressed on account of sampling error, but rather that the words were truly outside the naming vocabulary for these patients. On this reasoning, regression to the mean is an unlikely explanation for the improvement seen on the post-test. More likely, it reflects generalisation of treatment gains to a new test environment.

(3) There are indications that for some patients the benefits of treatment also generalised to other words and other production tasks. Thus, a few subjects, most notably EL and AS, showed measurable improvement on Set 2 during the training of Set 1. While these changes could be the result of repeated opportunities to produce those words, the

fact that the Set 2 baseline remained stable[6] until Set 1 treatment was initiated, suggests that for these subjects, there was some generalised effect of Set 1 treatment on the (untrained) words of Set 2.

(4) On the 339-item post-test, two of the six patients (GM and AS), showed significant improvement on the items of that test that had never been trained. Note that AS was also one of the patients who showed generalisation to Set 2 words on the repeated measure. At least for this patient, one can say with some assurance that the benefits of training were not restricted to the trained words. Table 5 summarises the evidence for limited generalisation to repetition and oral reading, once again on untrained words.

Findings 1–4 attest to the benefits of computer-assisted cued naming therapy, relative to general motivational and attentional effects associated with computer use. (Recall that the subjects performed a nonverbal computer game during the Baseline phase.) These benefits are strongest for acquisition and maintenance of trained words, and generalisation of trained words to a new context. The evidence for generalisation to untrained words, in naming or other production tasks, is more variable, but still significant in some patients.

(5) The implemented cueing protocol proved effective for patients in both the CG and PSG conditions. Although average effect sizes indicating change in Set 1 somewhat favoured the CG group, it is noteworthy that two of the four stronger performers (EL & EG) were in the PSG group and that most effect size estimates for the PSG subjects were in the medium to large range. This is a key finding, suggesting that independent work on the computer can be an effective adjunct to clinician-guided therapy.

Phonological cueing treatments: findings and questions

In the remaining sections we will review questions raised by this study and related studies. Our review of the relevant literature will primarily focus on the small set of studies that have used phonological cueing techniques to improve word retrieval and that have characterised the subjects with respect to subtype of naming deficit. Table 6 summarises these studies with respect to type of patient and treatment procedures. For a more detailed review and discussion of naming treatments (semantic and phonologic) please refer to Nickels and Best, 1996, a & b, Wilshire and Coslett, 2000, or to the original manuscripts cited.

First, a caveat about phonological cueing treatments. Most are not "pure" in the sense of excluding semantic processing. For example, our cueing hierarchy, as well as the one used by Thompson and Kearns (1981) and Hillis and Carramazza (1994, Study 2) included a sentence completion cue; and many "phonological" treatments (e.g., Raymer et al., 1993; Thompson et al., 1991) present a picture along with the phonological cue. What qualifies these, in our mind, as "phonological" treatments is that they aim to (1) facilitate phonological retrieval by providing information about the word form (e.g., via phoneme cues, oral reading, or repetition) and (2) provide repeated practice in producing

---

[6] Our laboratory uses the following heuristic to check on whether a baseline has stabilised at the point of initiation of treatment. For a three-data-point baseline (our minimum) the third score should be no higher (better) than the previous two. For longer baselines, the final data point should be within 10% of the average of the three preceding data points and should not indicate a rising trend. By this criterion, our subjects all demonstrated stable baselines on Set 2 words prior to the initiation of Set 1 training.

TABLE 6

Phonological cueing case studies: Subjects and procedures

Study	Subjects	Naming subtype[a]	Phonologic Treatment
Miceli et al., 1996	RBO	Phonological retrieval	Phonological (no pictures) Set 1: reading; Set 2: repetition
	GMA	Phonological retrieval	Set 1: picture + reading; Set 2: reading (no picture) Set 3: picture + phoneme cue
Hillis and Caramazza, 1994			
Study 1	HW	Phonological retrieval	Cued reading (no picture) phoneme cue, repetition
Study 2	HW KE	Phonological retrieval Central Semantic	Cueing hierarchy (with picture) sentence completion, phoneme cue, repetition
Study 3	HW JJ	Phonological retrieval Central Semantic	Cued reading (no picture) phoneme cue, repetition
Thompson and Kearns, 1981	#1	Phonological retrieval	Cueing hierarchy (with picture) sentence completion, phoneme cue, repetition
Thompson et al., 1991	CG RJ	Phonological retrieval & encoding Phonological retrieval (see Raymer et al., 1993)	Cueing hierarchy (with picture) phoneme cue, rhyme cue, repetition
Raymer et al., 1993	CG RJ MT RE	Phonological retrieval & encoding Phonological retrieval & Semantic Phonological retrieval & Semantic Phonological retrieval & Semantic	Cueing hierarchy (with picture) phoneme cue, rhyme cue, repetition
Greenwald et al., 1995			
Study 1	SS MR	Phonological retrieval & Semantic Phonological retrieval & Semantic	Cueing hierarchy (name to definition–no picture) phoneme cue, rhyme cue, repetition
Study 3	SS MR	Phonological retrieval & Semantic Phonological retrieval & Semantic	Repetition (with picture)

[a]Not all authors classified their patients in this way. Where they did not, we assigned naming subtypes to patients based on the descriptions and data provided.

the word. We will return to these issues in the section entitled "What is the active ingredient in phonological cueing treatments?". We begin with our results.

Acquisition, maintenance and generalisation

First and foremost, our results add to the small body of studies attesting to the effectiveness of phonological cueing protocols for the treatment of naming impairments. For example, Thompson et al. (1991) used a phonological cueing hierarchy modelled after Howard et al.'s (1985b) phonological treatment, with two patients who exhibited deficits "primarily in phonological word form selection" (one in accessing phonology from semantics and one in phonological encoding.) Following treatment, both subjects showed improved naming, with degrees of generalisation to untrained items that rhymed or were semantically related. Raymer et al. (1993), used a similar hierarchy with four Broca's patients theorised to have phonological/or mixed deficit patterns (three patients exhibited varying degrees of semantic involvement). The treatment, which was intended to improve access to phonology via semantics, resulted in generally successful acquisition of naming targets for all subjects, and varying patterns of maintenance and generalisation to untrained related items. Thompson and Kearns (1981) and Hillis and Caramazza (1994, Study 2, patient HW), using a slightly different cueing hierarchy to facilitate phonological access, found strong acquisition and maintenance effects but no generalisation to untreated words for their subject with primarily phonological deficits.[7]

Although it pays to be cautious when drawing conclusions from studies with differing methods, it seems clear that phonological cueing techniques have the potential to produce long-lasting effects and some degree of generalisation. This is contrary to the results of earlier facilitation studies of Howard et al. (1985a) and Patterson, Purell, & Morton (1983), which reported short-term effects of phonological techniques. A lesson to be drawn is that negative findings from facilitation studies should not dissuade investigators from exploring the benefits of a protocol in a more extended treatment design.

Who is a good candidate for phonological cueing treatments?

Although all our subjects showed improvement in acquiring the naming targets, there were clear differences within both groups, in how patients responded to this therapy protocol. One subject from each group (GM and EL) reached criterion performance, one subject from each group (AS and EG) showed moderately strong improvement, although performance fell short of criterion, and one subject from each group (BM and RH) showed only small gains. Interestingly, these differences are not explained by initial severity of the naming deficit. EG, who had the lowest naming score on the PNT (17% correct) was a moderately strong performer, whereas RH, who had a high naming score (69%), was a poor performer.

An obvious possibility is that the differences among patients may relate to the details of their language deficits. We noted earlier that our patients differed in the locus of the phonological disruption—retrieval vs encoding. However, this does not appear to explain the findings; among the stronger performers, GM and EG tested out as having a

---

[7] In contrast, a second patient (KE) with a deficit in semantics did show generalisation to untrained items in the same semantic category, leading the authors to conclude that the same treatment (which contained multiple components) can work at different levels for patients. For HW, repeated production of the target may have been the key element in the task, whereas for KE, the semantic information provided by the sentence completion cue may have been critical.

phonological encoding problem, AS a phonological retrieval problem, and EL a combination of the two.

Differences with respect to lexical-semantic processing may be of greater relevance. Although none of our patients exhibited significant semantic involvement, the weakest performers, BM (CG group) and RH (PSG group) were the only ones to make errors on the lexical comprehension sub-test of the PCB. BM also scored lowest on the picture-name verification test. Raymer et al. (1993) also noted that acquisition effects were stronger for patients with less semantic involvement.

On the other hand, prior studies involving phonological-based treatments have sometimes included patients with more severe semantic involvement, and this has not prevented those patients from making strong gains. For example, Greenwald et al. (1995) studied two patients with impaired phonological retrieval, whose deficits also included poor extraction of semantic information from pictures and in one case, poor picture–word matching. Using a phonological cueing protocol (Treatment 1-name to definition), they obtained strong acquisition and generalisation to the untrained task of picture naming and, with one subject, generalisation to untrained vocabulary. Hillis and Caramazza (1994, Study 2) described a patient (KE), who had a central semantic deficit, yet demonstrated strong acquisition and generalisation with a phonological cueing protocol.

These findings demonstrate that some degree of semantic involvement does not preclude patients from making strong gains using phonologically based treatments. This leaves us without a compelling account of why BM and RH benefited less than the other patients in our study. More generally, the available evidence does not answer the critical question of who is and is not a good candidate for phonological cueing treatment. Answering these questions may require looking beyond characteristics of the patients' lexical processing. In our sample, for example, the two patients who reached criterion on Sets 1 and/or 2 (GM and EL) were least severe in terms of overall aphasia severity (see BDAE severity score, Table 1); and one of the poor performers (RH) may have been hampered by his intermittent difficulty in remembering how to navigate through the computer program.

What is the active ingredient in phonological cueing treatments?

Observation of PSG subjects' behaviour during the self-guided sessions revealed that they adhered more loosely to the hierarchical cueing procedure in those sessions, compared with the sessions that were clinician-guided. For example, EL consistently began with the first sound cue, skipped over the fill-in, and went straight to the whole word cues. In addition, she would often skip the most difficult items, especially during the second half of the session, as she tired. Patient EG tended to start with the most powerful cue—spoken or written word—and then progress to the fill-in and initial sound cues, in that order. As these patients made comparable gains to those in the CG group, we are led to conclude that strict adherence to an optimal cueing hierarchy was not required for a good treatment outcome.

What then is the active ingredient in our therapy protocol? One possibility is that the critical element was simply having the opportunity to read and/or repeat the names of the treated items. Support for this comes from a naming treatment study conducted by Miceli and colleagues (Miceli, Amitrano, Capasso, & Caramazza, 1996). That study examined several approaches to the treatment of two individuals with phonologically based naming impairments, all of which involved giving subjects intensive practice in producing target names (i.e., by reading aloud or repeating with and without picture stimuli, or by naming pictures with phonological cues). Each treatment task yielded strong acquisition and long-term maintenance. Hillis and Caramazza (1994, Study 1) used a cued oral reading approach with patient HW and also obtained strong acquisition effects. Although more work is needed to isolate the active ingredient in computer-assisted (and other) cued naming treatments, we may find that for individuals with phonologically based naming impairments, the critical element for improving acquisition is that the cue successfully and repeatedly elicits the word's name in conjunction with subsequent opportunities to name the picture. On the other hand, the cueing hierarchy may provide critical support for patients with multiple levels of impairment (which clinicians are more likely to find in the clinical setting) and for maximising generalisation, as we discuss next.

What accounts for the limited generalisation to untrained words?

Although this was not a major focus of our study, the results of the repeated- and pre–post generalisation probe yielded convincing evidence that the treatment generalised to untrained words in a few patients. Such generalisation is surprising if one takes the view that the treatment involved strengthening specific connections from a word's semantic specification to its phonological code, and/or that it enhanced item-specific procedures for retrieval or assembly of the phonological segments (see Miceli et al., 1996). On the other hand, some degree of generalisation is consistent with the assumptions of interactive activation models of naming (e.g., Dell et al., 1997). Such models postulate two-way connections between semantic feature nodes and syntactic-semantic word forms (lemmas) and between lemmas and phonological segments. Activation of lemmas (by pictures, cues, or words) spreads up to semantic features and down to phonological segments; and in both cases, the spread is one-to-many (i.e., one lemma node activates multiple semantic features and multiple segments). This property, along with feedback from lower to higher levels, ensures that phonological and semantic neighbours of the target also achieve some degree of activation and, conceivably, some long-term strengthening of connection weights. Our materials were not designed to track the spread of generalisation along phonologic and/or semantic dimensions. However, two studies have demonstrated some degree of generalisation to both semantically and phonologically related words after a phonologically based cueing treatment (Raymer et al., 1993; Thompson et al., 1991). And two others have shown generalisation to semantically related words following phonological treatment in patients with semantic involvement (Greenwald et al., 1995, Treatment 1, Patient SS; Hillis & Caramazza, 1994, Study 2, Patient KE). On the other hand, a number of similar phonological cueing studies have tested for generalisation in patients with phonological deficits and have not found it (Hillis & Caramazza, 1994, Study 2, Patient HW; Thompson & Kearns, 1981).

In contrast to these mixed generalisation results from cueing hierarchy studies, no study employing a single phonological cue (repetition or oral reading) has produced evidence of generalisation to untrained words either in patients with phonological impairments (e.g., Hillis & Caramazza, 1994, Study 1; Miceli et al., 1996) or in a patient with multilevel impairments (Greenwald et al., 1995, Study 3). It may be that the active ingredient for generalisation is having some opportunity to strengthen the semantic–phonological link. This is an interesting avenue for further research.

There is another, less mechanistic, explanation for the observed generalisation, which is that subjects learned to generate and use cues effectively on their own (Best, Howard, Bruce, & Gatehouse, 1997, study 2; Greenwald et al., 1995; Linebaugh & Lehner, 1977; Nickels, 1992; Robson, Marshall, Pring, & Chiat, 1998). This is the hope that lies behind the use of cue-based treatments. For subjects who learn to self-cue, there is the possibility of unlimited generalisation, not just to new items, but also to new production tasks. Although the evidence indicating that subjects become proficient at self-cueing is weak at best, the possibility exists that AS and the others in our study who showed some item and/ or task generalisation may have acquired such proficiency, to a limited degree.

CONCLUSIONS

The results of this study indicate that chronic aphasic subjects with moderate-to-severe phonologically based naming impairment can benefit from a computerised cued-naming protocol and that independent work on the computer can be an effective adjunct to clinician-guided therapy. We did not attempt to determine what the optimal balance of clinician vs self-guided practice looks like. This and other topics discussed earlier (e.g., Who benefits? What is the active ingredient? How does generalisation come about?) are important topics for future study. We are optimistic about the use of computer treatment to extend the period of speech-language re-training and also to facilitate the model-driven approach, which is so difficult to realise in today's cost-cutting rehabilitation environment (Schwartz, 1998).

REFERENCES

Aftonomos, L.B., Steele, R.D., & Wertz, R.T. (1997). Promoting recovery in chronic aphasia with an interactive technology. *Archives of Physical Medicine & Rehabilitation, 78*, 841–846.

Baayen, R.H., Piepenbrock, R., & Van Rijn, H. (1993). *The CELEX Lexical database [CD-ROM]. Philadelphia: University of Pennsylvania, Linguistic Data Consortium.*

Best, W., Howard, D., Bruce, C., & Gatehouse, C. (1997). A treat for anomia combining semantics, phonology and orthography. In S. Chiat, J. Law, & J. Marshall (Eds.), *Language disorders in children and adults* (pp. 102–129). London: Whurr.

Bluestone, R. (1998). *Computer applications for patients and clinicians.* Paper presented at the Tenth Annual Stroke Rehabilitation Conference, October, Cambridge, Massachusetts.

Cohen, J. (1988). *Statistical power analysis for the behavioral sciences.* Hillsdale, NJ: Lawrence Erlbaum Associates Inc.

Crosbie, J. (1993). Interrupted time-series analysis with brief single-subject data. *Journal of Consulting and Clinical Psychology, 61*, 966–974.

Crosbie, J. (1995). Interrupted time-series analysis with short series: Why is it problematic; how can it be improved. In J.M. Gottman (Ed.), *The analysis of change.* Mahwah, NJ: Lawrence Erlbaum Associates Inc.

Dell, G.S., Schwartz, M.F., Martin, N., Saffran, E.M., & Gagnon, D.A. (1997). Lexical access in aphasic and nonaphasic speakers. *Psychological Review, 104*, 801–838.

Faith, M.S., Allison, D.B., & Gorman, B.S. (1997). Meta-analysis of single-case research. In D.R. Franklin, D.B. Allison, & B.S. Gorman (Eds.), *Design and analysis of single-case research.* Mahwah, NJ: Lawrence Erlbaum Associates Inc.

Fink, R.B., Brecher, A.R., Montgomery, M., & Schwartz, M.F. (2001). *Moss Talk Words* [computer software manual]. Philadelphia: Albert Einstein Healthcare Network.

Gorsuch, R.L. (1983). Three methods for analyzing limited time-series (N of 1) data. *Behavioral Assessment, 5*, 141–154.

Gottman, J.M. (1981). *Time-series analysis: A comprehensive introduction for social scientists.* London: Cambridge University Press.

Greenwald, M.L., Raymer, A.M., Richardson, M.E., & Rothi, L. (1995). Contrasting treatments for severe impairments of picture naming. *Neuropsychological Rehabilitation, 5*, 17–49.

Hillis, A.E. (1991). Effects of separate treatments for distinct impairments within the naming process. In T. Prescott (Ed.), *Clinical Aphasiology, 19* (pp. 255–265). Austin, TX: Pro-Ed.

Hillis, A.E., & Caramazza, A. (1994). Theories of lexical processing and rehabilitation of lexical deficits. In M.J. Riddoch & G.W. Humphreys (Eds.), *Cognitive neuropsychology and cognitive rehabilitation*, (pp. 449–484). Hove, UK: Lawrence Erlbaum Associates Ltd.

Howard, D., Patterson, K., Franklin, S., Orchard-Lisle, V., & Morton, J. (1985a). The facilitation of picture naming in aphasia. *Cognitive Neuropsychology, 2*, 49–80.

Howard, D., Patterson, K., Franklin, S., Orchard-Lisle, V., & Morton, J. (1985b). Treatment of word retrieval deficits in aphasia: A comparison of two therapy methods. *Brain, 108*, 817–829.

Katz, R., & Wertz, R. (1997). The efficacy of computer-provided reading treatment for chronic aphasic adults. *Journal of Speech, Language & Hearing Research, 40*, 493–507.

Kay, J., Lesser, R., & Coltheart, M. (1992). *PALPA: Psycholinguistic Assessments of Language Processing in Aphasia*. Hove, UK: Lawrence Erlbaum Associates Ltd.

Kromrey, J.D., & Foster-Johnson, L. (1996). Determining the efficacy of intervention: The use of effect sizes for data analysis in single-subject research. *The Journal of Experimental Education, 65*, 73–93.

Linebarger, M.C., Schwartz, M.F., & Kohn, S.E. (2001). Computer-based training of language production: An exploratory study. *Neuropsychological Rehabilitation, 11*, 57–96.

Linebaugh, C., & Lehner, L. (1977). Cueing hierarchies and word retrieval: A treatment program. In R.H. Brookshire (Ed.), *Clinical Aphasiology: Conference proceedings* (pp. 19–31). Minneapolis: BRK Publishers.

McReynolds, L.V., & Kearns, K.P. (1983). *Single-subject experimental designs in communication disorders*. Baltimore: University Park Press.

Micelli, G., Amitrano, A., Capasso, R., & Caramazza, A. (1996). The treatment of anomia resulting from output lexical damage: Analysis of two cases. *Brain and Language, 52*, 150–174.

Nettleton, J., & Lesser, R. (1991). Therapy for naming difficulties in aphasia: Application of a cognitive neuropsychological model. *Journal of Neurolinguistics, 6*(2), 139–157.

Nickels, L. (1992). The autocue? Self generated phonemic cues in the treatment of a disorder of reading and naming. *Cognitive Neuropsychology, 9*, 155–182.

Nickels, L., & Best, W. (1996a) Therapy for naming disorders (Part 1): Principles, puzzles and progress. *Aphasiology, 10*, 21–47.

Nickels, L., & Best, W. (1996b). Therapy for naming disorders (Part 2): Specifics, surprises and suggestions. *Aphasiology, 10*, 109–136.

Patterson, K.E., Purell, C., & Morton, J. (1983). Facilitation of word retrieval in aphasia. In C. Code and D.J. Muller (Eds.), *Aphasia Therapy* (pp. 76–87). London: Edward Arnold.

Raymer, A.M., Thompson, C.K., Jacobs, B., & Le Grand, H.R. (1993). Phonological treatment of naming deficits in aphasia: Model-based generalization analysis. *Aphasiology, 7*, 109–136.

Roach, A., Schwartz, M.F., Martin, N., Grewal, R.S., & Brecher, A. (1996). The Philadelphia Naming Test: Scoring and rationale. In M.L. Lemme (Ed.), *Clinical Aphasiology, 24*, (pp. 121–133). Austin, TX: Pro-Ed.

Robertson, I. (1990). Does computerized cognitive rehabilitation work? A review. *Aphasiology, 4*, 381–405.

Robey, R.R., Schultz, M.C., Crawford, A.B., & Sinner, C.A. (1999). Single-subject clinical-outcome research: Designs, data, effect sizes, and analyses. *Aphasiology, 13*, 445–473.

Robson, J., Marshall, J., Pring, T., & Chiat, S. (1998). Phonological naming therapy in jargon aphasia: Positive but paradoxical effects. *Journal of International Neuropsychological Society, 4*, 675–686.

Saffran, E.M., Schwartz, M.F., Linebarger, M., Martin, N., & Bochetto, P. (1988). *Philadelphia Comprehension Battery*. [Unpublished test battery.]

Schwartz, M.F. (1998). *Cognitive theory in the aphasia clinic: When worlds collide*. Presented at the Academy of Aphasia, Santa Fe, NM, November 2.

Thompson, C.K., & Kearns, K.P. (1981). An experimental analysis of acquisition, generalization and maintenance of naming behavior in a patient with anomia. In R.H. Brookshire (Ed.), *Clinical Aphasiology: Conference Proceedings* (pp. 35–42). Minneapolis: BRK Publishers.

Thompson, C.K., Raymer, A.M., & Le Grand, H.R. (1991). The effects of phonologically based treatment on aphasic naming deficits: A model-driven approach. In T.E. Prescott (Ed.), *Clinical Aphasiology* (pp. 239–261). Austin, TX: Pro-Ed.

Wilshire, C.E., & Coslett, H.B. (2000). Disorders of word retrieval in aphasia: Theories and potential applications. In S.E. Nadeau, L.J. Gonzalez Rothi, & B. Crosson (Eds.), *Aphasia and language: Theory to practice* (pp. 82–107). New York: Guilford Press.

APHASIOLOGY, 2002, *16* (10/11), 1087–1114

Generalised improvement in speech production for a subject with reproduction conduction aphasia

Sue Franklin, Frauke Buerk, and David Howard

University of Newcastle-upon-Tyne, and Newcastle Integrated Older People's Services, UK

Background: Reproduction conduction aphasia is a disorder of phonological production characterised by phonological errors occurring particularly with longer words in all tasks requiring spoken output. There have been few previous studies of therapy for subjects with this disorder.
Aims: The study investigates the effects of a treatment procedure involving the detection and correction of the errors in speech production with a single subject, MB. We also seek to establish the nature of MB's underlying deficit, and show how it changes as a result of treatment.
Methods & Procedures: Treatment effects were investigated in a single case study using multiple baselines over tasks, materials, and time. An in-depth cognitive neuropsychological case study was used to investigate the nature of MB's speech production deficit.
Outcomes & Results: MB had impaired naming, repetition, and oral reading particularly with longer words, but good word comprehension. Her errors were primarily phonological, with many repeated attempts (*"conduite d'approche"*). Production of non-words was less accurate than real words. The treatment improved production in all modalities and across a variety of tasks (including non-word reading). Further analysis of assessment results suggested that MB's impairment was at the level of phonological encoding and that therapy had improved phoneme production across all word positions.
Conclusions: Treatment was successful and generalised across items and to connected speech. MB's deficit could be characterised as a difficulty in the process of phoneme retrieval, and this improved as a result of the treatment.

INTRODUCTION

Individuals with phonological errors in speech production have been described by several researchers (e.g., Caplan, Vanier, & Baker, 1986; Shallice & Warrington, 1977). Typically these patients have relatively well-preserved (or even normal) auditory comprehension, but severely impaired repetition of words and sentences. Conversational speech is fluent including normally articulated words and generally preserved use of grammar and syntax, but with some phonological errors. In tasks requiring production of specific words, speech production is primarily characterised by frequent errors in selecting and sequencing phonemes and syllables, which may be omitted, substituted, or transposed, creating "literal paraphasias" (Goodglass & Kaplan, 1972). Very often attempts at naming will result in repeated, phonologically related attempts (*conduit d'approche*, e.g. tweezers → /dlɪtəs ... klɪtə ... klɪtəs/), which may get nearer the target (Joanette, Keller, & Lecours, 1980; Valdois, Joanette, & Nespoulous, 1989). However

---

Address correspondence to: Sue Franklin, Department of Speech, University of Newcastle-upon-Tyne, Newcastle-upon-Tyne NE1 7RU, UK. Email: s.e.franklin@ncl.ac.uk

---

http://www.tandf.co.uk/journals/pp/02687038.html   DOI:10.1080/02687030244000491

some patients do not get nearer to target in their repeated attempts (e.g., Miller & Ellis, 1987), or continue to try to produce the name despite having produced it correctly (Kohn & Goodglass, 1985). In severely affected cases output will be sufficiently disturbed to produce strings of phonemes unrelated to the target as well as target-related phoneme strings.

Shallice and Warrington (1977) distinguished repetition conduction aphasia and reproduction conduction aphasia. Repetition conduction aphasia is a phonological short-term memory deficit, with good comprehension and good single-word production. Reproduction conduction aphasia is a phonological impairment of production at the single-word level, again with good comprehension. Caplan et al. (1986) and others (Dubois, Hecaen, Angelergues, Maufras de Chatelier & Marcie, 1964; Kinsbourne, 1972; Strub & Gardner, 1974) assume a disturbance at some stage of planning of phonemic content of words (and non-words). Shallice and Warrington (1977) explained it in terms of a breakdown in formulating the phonological form and the sequence of articulatory gestures associated with a single word. This disturbance impairs speech production in all modalities including oral reading, naming, repetition, and conversational speech.

In terms of current theories of speech production (e.g., Levelt, Roelofs, & Meyer, 1999) there are a number of possible underlying deficits that could be responsible for phonological errors (see Nickels & Howard, 2000). The impairment may be specific to an impairment of lexical-phonological representations or a post-lexical impairment in the processes of phonological encoding. Models of phonological encoding have been elaborated in the past decade into several possible layers; if the deficit is at this level, which particular mechanisms of encoding are impaired?

Speech production models

Levelt et al. (1999) suggest that there are functionally separable levels of lexical semantic representation, phonological semantic representation, and phonological encoding. Within this model, information is processed serially so that only one output is fed forward from each processing level to the next. Word frequency affects access to phonological word forms from semantic word forms. A phonological lexical deficit should therefore be sensitive to word frequency and would affect naming, but not repetition, at least in those cases where repetition can be performed sub-lexically. A deficit of phonological encoding would not result in a word frequency effect (because of the serial nature of the model), but in this case all output modalities would be affected (oral reading, repetition, and naming). Individuals with either lexical or phonological encoding deficits have certainly been reported, with word frequency being the critical lexical variable (Howard, 1995; Kay & Ellis, 1987), and word length for phonological encoding (Caplan et al., 1986).

Dell, Schwartz, Martin, Saffran, and Gagnon (1997) proposed a rather different model of speech production. This is an interactive activation model that contains three layers corresponding to semantic feature nodes, lexical nodes, and phonemes. The model was "lesioned" by globally changing either the connection weights or the decay rates. Reducing the values of the weights tended to produce many non-word errors (other error types were produced in smaller proportions). Increased decay produced related errors (semantic or phonological) with a tendency for the phonological errors to be real words. These error patterns were fitted to error data produced by people with aphasia. However the existence of a bias towards the production of real word phonological errors is open to question. A limited number of subjects have been reported with a substantial proportion of formal errors (e.g., Best, 1996; Blanken, 1990). However, Nickels and Howard (1995) found that the number of real word errors (as oppose to non-word errors) were produced at no greater than chance rates, for any of 15 patients who made phonological errors in production, suggesting there is little evidence for a general lexical bias in error production.

In their original characterisation of reproduction conduction aphasia, Shallice and Warrington described production as being affected by both length and frequency. Shallice, Rumiati, and Zadini (2000) conclude that this pattern is typical of the patients since reported, and suggest that patients who do not demonstrate a word frequency effect have an impairment at a "more peripheral stage of processing" (p. 528). However there are patients reported whose impairments appear to conform to the characteristics of reproduction conduction aphasia rather than apraxia, whose naming is not affected by frequency (e.g., Wilshire & McCarthy, 1996).

Dell et al. (1997) did not account for word frequency effects in their model, and they only used words that were three phonemes in length. In the case of such a highly interactive model it is likely that if word frequency were built in at any level, "lesioning" would invariably cause strong effects of word frequency. It is not clear what would happen for words of different phoneme length. In the current formulation of the model, connections from the lexical level to the phoneme level, and from the phoneme level to the lexical level, are equal in their connection strength. If this were to apply irrespective of word phoneme length, longer words would benefit because of more feedback from the richer representation at the phoneme level. This would result in a greater probability of the correct lexical item being selected with longer words. Set against this, longer words would require more phonemes to be correctly activated; difficulties in phoneme selection will therefore result in poorer performance with longer words. The length effects that would be anticipated will therefore depend on the nature of the lesion. With increased decay of activation, a lesion that results primarily in real word errors, there should be a reverse word length effect (better performance with longer words). With reduced connection strength that causes target-related phonological errors and neologisms, performance should be worse with longer words.

One possible source of phonological errors in production is rapid decay of a phonological representation during the process of phonological assembly (Miller & Ellis, 1987). If this were the case in reproduction conduction aphasia, it would explain the tendency for more errors with longer words, and would also suggest that phonological errors should be most likely to occur towards the end of words. In fact, when Miller and Ellis (1987) looked at position of error within the word for their patient RD, errors were evenly distributed across positions. This is, perhaps, not surprising given that RD's naming was affected by frequency rather than word length, suggesting that his primary difficulty may have been in word retrieval rather than phonological assembly. However a lack of effect of position in the word could be found with a length effect where a constant probability of mis-selection for each phoneme would produce more errors in words with more phonemes.

Several patients have been reported with intact repetition and oral reading of real words, and impaired repetition and oral reading of non-words (e.g., Bub, Black, Howell, & Kertesz, 1987; Caramazza, Miceli, & Villa, 1986). Caramazza et al., taking this to be evidence of a strong dissociation between word and non-word production, suggested different processes for the phonological encoding of real and non-words. Shallice et al. (2000) challenged this notion, suggesting that a phonological encoding impairment will produce a greater impairment for non-words. They show that patients with phonological errors in speech production, who are also impaired at real words, are correspondingly worse at producing non-words than the patients showing the apparent dissociation. All of these patients have the same underlying impairment, and the apparent dissociation is, Shallice et al. argue, a severity continuum.

Monitoring accounts

An alternative account of phonological errors in speech production assumes that fluent, correctly formed speech is only achieved by covert repairs being carried out in response to a constant monitoring of the output (Schlenk, Huber, & Willmes, 1987). Thus an impairment in "inner speech"—the process of internal monitoring—would produce phonologically disordered speech (Goldstein, 1948). To suggest that such a monitoring deficit is the sole explanation for errors in a relatively simple task such as single word repetition seems unconvincing. According to Levelt (1989) self-monitoring is carried via the perceptual system. Recent phoneme monitoring experiments carried out by Wheeldon and Levelt (1995) have suggested that representations formed at a late stage of phonological encoding (post syllable assembly) feedback into the perceptual system for error monitoring. Butterworth (1992), on the other hand, proposed that there are control processes monitoring directly at an output level.

Miller and Ellis (1987) described a person, RD, who produced phonological errors and multiple phonological attempts. As RD had severely impaired auditory comprehension, it is plausible that his repeated naming attempts (which did not get closer to the target) were caused by an anomia exacerbated by poor monitoring. This would be in line with Levelt's perceptual monitor.

Phonological encoding

Speech error data and, more recently, priming experiments with normal subjects have led to more sophisticated conceptualisations of the phonological encoding process. Fromkin (1971) has argued that naturally occurring errors provide evidence for the psychological reality of the syllable, while Shattuck-Hufnagel (1992) suggests word-initial rather than syllable-initial segments are particularly prone to transposition errors. Priming experiments by Meyer (1990) suggested that phoneme segments are accessed before syllables. Most phonological encoding models suggest some kind of frame is set up which is filled with phoneme segments. A model of speech production, based on Levelt et al. (1999) is shown in Figure 1. The model begins at the point of lexical retrieval. At this point phoneme segments and the metrical information are processed in parallel (metrical aspects of phonological encoding will not be considered in this paper). The phoneme segments are then inserted into a frame and this information is used to form syllables (retrieved from a store of syllable plans in the case of frequently occurring syllables).

Post-lexical phonological errors in production could be due to impairments at the phoneme or the syllable level. In Roelofs' (1997, 2000) WEAVER++ model, all of the segments in a word have to be correctly activated to generate a syllable specification. With longer words, more phonemes need to be activated; a difficulty in activating the phonemes will therefore result in poorer performance with longer words. Levelt and Wheeldon (1994) and Levelt et al. (1999) suggest that higher-frequency syllables (perhaps the 1000 most frequent syllables in English) may be stored as pre-programmed wholes in a syllabary. The articulatory motor programs for these syllables will only need to be retrieved; for the remaining syllables the programme is assembled on line. If the syllabary is intact but there is a difficulty in assembling the articulatory motor program,

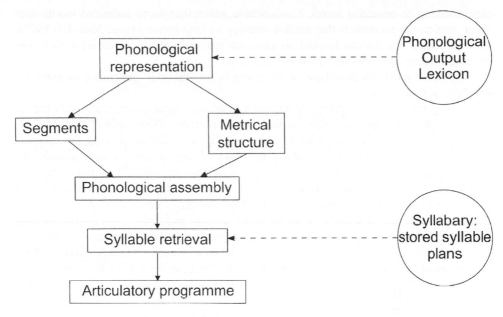

Figure 1.   Model of phonological encoding based on Levelt et al. (1999).

errors will occur with lower-frequency syllables. Because syllable frequency is confounded with syllable length (syllables with more phonemes tend to have lower frequency), this will result in more errors with longer syllables. If there is an impairment to the syllabary, or in retrieval from it, the syllables will have to be assembled; where the assembly process is unimpaired no effects of syllable frequency would be predicted.

Treatment studies

Therapy for subjects with phonological errors in speech production is somewhat problematic. Given that it is often not possible to elicit the target word (or non-word) from any modality, treatment that relies on eliciting and practising the target word is unlikely to be effective. Kohn, Smith, and Arsenault (1990) treated a patient with phonological errors in speech production using sentence repetition. The emphasis was on repeating the whole sentence rather than producing individual phonemes correctly. They found that both sentence repetition and picture description improved following therapy. Le Dorze (1991) worked on picture naming with a person with phonological errors in speech production. The written word and the first letter were given with the picture to assist naming. Naming of treated words improved and this improvement generalised to untreated words. Both these studies suggest that therapy for subjects with phonological errors in speech production may produce results that generalise beyond the specific words treated—a finding that is consistent with improvement in the *process* of phonological assembly rather than improvement in specific phonological representations.

The many successful treatments for lexical/semantic-level naming impairments tend to fall into two types. One is so-called "facilitation" therapy (Howard, Patterson, Franklin, Orchard-Lisle, & Morton, 1985a,b) where the words to be treated are in some way primed by word-picture matching, phonemic cueing etc. This type of therapy has generally had item-specific effects; that is the words worked on in treatment improve, but there is no generalisation to untreated words. Cases where generalisation to untreated words does occur tend to use treatments that teach a strategy to help naming (e.g., Nickels', 1992a, autocue where the patient learned to generate his own phonemic cues) rather than targeted directly at improving the naming process.

Clearly the most effective type of treatment is one that will generalise to untreated words.

In this paper we will describe one patient with phonological errors in all modalities of speech production—naming, oral reading, and repetition. First we will describe and evaluate an intervention programme that has, broadly, as its aim improving the subject's self-monitoring. We address particularly the issue of item-specificity in treatment. We might expect this therapy to generalise for one of two reasons. First, improving self-monitoring might be seen as a strategic change in word production rather than an improvement in actual phonological assembly. In this case we might expect the improvement to be in covert monitoring of errors, and more successful *conduite d'approche*. Alternatively the nature of the processes being treated—that is the fact that they are processes of assembly rather than specific lexical items—should mean that direct improvement at this level would generalise. In either case the aim of the therapy is to decrease the patient's phonological errors overall, and as a result, to improve her ability to communicate effectively.

Having established the success of therapy, the second half of the paper will investigate the source of the patient's phonological errors in speech production in more depth, in order to locate the impairment within a model of phonological encoding, and to establish what aspects of encoding had improved.

CASE HISTORY

MB is a retired 83-year-old widow with three children and several grown up grandchildren. In both January and October 1995 she had TIAs (transient ischaemic attacks), and then in June 1996 she suffered a left middle cerebral artery infarction that resulted in aphasia and a right hemiparesis.

MB received regular speech therapy during her stay in hospital and following discharge in July. Testing began in October 1996 by which time MB's auditory comprehension had significantly improved, and no difficulties were apparent in her comprehension of everyday speech. She showed marked expressive problems (verbal and written) that made communication difficult for her. Spontaneous speech was characterised by many phonemic paraphasias as well as neologistic words or phrases. She was able to produce some social and automatic phrases correctly. Her written skills were also limited, with many spelling errors and omissions.

As the focus of speech intervention was to improve MB's spoken output, a series of tests concentrating on speech production was carried out. Auditory input was briefly assessed to investigate its influence on any improvement in MB's spoken output.

Baseline tests

To establish whether spontaneous recovery was occurring, MB was given the Nickels Naming Test (see later) on two occasions 1 month apart. She scored 59/130 and 55/130 respectively (taking the final response) indicating that her naming performance was stable before treatment 1. On the same two occasions written sentence comprehension was assessed, using the TROG (Test for the Reception of Grammar; Bishop, 1982). MB made more errors in the second half of the test, suggesting a sentence-level deficit. On the whole test she scored 58/80 and 56/80 correct respectively. This test was used as a control task throughout the therapy study as no improvement would be expected on written sentence comprehension while undergoing therapy for a phonological deficit.

Auditory/phonological processing

In order to assess auditory input processing, we used a spoken word-to-picture matching test, a matching span task, and spoken rhyme judgements. This was to establish whether input processing deficits were compromising MB's monitoring abilities.

(i) *Spoken word to picture matching* (Comprehensive Aphasia Test; Swinburn, Baker, & Howard, unpublished): The CAT spoken word-to-picture matching test has phonological and semantic picture foils. MB scored within the normal range (29/30; normal subjects mean 29.2 range 25–30).

(ii) *Auditory Matching Span* (PALPA; Kay, Lesser, & Coltheart, 1992): MB was given two sequences of numbers one after the other, and she had to judge whether they were the same or different. The assessment involved sequences of from two numbers to seven numbers in length. Digit repetition span was not used because results would have been compromised by MB's output difficulties. MB performed well on this task, being able to correctly compare strings of six digits.

(iii) *Auditory rhyme judgements* (PALPA; Kay et al., 1992): Two spoken words were presented to MB and she had to judge whether they rhymed or not. This task investigates the integrity of the input phonological system, as well as segmentation skills. MB scored 41/60 (Table 1); this score is much better than chance (A' – 0.842, Fisher exact, $p =$ .0002) but very poor. Her responses were abnormally slow, and she produced only false positive errors. There was a tendency to make more errors to visually similar non-rhymes, which would suggest she was consulting orthography in this task, but this did not reach significance (Fisher exact, $p -$ .064, one-tailed).

Single word and non-word production

Word naming, oral reading, and repetition.   Nickels' naming test (1992b) was used for naming and the corresponding words were used for oral repetition and reading. The test consists of 130 words with orthogonal contrasts for frequency (high and low) and number of syllables (one, two & three syllables). A set of 26 abstract words, matched in frequency, phoneme and syllable length, and number of clusters was used to investigate imageability effects in repetition and oral reading (a reduced set derived from Nickels, 1992b). The results are shown in Table 2.[1] MB performed poorly in all modalities; in both reading and repetition, low-imageability words were no worse affected than high-

TABLE 1
Rhyme judgements (auditory presentation)

Rhyme, visually similar	15/15
Rhyme visually dissimilar	15/15
Non-rhyme, visually similar	3/15
Non-rhyme, visually dissimilar	8/15

---

[1] In this paper the results and statistical tests reported are all based on the final response, except where stated otherwise.

TABLE 2
Effects of length, frequency, imageability, and lexicality in naming, reading, and repetition before therapy

| | | Real words | | | | | | | Non-words | | | |
| | | Syllables | | | Frequency | | Imageability | | Syllables | | | Total |
Task	Date	1 n = 50	2 n = 50	3 n = 30	High n = 65	Low n = 65	High n = 130	Low n = 26	1 n = 25	2 n = 25	3 n = 15	n = 65
Naming 1	13 Sep 1996	0.500 (0.220)	0.500 (0.260)	0.300 (0.100)	0.508 (0.200)	0.400 (0.215)	0.454 (0.208)					
Naming 2	18 Oct 1996	0.520 (0.180)	0.500 (0.240)	0.133 (0.133)	0.462 (0.215)	0.385 (0.169)	0.423 (0.192)					
Oral reading	16 Sep 1996	0.780 (0.520)	0.640 (0.360)	0.367 (0.200)	0.615 (0.292)	0.646 (0.477)	0.631 (0.385)	0.615 (0.346)	0.360 (0.320)	0.080 (0.000)	0.000 (0.000)	0.169 (0.123)
Repetition	18 Sep 1996	0.620 (0.460)	0.680 (0.520)	0.200 (0.133)	0.569 (0.462)	0.523 (0.354)	0.546 (0.408)	0.731 (0.538)	0.200 (0.160)	0.240 (0.200)	0.000 (0.000)	0.169 (0.138)

Proportions of final responses correct are given; the proportion of initial responses correct is given in parentheses. (The breakdown by syllables and frequency is based on the 130 real words in the naming set.)

TABLE 3
Examples of MB's error types in single word and non-word production

Task	Target item	MB's response
Naming	tweezers	dlɪtəs, klɪtə, klɪtəs
	signal	sɪgələt
	axe	hammer
Repetition of words	violin	vɛl, vɛlə, vɛlɛt, vɛl, veli, vɛlinət
	brush	blʌs
Repetition of non-words	flet	fleɪk
	spollenit	kɔ, kɔ, dɔrɛk
Reading of words	trumpet	tʌpət, tʌmət, tʌtʌm, tʌmʌt, tʌmpət, tʌpət
	grave	gleɪf
Reading of non-words	adiby	ɛ, ɛdɛibə, ɛləvɛ, bilə, bid,
	timpy	tɪmpt

imageability words ($z = 0.07$, ns, and $z = -1.52$, ns, respectively). In all versions of the test, MB produced primarily phonemic errors, characterised by both omissions and substitutions. Some of these errors were repeated attempts, conforming to the label *"conduite d'approche"*. In naming MB also produced a small number of semantic errors, but no more than the elderly control subjects tested by Nickels (1992b). Examples of errors produced in the different versions of the test are given in Table 3 and the frequency of different types of response is given in Table 4.

As words get longer, MB produces fewer correctly. Although the effect of syllable length fails to reach significance in the first administration of the naming test, it is significant for the second administration and for repetition and reading of the same words. (Naming 1 $z = 1.39$, $p = .08$; Naming 2 $z = 2.86$, $p < .002$; Oral reading $z = 3.42$, $p < .001$; Repetition $z = 3.07$, $p < .001$). On the 130 items, MB's accuracy in both reading

TABLE 4
The incidence of different types of response

Response type	Naming 1 pre-therapy	Naming 2 pre-therapy	Repetition pre-therapy	Reading pre-therapy
Immediate correct	27	25	53	50
Conduite d'approche:				
finally correct	28	21	11	32
nearer target	25	23	18	21
no nearer target	9	1	3	4
Phonologically related non-words	20	28	31	20
Phonologically related real words	2	4	7	3
Semantically related	11	15	0	0
Other*	8	13	7	0

Total N = 130
* Other includes corrected semantic errors, no responses and visual errors.

and repetition is significantly better than naming (McNemar, $p < .0001$ and $p = .019$ respectively); accuracy in reading is marginally, but not significantly, better than in repetition (McNemar, $p = .13$ two-tailed).

Repetition and oral reading of non-words. To assess non-word repetition and reading, 65 non-words matched to the words from the Nickels naming test were used. They were matched in terms of number of syllables, phonemes and number of clusters (Nickels, 1992b). In both tasks, MB had much greater difficulty with non-words than real words (reading: $z = 6.06$, $p < .001$; repetition: $z = 5.38$, $p < .001$). Errors were again phonologically related. There was a significant effect of syllable length for oral reading of non-words ($z = 2.97$, $p < .002$), but the effect of syllable length in repetition failed to reach significance, possibly due to floor effects ($z = 1.10$, $p = .14$).

Connected speech

MB was asked to re-tell the story of Cinderella (Saffran, Berndt, & Schwartz, 1989); the first 100 words are transcribed in Appendix 1. A broad phonological transcription indicated that generally intelligibility was very poor. MB produced primarily neologisms and phonemic paraphasias, as well as long phonological searches that rarely led to any success. Many filled pauses (usually "eh") were apparent.

Summary of pre-therapy assessments

The assessments show that MB produces mainly phonological errors. All output tasks are affected by word length and are characterised by phonological searching and *conduite d'approche*. Poor performance on auditory rhyme judgements may indicate some concomitant auditory processing problems, but may be a specific segmentation problem given MB's good performance on digit matching span and spoken word-to-picture matching. From the assessment results we hypothesise that MB has a post-lexical, phonological output deficit.

DESIGN OF THE TREATMENT STUDY

Testing of MB fell into five phases (Table 5):

(i) *First pre-test.* This involved naming of the 130 items in Nickels' naming test. On the basis of performance on this first pre-test, items were divided randomly into two sets, matched for performance in this test as well as frequency, number of phoneme clusters, and the number of syllables. One set was targeted in treatment (treatment items), whereas the other, control set, was not used in treatment.Written TROG, used as a control task, involving written sentence comprehension but not speech production, was also presented.The 130-item naming test was also used for both repetition and reading. In addition MB was also tested in repetition and reading of the matched set of 26 low-imageability words, and in repetition and reading of the set of 65 matched non-words. To assess spontaneous speech production, MB was asked to tell the story of Cinderella.

(ii) *Second pre-test.* The 130-item naming test and written TROG were re-presented. If MB was still undergoing spontaneous recovery at this point we would anticipate improvement in both the naming test and the TROG.

(iii) *After the first phase of therapy.* At the end of the first phase of therapy, we re-presented (a) the Nickels naming test, and (b) a test of picture naming in sentences. In this

TABLE 5
Tests used to measure treatment effects

Pre-test 1	Pre-test 2	Post Phase 1	Post Phase 2	Follow-up
TROG	TROG		TROG	
Picture naming	Picture naming	Picture naming	Picture naming	Picture naming
Repetition			Repetition	
Reading			Reading	
Non-word reading			Non-word reading	
Cinderella			Cinderalla	
		Naming in sentences	Naming in sentences	

task, MB was presented with a composite picture developed from the pictures used in the naming test (for example, a picture of a monkey playing a saxophone) and asked to describe it. This test had not been used previously as it had only just been devised.

(iv) *After the end of the second phase of therapy.* At the end of the therapy, MB was tested in (a) naming, (b) repetition, (c) reading, and (d) naming in sentences for the full set of 130 items from Nickels' naming test. To evaluate improvement with non-words, the set of 65 non-words were presented for reading, and for changes in spontaneous speech MB was asked to re-tell the Cinderella story. To evaluate spontaneous improvement, the written TROG test was re-administered.

(v) *Follow-up.* Four months after the treatment programme had finished, MB was tested with the 130-item naming test to see whether the therapy effect was maintained.

The treatment we used aimed to improve MB's perceptual processing and monitoring skills in general, in the sense of a strategy. Therefore we hypothesised that both treated and untreated items would improve, but it would be possible that there would be some item-specific improvement for the words practised in addition to the general improvement.

TREATMENT

Treatment was designed to be carried out in two phases. As stated earlier, only picture naming was re-assessed after the first phase. Treatment was carried out twice a week at the patient's home. Therapy material was based on the names of half the pictures used in assessment, which had been divided into two equal matched sets.

Phase 1 of the treatment focused on phoneme discrimination tasks, and therefore was aimed at the early auditory processing stages. Although MB did not show any obvious impairment in auditory input processing, her performance on auditory rhyme judgement suggested some mild impairment in manipulating phonemes. Treatment in this phase used the 65 treatment words in a number of auditory discrimination tasks. Sessions were approximately 45 minutes long and seven sessions were given over three and a half weeks. The first tasks were MB deciding whether heard words were short or long (initially errorful, but perhaps a slightly odd task), and then spoken-to-written phoneme matching, at which she was 90% correct at the beginning of the treatment. The next task to be introduced was listening to the therapist saying a word, MB had to point to the initial sound (94% correct initially). The next two tasks concentrated on listening to the ends of words. MB was initially at chance on deciding whether two words had the same final phoneme, but had improved to 95% by the fifth session. Listening to a word and selecting the final phoneme was less problematic (90% initially). In the final sessions MB heard a word and had to point to the written word that rhymed (85% initially).

Phase 2 comprised the actual work on self-monitoring, and in contrast to Phase 1 involved speech production. There were three successive stages (a, b, c) with increasing task complexity that followed each other sequentially. Each session used 20 words from the treatment set of 65 items and lasted approximately 30 minutes. A 90% criterion was used for moving on to a new set of words.

Phase 2a involved "external monitoring" or "examiner-off-line judgement" (Maher, Gonzalez Rothi, & Heilman, 1994). In this task the therapist produced a word to a given picture where MB had to judge whether the word was correct or incorrect. When she recognised an incorrect word (e.g., "bouse" for "blouse", or "harrot" for "carrot"), MB was asked to identify the location of the error (i.e., initial, medial, or final position). Finally MB was asked to produce the correct word to the target picture. This phase lasted for six sessions.

Phase 2b was "indirect monitoring" or "off-line judgement" (Maher et al., 1994). Here MB had to name the pictures from the treatment set. The recorded responses were played back to MB and she had to make the same judgements as in Phase 2a (i.e., successively: judging whether correct or incorrect; identification of the location of error; production of the correct word). This phase lasted for four sessions.

Phase 2c was "direct internal monitoring" or "on-line judgement" (Maher et al., 1994), using the same monitoring procedures as in Phases 2a and 2b, but MB was given a picture and asked to produce the correct word for the picture (and later she was asked to build a sentence); immediately after each production she was asked whether her response was correct, and if she made an error she was asked to judge where it occurred, and then produce it correctly. These tasks were carried out over four sessions.

RESULTS

The results are summarised in Table 6 and Figure 2. Performance on the control task, written sentence comprehension in the TROG, did not change over the intervention period, suggesting that generalised spontaneous recovery was not occurring.

Only naming was re-assessed after the first phase of treatment and showed significant improvement (McNemar Test, $p = .0028$, one-tailed). Improvement in treated and control items did not differ significantly ($z - 0.06$, $p - .48$, one-tailed). Results of the naming and control task for the other testing periods are shown in Figure 2. Re-assessment after the second treatment phase, which lasted for 14 sessions, showed further significant improvement of MB's naming skills when compared to the assessment after Phase 1 (McNemar Test, $p = .0002$). Improvement in treated and control items did not differ ($z = 1.31$, $p = .095$). Improvement was maintained at 4-month follow-up with no significant difference in naming at follow-up compared with performance after Phase 2 ($p = .0631$; change in control versus treated $z = 0.30$, $p = .38$).

Although naming responses were not timed, following therapy MB named a greater number of pictures correctly and immediately. As can be seen in Table 7, MB produced fewer *conduite d'approche* errors overall following therapy. The ratio of immediately

TABLE 6

Results of assessments on the 130 picturable items at each phase in the study

Assessment phase	Task	Date	Syllables			Frequency		
			1 n = 50	2 n = 50	3 n = 30	High n = 65	Low n = 65	Total n = 130
Pre therapy	Naming 1	13 Sep 1996	0.500 (0.220)	0.500 (0.260)	0.300 (0.100)	0.508 (0.200)	0.400 (0.215)	0.454 (0.208)
	Naming 2	18 Oct 1996	0.520 (0.180)	0.500 (0.240)	0.133 (0.133)	0.462 (0.215)	0.385 (0.169)	0.423 (0.192)
	Oral reading	16 Sep 1996	0.780 (0.520)	0.640 (0.360)	0.367 (0.200)	0.615 (0.292)	0.646 (0.477)	0.631 (0.385)
	Repetition	18 Sep 1996	0.520 (0.460)	0.680 (0.520)	0.200 (0.133)	0.569 (0.462)	0.523 (0.354)	0.546 (0.408)
Post therapy Phase 1	Naming	21 Nov 1996	0.760 (0.540)	0.560 (0.260)	0.333 (0.167)	0.646 (0.385)	0.523 (0.308)	0.585 (0.346)
	Naming in sentences	28 Nov 1996	0.500 (0.340)	0.340 (0.160)	0.267 (0.233)	0.415 (0.292)	0.354 (0.200)	0.385 (0.246)
Post therapy Phase 2	Naming	19 Feb 1997	0.840 (0.660)	0.820 (0.560)	0.533 (0.333)	0.677 (0.523)	0.846 (0.569)	0.762 (0.546)
	Naming in sentences	17 Feb 1997	0.720 (0.480)	0.680 (0.420)	0.567 (0.300)	0.723 (0.446)	0.615 (0.385)	0.669 (0.415)
	Oral reading	24 Feb 1997	0.920 (0.820)	0.900 (0.620)	0.600 (0.500)	0.846 (0.615)	0.831 (0.723)	0.838 (0.669)
	Repetition	20 Feb 1997	0.820 (0.780)	0.880 (0.820)	0.700 (0.600)	0.800 (0.723)	0.831 (0.785)	0.815 (0.754)
Follow-up	Naming	19 Jun 1997	0.880 (0.700)	0.880 (0.680)	0.700 (0.433)	0.892 (0.708)	0.785 (0.554)	0.838 (0.631)

Proportions of final responses correct are given; the proportion of initial responses correct is given in parentheses.

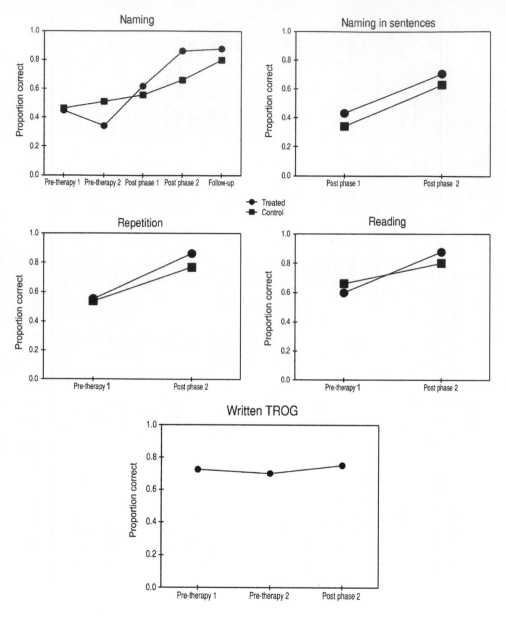

Figure 2.   The effects of treatment.

correct responses to conduite sequences is 27:62 and 25:45 in the two pre-therapy naming assessments, but 71:23 after Phase 2. Furthermore, when MB did produce *conduite* sequences, they were more likely to be successful after therapy (see Table 7; Wilcoxon two-sample tests show that the post-Phase 2 *conduite* responses are significantly better in their outcome than at the first pre-test, $z = 2.21$, $p = .013$, and the second pre-test, $z = 1.79$, $p = .037$). It is also noticeable that, before therapy, the majority of MB's successive approximations moved closer to the target, suggesting that she was already able to self-correct quite efficiently.

TABLE 7
Conduite d'approche errors in naming

	Pre-therapy 1	Pre-therapy 2	Post Phase 2
No nearer	9	1	1
Nearer	25	23	5
Correct	28	21	17

Further, as shown in Table 6 and Figure 2, significant improvement was achieved in both oral reading of words (McNemar Test, $p < .001$) and word repetition (McNemar Test, $p < .001$). For repetition there was no significant difference between treated and control items ($z = 0.92$, $p = .18$). The difference in improvement between treated and control items did reach significance for oral reading ($z = 1.71$, $p = .043$, one-tailed). To investigate whether there was generalisation to more complex tasks incorporating the single-word items used in the output tasks, we used the task of naming in sentences. This was first tested at the end of Phase 1 of treatment, and re-tested at the completion of the second phase. As can be seen in Figure 2, MB showed significant improvement on naming in sentences after therapy Phase 2 (McNemar Test, $p = .0008$). Improvement in the treated and control items did not differ significantly ($z = 0.56$, $p = .29$).

A general pattern emerged in the results; both treated and non-treated words improved significantly and to the same extent (except for oral reading where there was a small additional benefit for treated items), and had improved for all speech output modalities. It should be noted, however, that improvement has so far been demonstrated only on the items from the naming test in all tasks. By the end of the study the items from this test had been administered several times, so it might be argued that the apparent generalisation is actually an effect of practice from these repeated administrations. MB's performance in spontaneous speech and non-word reading was assessed before and after therapy to establish whether performance generalised to a different vocabulary set and to non-lexical phonology.

The non-word reading test was re-administered following therapy. Although the number of non-words read correctly had not changed (11 vs 10), significantly more phonemes were produced correctly. The 65 non-words used had an average length of 5 phonemes. MB improved from a mean of 2.94 of these phonemes presented in her most accurate attempt before therapy to 3.63 phonemes following therapy. The improvement is significant (Wilcoxon matched pairs test, exact $p = .0002$).

Another sample of MB's speech using the telling of the Cinderella story was recorded following therapy. This was transcribed and compared with the pre-treatment sample. In Table 8 the results are shown in terms of number of non-words, real words, and filled pauses (e.g., er, ah, um) used. The first sample taken in September 1996 showed predominantly non-words, i.e., neologisms and phonemic paraphasias. MB also produced many long phonemic searches. In the second sample her phonemic errors were more target-oriented. The comparison between the two samples shows that MB produced more phonemically accurate real words in the post-therapy sample (Fisher exact, $z = 3.85$, $p < .001$). On closer examination MB also produced many more content words in the later sample (pre-therapy = 21 types; post-therapy = 41 types). A final indication of improvement in the story telling was the decrease of filled pauses by about 50% from the first to the second sample. This makes her speech appear more fluent. The first hundred words for each of the two samples are shown in Appendix 1.

TABLE 8
Results of the Cinderella story telling

Date	Non-words (tokens)	Real words (types)	Real words (tokens)	Filled pauses (e.g., eh, mhm)
September 1996	361 (61%)	21	231 (39%)	63
February 1997	311 (50%)	41	313 (50%)	35

CONCLUSIONS

The results of the study showed that the therapy was successful. There was significant improvement in all output modalities. Further, there was generalisation to words not used in therapy (i.e., generalisation from treated to untreated items and to non-words), and there was evidence of generalisation of the improvement to other tasks involving speech production (i.e., improvement in naming in sentences and story telling). The improvements in the story-telling sample and in non-word reading were particularly important, as this rules out practice effects on the control items as a possible explanation. The therapy effect was maintained over a 4-month period following treatment.

Further analysis of the phonological output deficit

Having established that the therapy was successful, is it possible to identify more closely the level of breakdown in MB's speech production, and how therapy had improved performance? Using the model of naming described earlier in Figure 1, MB's naming impairment and its pattern of improvement are considered in terms of impairments to lexical selection, phonological encoding, and syllable assembly.

A lexical or post-lexical deficit?   We have argued earlier that MB has a deficit in the processes of phonological output, but given the strong lexicality effect could there be some additional damage at the lexical level? Studies demonstrating therapeutic improvement for this level of deficit are common (e.g., Miceli, Amitrano, Capasso, & Caramazza, 1996). However they generally demonstrate a pattern of item-specific improvement (Howard, 2000); our finding that MB's improvement was not item-specific therefore suggests that improvement is unlikely to be due to improved lexical access. We also need to address the question of whether an impairment in lexical access or representation contributes to MB's underlying deficit. Nickels' naming test compares words of high and low frequency; a lexical deficit would predict that MB would be worse at naming low-frequency words—is this the case?

A series of logistic regressions were carried out on naming, repetition, and reading of the 130 items in the naming test, administered prior to therapy. Using performance on immediately correct responses, for the two naming tests, word frequency, number of syllables (syllable length), and number of phonemes (phoneme length) were entered into the analysis. The effect of word frequency was not significant, Wald (1) = 1.97, p = .16, phoneme length was significant, Wald (1) = 13.92, p = .002, and syllable length was not significant, Wald (1) = 1.60, p = .21. For repetition and reading, word frequency, imageability, and syllable length were entered into the analysis. There were no main effects of frequency, Wald (1) = 0.24, p = .61, imageability, Wald (1) = 1.47, p = .23, or task, Wald (1) = 2.68, p = .10, but there was an effect of syllable length, Wald (1) = 10.65, p = .0011.

When naming (first pre-test), reading, and repetition for the 130 core items are entered into a single simultaneous logistic regression, with frequency, number of syllables, number of phonemes, and task as predictors, there is no effect of frequency, Wald (1) = 0.35, $p = .55$, or of the number of syllables, Wald (1) = 1.49, $p = .22$. There is a main effect of task, Wald (2) = 9.95, $p = .007$, reflecting MB's better production in repetition and reading than in naming, and a highly significant effect of the number of phonemes, Wald (1) = 20.60, $p < .0001$. There are no significant interactions between task and any of the other predictor variables ($p = .38$ or greater).

Taken together, these regressions show that the same factor affects MB's performance in all output tasks: the number of phonemes in the word. There is, in contrast, no effect of imageability, frequency, or the number of syllables in the target.

Word frequency did not significantly affect performance in reading, repetition, or naming. A problem in producing low-frequency words cannot therefore account for the equivalent output deficit across all tasks. Because, following therapy, all modalities improved, it is clear that the therapeutic effect was occurring at an output level common to all modalities. MB's speech production is very much worse for non-words (reading and repetition) than for real words (reading, repetition, and naming). As well as improved word production, MB demonstrates a modest, but significant, improvement in the oral reading of non-words. Both the deficit, and its improvement, is at a post-lexical level.

A syllable or a phoneme deficit?   We have already shown that word length affected MB's performance in all output tasks. Pate, Saffran, and Martin (1987) show that for their patient the important predictor of naming success is the number of syllables rather than the number of phonemes in the target word. Levelt et al. (1999) suggested that there are syllable assembly processes following phonological encoding. The logistic regressions described earlier showed that when both syllable length and phoneme length are entered into the analysis, only phoneme length has a significant effect.

That MB's accuracy in word production is determined by the number of phonemes in the target, rather than the number of syllables, strongly suggests that the problem was not at a level at which syllables are the defining unit.

Syllable frequency

Levelt et al.'s (1999) model proposes that the most commonly used syllables are represented in a syllabary (which might contain, in pre-programmed form, the 1000 most frequent syllables in English). Lower-frequency syllables would have to be assembled into articulatory programs on-line.

We therefore investigated whether syllable frequency affected MB's errors in naming. Two questions were investigated: first, whether errors were more likely to occur on less frequent syllables, and second whether, in error responses, substituted syllables were higher in frequency than the target syllables. Syllable frequency was calculated using the CELEX database (Baayen, Piepenbrock, & Gulikers, 1995), and all analyses used log-transformed frequencies. Because syllable frequencies are strongly related to the ordinal position in the word, the analyses were conducted separately for the first, second, and third syllable in the word.

The results for the pre-therapy naming assessments are shown in Table 9. They show that syllable frequency was not an important factor in determining MB's errors. First the stimuli resulting in errors are typically higher in syllable frequency than both the errors and the words produced correctly. Second, when the 19 first syllables that do not occur in

TABLE 9
Syllable frequency

		Log syllable frequencies		
		Syllable 1	Syllable 2	Syllable 3
Naming pre-test 1				
Errors	Mean	1.89	2.27	1.97
	sd	1.29	1.2	1.04
Stimuli resulting in errors	Mean	2.22	2.97	2.36
	sd	0.93	0.73	1.01
Stimuli correct	Mean	2.10	2.86	3.22
	sd	0.93	0.57	0.64
Errors vs their stimuli		$t(78) = 0.29$	$t(32) = -2.53$	$t(9) = -0.28$
Stimuli correct vs stimuli resulting in errors: $t(128)$		0.61	0.60	-1.18
Naming post Phase 2				
Errors	Mean	1.94	2.72	1.41
	sd	1.37	1.08	1.18
Stimuli resulting in errors	Mean	2.38	3.02	2.11
	sd	0.90	0.66	0.95
Stimuli correct	Mean	2.06	0.87	3.17
	sd	0.94	0.72	0.71
Errors vs their stimuli		$t(41) = -0.53$	$t(23) = -0.59$	$t(7) = -1.37$
Stimuli correct vs stimuli resulting in errors: $t(128)$		1.97	0.93	-2.85

real words in the CELEX corpus in her errors are excluded, the mean frequency of first syllables in her errors (2.34) is no higher than the mean frequency of first syllables in the stimuli resulting in these errors (2.22). Taken together, these results show that MB has no particular difficulty with low-frequency syllables, and no tendency to replace syllables with others of higher frequency. This strongly suggests that her difficulty is not one of assembling lower-frequency syllables into an articulatory programme, nor of retrieving pre-assembled articulatory specifications of more frequent syllables from a syllabary.

Characteristics of the phoneme deficit

The previous analysis showed that the number of phonemes in a word predicts naming success. There are at least two possible explanations for the effect of phoneme length. If the system is working noisily or inefficiently, with a percentage of phonemes incorrectly specified, then the more phonemes there are in the word, the greater the probability of errors. Alternatively phoneme encoding could be being affected by abnormally fast decay: in this case, errors should occur towards the end of the word.

Further investigation of the phoneme length effect

The primary determinant of MB's accuracy in speech production in all tasks (naming, reading, and repetition) is the number of phonemes in the word, even when word syllable length is taken into account. This applies both to the production of real words and non-words.

The simplest model for these phoneme length effects is to assume that the probability of producing a phoneme in a word correctly is constant. Calling the probability of correctly producing an individual phoneme p, the probability of producing a word correctly (C) is the probability of producing all of its constituent phonemes correctly. For a word with n phonemes, $C = p^n$. Taking logarithms, $log\ C = n\ log\ p$. Thus, the log transformed probability of correct word production should be linearly related to the numbers of phonemes in the word, with a line through the origin with a gradient of $log\ p$.

The relationship between MB's pre-therapy performance and the stimulus phoneme length was analysed on this basis varying p (the only free parameter) to minimise χ^2. The results of this are shown in Table 10, and the results of the fitting procedure for the first naming pre-test are illustrated in Figure 3.

From the results in Table 10, a number of points are evident. First, in each of the regressions, the resulting value of χ^2 does not reach the critical value when this is Bonferroni corrected for the 26 comparisons. This shows that this model provides an adequate account of the relationship between the stimulus phoneme length and the accuracy of its production. Two of the three χ^2 tests that are significant at $p < .05$ uncorrected are the initial attempts at production of names in sentences. This finding is predictable; the relevant unit for phonological coding in sentence production is greater than a single word, most probably the phonological phrase (Howard & Smith, 2002; Levelt et al., 1999; Roelofs, 2002). The predicted relationship between word phoneme length and production accuracy will only be found in single-word production. The size of the unit in sentence production will be larger than the individual word, but will vary in size depending on the phonological phrase; as a result the phoneme length of the target noun will not itself determine MB's production accuracy. The model fits the final responses in naming in sentences adequately. This is because, when self-correcting, MB almost always attempts only the target word; the unit of phonological production is then the single word.

Second, the estimated probability of a phoneme being produced correctly is higher for real words than non-words in both reading and repetition; this reflects the lexicality effect

TABLE 10
The results of fitting a model where the probability of each phoneme in a word is correct is p

Task	Test	Initial response		Final response	
		p	$\chi^2(5)$	p	$\chi^2(5)$
Naming	Pre-test 1	0.711	3.64	0.839	1.55
Naming	Pre-test 2	0.706	8.96	0.829	6.80
Naming	Post Phase 1	0.808	11.78	0.891	7.49
Naming	Post Phase 2	0.880	11.23	0.941	5.30
Naming	Follow-up	0.906	7.32	0.960	5.55
Naming in sentences	Post Phase 1	0.757	16.58	0.817	7.75
Naming in sentences	Post Phase 2	0.831	14.98	0.915	3.94
Non-word reading	Pre-test 1	0.651	4.29	0.691	4.43
Non-word repetition	Pre-test 1	0.676	3.81	0.703	4.01
Reading	Pre-test 1	0.807	2.26	0.902	7.31
Reading	Post Phase 2	0.913	14.60	0.959	6.13
Repetition	Pre-test 1	0.832	7.79	0.886	10.04
Repetition	Post Phase 2	0.939	6.15	0.955	5.24

Critical values for χ^2 with 5 df: 11.07 for $p = .05$ and 15.09 for $p = .01$. Bonferroni corrected for 26 different comparisons the critical value is 18.91 for $p = .05$.

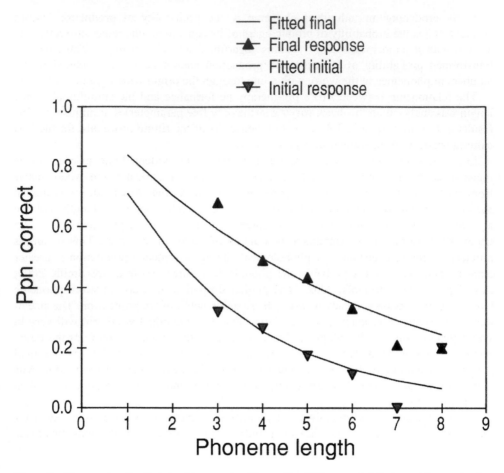

Figure 3.   Phoneme length effects in picture naming: The results of fitting a probabilistic model to naming data from pre-test 1.

we have already demonstrated in these tasks. Third, the estimated value for *p* is higher in repetition and oral reading than in naming.

The fitted *p* values can give us some indication whether the real word and non-word production values are at a common level or are the result of independent processes. Consider the following two possibilities:

(i)   There are separate impairments to real word and non-word production. Word repetition is better than naming because a word can be produced either lexically or sub-lexically. The fitted *p* value for naming is p_{nam}, which we take to be an estimate of the accuracy of phoneme production with real words. The fitted *p* value for non-word repetition is p_{nwd}—an estimate of the sub-lexical production accuracy. On the assumption that these represent independent deficits, the expected fitted *p* value for real word repetition p_{rwd} then is

$$p_{nam} + p_{nwd} - p_{nam}\, p_{nwd}\,.$$

(ii)   There is impairment to a common process of phonological assembly. The input to the process is more strongly or richly represented with real words than non-words: hence $p_{nam} > p_{nwd}$. The input in repetition is stronger than in naming, because the phonological representation is specified both lexically and sub-lexically: hence $p_{rwd} > p_{nam}$. But because the impairment is to a common process, the effects of the double input should be less than that predicted by the first model.

Take the comparison of repetition and naming for initial responses at pre-test 1. The fitted values are $p_{nam} = 0.711$, $p_{nwd} = 0.676$. The predicted value of p_{rwd}, under the independent deficits model is then $0.711 + 0.676 - 0.711 \times 0.676 = 0.906$. But the fitted value is 0.832, considerably less. The same underadditivity is also found for the final response and for both initial and final responses in reading. This finding then supports the second model in which the impairments to real word and non-word production occur at a common level of phonological assembly.

Do the data accord with the decay theory? For a simple, left-to-right model of decay, errors should be more frequent at the end of words (Miller & Ellis, 1987). For a more complex, parallel system, decay might mean that the longer the word, the more errors in every word position compared to shorter words. For four of the naming tests (post-Phase 1 naming was not used in this analysis) the proportion of errors was calculated separately for the first, second, and third syllables (targets that had produced semantic errors were omitted), for the one-, two-, and three-syllable words (see Table 11). Over all syllable lengths and positions there were significant differences in the probability of phonemes being produced in error: Naming pre-test 1, $\chi^2(5) = 14.42$, $p = .013$; naming pre-test 2, $\chi^2(5) = 7.96$, $p = .158$; naming post Phase 2, $\chi^2(5) = 29.30$, $p < .001$; naming follow-up, $\chi^2(5) = 30.68$, $p < .001$. However, errors might occur later in the word because MB detects an error and, as a result, abandons the production of the word. The critical comparison is her accuracy in producing the first syllable in the word. Here analysis shows no significant difference: Naming pre-test 1, $\chi^2(2) = 1.02$, $p = .60$; naming pre-test 2, $\chi^2(2) = 1.03$, $p = .60$; naming post phase 2, $\chi^2(2) = 1.04$, $p = .59$; naming follow-up, $\chi^2(2) = 5.84$, $p = .054$.

The more complex pattern of decay can be ruled out, but the data appear consistent with the idea of simple decay and more errors occurring later in words. However, another explanation for this pattern is that MB abandons words that are incorrect during or after the first or second syllable, which would mean that errors later in the word would tend to be omissions rather than substitutions. For the two naming pre-tests, the percentage of omission and substitution errors were therefore plotted for the first, second, and third syllables, and are shown in Figure 4. It can be seen that, as predicted, omission errors tend to occur in later syllables. Substitution errors do not show any effect of word position; there are a constant number of errors across the syllable positions. What then happens after therapy? Percentage omission and substitution errors in the two naming post-tests are also shown in Figure 4. The number of omission errors has not changed following therapy but the number of substitution errors shows an equal decrease across all syllable positions. The probabilistic model of the deficit in phoneme retrieval (or activation) seems the best explanation for MB's impaired speech production; treatment has increased the overall probability that phonemes will be produced correctly.

Analysis of MB's speech production demonstrated that word frequency and imageability did not affect performance. Phoneme length rather than syllable length predicted the number of errors. Syllable frequency did not affect naming. Omission errors increased later in a word, suggesting that MB abandoned words she was producing

TABLE 11
The proportion of phonemes correctly produced in each syllable of the word in picture naming

Test	Word length	Syllable		
		First	Second	Third
Pre-test 1	One syllable	0.762		
		(126)		
	Two syllables	0.736	0.660	
		(91)	(103)	
	Three syllables	0.683	0.595	0.500
		(41)	(37)	(52)
Pre-test 2	One syllable	0.695		
		(151)		
	Two syllables	0.745	0.737	
		(106)	(114)	
	Three syllables	0.821	0.667	0.580
		(39)	(36)	(50)
Post Phase 2	One syllable	0.950		
		(161)		
	Two syllables	0.943	0.890	
		(105)	(118)	
	Three syllables	0.837	0.750	0.754
		(43)	(44)	(57)
Follow-up	One syllable	0.899		
		(159)		
	Two syllables	0.980	0.922	
		(99)	(115)	
	Three syllables	0.833	0.738	0.754
		(48)	(42)	(61)

Only target-related initial responses are analysed. The number of phonemes for each word length and syllable position is given in parentheses.

incorrectly. However, substitution errors were constant across word positions, and it was substitution errors that reduced following treatment.

MB's production difficulty can, therefore, be accounted for by a difficulty in phoneme production. In Roelofs' WEAVER model, each phoneme needs to be independently activated for production. The more phonemes in the word the less likely it is that all the phonemes in the word are correctly activated.

Word production is better in reading and repetition than in naming because the phonological specification of the word is activated both lexically and sub-lexically. The accuracy of non-word production in reading and repetition is lower than with real words because the target phonology is specified only by sub-lexical routines.

Discussion

MB's impaired speech output appears to be attributable to a post-lexical deficit in phonological encoding. The impairment is related only to word phoneme length, and independent of syllable structure or syllable frequency. It applies both to words and non-words, but is more severe for non-words. The phoneme length effect is explicable in terms of a constant probability of incorrect phoneme production; following therapy this

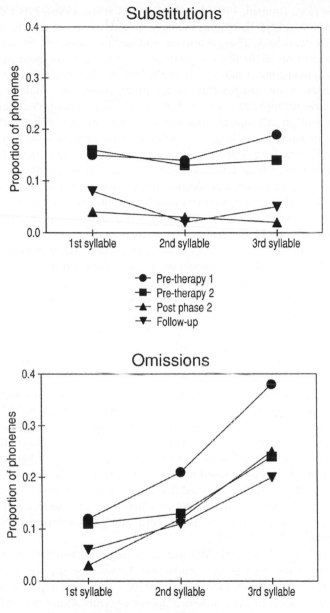

Figure 4. Omissions and substitutions in naming.

probability is reduced. It is then predictable that the effects of therapy have generalised; phoneme access is not a word-specific process.

GENERAL DISCUSSION

MB makes phonological errors in reading, repetition, and naming, with naming being the most impaired. She produces copious numbers of phonologically related errors, many of them non-words. Repeated self-correcting attempts at producing a word are often successful (*conduite d'approche*). As with several other patients with phonological errors in production (e.g., Romani, 1992; Wilshire & McCarthy, 1996), MB's difficulty cannot be attributed to a severe short-term memory deficit, as she is able to match strings of digits up to six items long. There is also no evidence of a semantic impairment that might be contributing to her difficulties in production. She makes no more semantic errors in picture naming than control subjects (Nickels, 1992b). Her single-word comprehension is good and there is no imageability effect in repetition or reading. This case is a particularly clear example of a deficit of phonological encoding. Phoneme length affects word production in all output modalities. There are no effects of frequency or imageability in naming, reading, or repetition. This pattern is in marked contrast to patients investigated, for example, by Kay and Ellis (1987) and Howard (1995) who have lexical-level deficits, strong effects of frequency, and good repetition. This contrast is consistent with a serial speech-production model that distinguishes between a level of phonological lexical representation and post-lexical processes of phonological assembly (Levelt et al., 1999). Assuming word frequency is a lexical property, it is unlikely that a more interactive model with feedback between phonological and lexical layers would produce length effects without effects of word frequency. Many individuals described as having reproduction conduction aphasia are affected by word frequency as well as word length (Shallice et al., 2000). This may be an indication that these individuals have a lexical-level deficit in addition to one of phonological encoding.

MB is very much worse at producing non-words than real words, but both words and non-words show a similar qualitative impairment in terms of error type and length. Like Shallice et al.'s (2000) patient LT, MB has a more severe impairment in non-word production than the patients who show an apparent dissociation between non-word and word production (e.g., IGR, Caramazza et al., 1986; MV, Bub et al., 1987). MB's non-word and word impairment is consistent with the notion that this one-way dissociation is in fact a severity continuum as suggested by Shallice et al. A mild impairment will produce errors in non-words only. A more severe impairment will produce more non-word errors and some (but fewer) word errors. All of these patients could have the same disorder of phonological encoding, but of varying severity. Further evidence for this notion is that MB's therapy, carried out on a set of real words, generalised to non-word production. In addition, we have argued that the fitted probabilities in repetition, reading, and naming do not accord with a model in which there are independent impairments to lexical and non-lexical processes, but accord better with impairment in a common process of phonological assembly.

The therapy carried out with MB had, as a major component, development of her ability to monitor her own speech production. Monitoring therapy might improve her speech for one of two reasons. First, MB might have had some impairment of monitoring. In fact, an examination of her *conduite d'approche* errors shows that MB could monitor her speech quite efficiently—she stopped producing attempts once the correct word had been produced. In the four pre-tests (naming × 2, repetition, and reading), MB produced 267 correct responses. On only four occasions (1.5%) did she produce a response that could possibly be described as an attempt to repair a correct response: twice she repeated a correct response; once she followed a correct response with "no"; and once she followed a correct response with a phonologically related error. The justification for the therapy was that it would give MB a conscious strategy for editing out repeated attempts and make speech more comprehensible, though perhaps more halting. There was no indication that this actually happened following therapy; speech was still fluent and correct names were more often produced immediately. *Conduite d'approche* behaviours reduced overall following therapy (although a higher proportion of them were successful;

see Table 7). Monitoring does not seem strongly implicated in MB's impaired production. A deficit in phonological encoding appears a much more plausible and sufficient explanation.

Both before and after therapy, MB's *conduite d'approche* demonstrated an excellent ability to produce self-corrections (either correct or closer to the target). For an impaired process, how is self-correction possible? It has been argued that MB's lexical processing is intact. An obvious mechanism for successful self-correction would be repeated activation proceeding from the lexical to the phonological level, refreshing and adding information. In an interactive model, where incorrect phoneme encoding will be constantly feeding back to the lexical level, it is not obvious how self-corrections might occur. RD (Miller & Ellis, 1987) did not self-correct over the course of his repeated naming attempts, which the authors attributed to his poor comprehension. An alternative account would be that RD had a lexical-level deficit (indicated by a word frequency effect), so was unable to add correct information for these multiple attempts. His poor comprehension explained why he continued making these fruitless attempts; monitoring *per se* is not an account of self-correction.

In Figure 1, we presented an elaborated model of phonological encoding (cf. Nickels, 1997). Is it possible to further specify MB's impairment(s) within this model? We have already argued that the deficit is post-lexical; could it be a deficit at the end of the encoding process, that is, an impairment in selecting/assembling syllables? When tests that manipulated syllable length were used, MB was always more impaired with words of more syllables. However, once phoneme length was introduced into the regressions there was no syllable length effect; only the number of phonemes in a word determined her production accuracy. MB's naming is affected by number of phonemes, not number of syllables. Neither was naming affected by syllable frequency; this was the case both before and after therapy. This case provides neither positive nor negative evidence for the existence of a syllabary; if there is a syllabary it does not appear to be impaired for MB.

Other possible levels of deficit are in selecting the required phonemes and assigning them to some kind of frame. Abnormally fast decay rates, at the phonological encoding level, could explain the length effect. An analysis of MB's errors by syllable does indicate a greater number of errors later in the word. She omits more phonemes in the third syllable than in the second, and least in the first syllable. However we have argued that the greater number of omission errors later in the word is rather an indication of MB abandoning the production of an incorrectly pronounced word. MB's substitution errors are not so obviously caused by decay—there are a constant number of errors for the first, second, and third syllable (note that this would still result in a length effect in the proportion of words produced correctly). This different pattern between omission and substitution errors is replicated over four administrations of the naming test. Following therapy, there was no obvious reduction of omission errors, and the distribution across word position remained the same, but numbers of substitution errors had reduced across all syllables. It appeared that MB's impairment was due to errors in phoneme encoding, and therapy directly reduced the proportion of these errors. Furthermore the effects of word phoneme length could be successfully modelled on the assumption that the probability of each phoneme being correctly retrieved was equal and independent. This would correspond naturally to the process of segment activation in production that occurs in parallel in Roelofs' (1997) WEAVER++ model, and serially in Dell et al.'s (1997; Foygel & Dell, 2000; Martin, Dell, Saffran, & Schwartz, 1994) models.

Therapy was successful both in the amount of improvement and in its generalisation across items and across tasks. Given that MB's ability to select phonemes has improved this is perhaps to be expected; more correct phonemes will affect all words (and non-words). We have established what improved in therapy, but we do not know how or why phoneme selection improved. Our therapy included tasks requiring and developing self-monitoring. It also included considerable practice in speech production. Given that, as we have argued, a difficulty in self-monitoring was not a prominent aspect of MB's difficulties in production before therapy (she repeatedly tried to correct phonological errors—*conduite d'approche*—and almost never attempted to correct a correct production), and there was no evidence that her improvement resulted from overt or covert self-correction, her improvement cannot be attributed to improved self-monitoring. Because the therapy included a variety of tasks and effectively required MB to produce words as well as practice monitoring, we have no way of knowing whether some elements of the therapy were more crucial than others. It would be interesting to treat further subjects with phonological errors in speech production, but using just particular aspects of the therapy used here. It is also worth noting that a therapy that used controlled, even meta-linguistic tasks appeared to have affected an automatic aspect of language processing.

In summary, this case report presents data that are compatible with an underlying post-lexical difficulty in phoneme activation (or retrieval) that cannot be attributed to a problem in decay in a phoneme buffer. Treatment resulted in generalised improvement in speech production reflecting improved phoneme activation.

REFERENCES

Baayen, R.H., Piepenbrock, R., & Gulikers, L. (1995). *The CELEX Lexical Database* (Release 2) [CD-ROM]. Philadelphia, PA: Linguistic Data Consortium, University of Pennsylvania.

Best, W. (1996). When racquets are baskets but baskets are biscuits, where do the words come from? A single word study of formal paraphasic errors in aphasia. *Cognitive Neuropsychology, 13*, 443–480.

Bishop, D.V.M. (1982). *TROG test for reception of grammar.* Newcastle upon Tyne: Medical Research Council.

Blanken, G. (1990). Lexicalisation in speech production: evidence from form-related word substitutions in aphasia. *Cognitive Neuropsychology, 15*, 321–360.

Bub, D., Black, S., Howell, J., & Kertesz, A. (1987). Speech output processes and reading. In M. Coltheart, R. Job, & G. Sartori (Eds.), *The cognitive neuropsychology of language.* Hove, UK: Lawrence Erlbaum Associates Ltd.

Butterworth, B. (1992). Disorders of phonological encoding. *Cognition, 42*, 261–286.

Caplan, D., Vanier, M., & Baker, C. (1986). A case study of reproduction conduction aphasia. I: Word production. *Cognitive Neuropsychology, 3*, 99–128.

Caramazza, A., Miceli, G., & Villa, G. (1986). The role of the (output) phonological buffer in reading, writing and repetition. *Cognitive Neuropsychology, 3*, 37–76.

Dell, G.S., Schwartz, M.F., Martin, N., Saffran, E.M., & Gagnon D.A. (1997). Lexical access in aphasic and nonaphasic speakers. *Psychological Review, 104*, 801–838.

Dubois, J., Hecaen, H., Angelergues, R., Maufras de Chatelier, A., & Marcie, P. (1964). Neurolinguistic study of conduction aphasia. *Neuropsychologia, 2*, 9–44.

Foygel, D., & Dell, G.S. (2000). Models of impaired lexical access in speech production. *Journal of Memory and Language, 43*, 182–216.

Fromkin, V. (1971). The nonanomalous nature of anomalous utterances. *Language, 47*, 27–52.

Goldstein, K. (1948). *Language and language disturbances.* New York: Grune & Stratton.

Goodglass, H., & Kaplan, E. (1972). *The assessment of aphasia and related disorders.* Philadelphia, PA: Lea & Febiger.

Howard, D. (1995). Lexical anomia (or the case of the missing entries). *Quarterly Journal of Experimental Psychology, 48*A, 999–1023.

Howard, D. (2000). Cognitive neuropsychology and aphasia therapy: The case of word retrieval. In I. Papathanasiou (Ed.), *Advances in acquired neurogenic language disorders: A clinical perspective* (pp. 76–99). London: Whurr.

Howard, D., Patterson, K.E., Franklin, S.E., Orchard-Lisle, V.M., & Morton, J. (1985a). The facilitation of picture naming in aphasia. *Cognitive Neuropsychology, 2,* 49–80.

Howard, D., Patterson, K.E., Franklin, S.E., Orchard-Lisle, V.M., & Morton, J. (1985b). The treatment of word retrieval deficits in aphasia: A comparison of two therapy methods. *Brain, 108,* 817–829.

Howard, D., & Smith, K. (2002). The effects of lexical stress in aphasic word production. *Aphasiology, 16,* 198–237.

Joanette, Y., Keller, E., & Lecours, A.R. (1980). Sequences of phoneme approximations in aphasia. *Brain and Language, 11,* 30–44.

Kay, J., & Ellis, A.W. (1987). A cognitive neuropsychological case study of anomia: Implications for psychological models of word retrieval. *Brain, 110,* 613–629.

Kay, J., Lesser, R., & Coltheart, M. (1992). *PALPA: Psycholinguistic assessments of language processing in aphasia.* Hove, UK: Lawrence Erlbaum Associates Ltd.

Kinsbourne, M. (1972). Behavioural analysis of the repetition deficit in conduction aphasia. *Neurology, 22,* 1126–1132.

Kohn, S.E., & Goodglass, H. (1985). Picture-naming in aphasia. *Brain and Language, 24,* 266–283.

Kohn, S.F, Smith, K.L., & Arsenault, J.K. (1990). The remediation of conduction aphasia via sentence repetition: A case study. *British Journal of Disorders of Communication, 25,* 45–60.

Le Dorze, G. (1991). Intervention for severe word retrieval problems in a patient with conduction aphasia. *Journal of Speech-Language Pathology and Audiology, 15,* 21–29.

Levelt, W.J.M. (1989). *Speaking: From intention to articulation.* Cambridge, MA: MIT Press.

Levelt, W.J.M., Roelofs, A., & Meyer, A.S. (1999). A theory of lexical access in speech production. *Behavioural and Brain Sciences, 22,* 1–75.

Levelt, W.J.M., & Wheeldon, L. (1994). Do speakers have access to a mental syllabary? *Cognition, 50,* 239–269.

Maher, L.M., Gonzalez Rothi, L.J., & Heilman, K.M. (1994). Lack of error awareness in an aphasic patient with relatively preserved auditory comprehension. *Brain and Language, 46,* 402–418

Martin N., Dell G.S., Saffran E.M., & Schwartz, M.F. (1994). Origins of paraphasias in deep dysphasia—testing the consequences of a decay impairment to an interactive spreading activation model of lexical retrieval. *Brain and Language, 47,* 609–660.

Meyer, A.S. (1990). The time course of phonological encoding in language production: The encoding of successive syllables of a word. *Journal of Memory and Language, 29,* 524–545.

Miceli, G., Amitrano, A., Capasso, R., & Caramazza, A. (1996). The remediation of anomia resulting from output lexical damage: Analysis of two cases. *Brain and Language, 52,* 150–174.

Miller, D., & Ellis, A.W. (1987). Speech and writing errors in 'neologistic jargonaphasia': A lexical activation hypothesis. In M. Coltheart, R. Job, & G. Sartori (Eds.), *The cognitive neuropsychology of language.* Hove, UK: Lawrence Erlbaum Associates Ltd.

Nickels, L.A. (1992a). The autocue? Self-generated phoneme cues in the treatment of a disorder of reading and naming. *Cognitive Neuropsychology, 9,* 155–182.

Nickels, L.A. (1992b). *Spoken word production and its breakdown in aphasia.* Unpublished PhD thesis, University of London.

Nickels, L.A. (1997). *Spoken word production and its breakdown in aphasia.* Hove, UK: Psychology Press.

Nickels, L.A., & Howard, D. (1995). Phonological errors in aphasic naming: Comprehension, monitoring and lexicality. *Cortex, 31,* 209–237.

Nickels, L.A., & Howard, D. (2000). When the words won't come: Relating impairments and models of speech production. In L. Wheeldon (Ed.), *Aspects of language production.* Hove, UK: Psychology Press.

Pate, D.S., Saffran, E.M., & Martin, N. (1987). Specifying the nature of the production deficit in conduction aphasia: A case study. *Language and Cognitive Processes, 2,* 43–84.

Roelofs, A. (1997). The WEAVER model of word-form encoding in speech production. *Cognition, 64,* 249–284.

Roelofs, A. (2000). WEAVER++ and other computational models of lemma retrieval and word-form encoding. In L. Wheeldon (Ed.), *Aspects of language production* (pp. 71–114). Hove, UK: Psychology Press.

Roelofs, A. (2002). Spoken language planning and the initiation of articulation. *Quarterly Journal of Experimental Psychology, 55A,* 465–483.

Romani, C. (1992). Are there distinct input and output buffers? Evidence from an aphasic patient with an impaired output buffer. *Language and Cognitive Processes, 7,* 131–162.

Saffran, E.M., Berndt, R.S., & Schwartz, M.F. (1989). The quantitative analysis of agrammatic production; Procedure and data. *Brain and Language, 37,* 440–479.

Schlenk, K-J., Huber, W., & Willmes, K. (1987). ''Prepairs'' and repairs. Different monitoring functions in aphasic language production. *Brain and Language, 30,* 226–244.

Shallice, T., Rumiati, R.I., & Zadini, A. (2000). The selective impairment of the phonological output buffer. *Cognitive Neuropsychology*, *17*, 517–546.

Shallice, T., & Warrington, E.K. (1977). Auditory-verbal short-term memory impairment and conduction aphasia. *Brain and Language*, *4*, 479–491.

Shattuck-Hufnagel, S. (1992). The role of word structure in segmental serial ordering. *Cognition*, *42*, 213–259.

Strub, R.L., & Gardner, H. (1974). The repetition deficit in conduction aphasia: Mnestic or linguistic? *Brain and Language*, *1*, 241–255.

Swinburn, K., Baker, G., & Howard, D (unpublished). *The Comprehensive Aphasia Test*.

Valdois, S., Joanette, Y., & Nespoulous, J-L. (1989). Intrinsic organisation of sequences of phonemic approximations: A preliminary study. *Aphasiology*, *3*, 55–73.

Wheeldon, L., & Levelt, W.J.M. (1995). Monitoring the time course of phonological encoding. *Journal of Memory and Language*, *34*, 311–334.

Wilshire, C.E., & McCarthy, R.A. (1996). Experimental investigations of an impairment in phonological encoding. *Cognitive Neuropsychology*, *13*, 1059–1098.

APPENDIX 1

MB's telling of the Cinderella story—pre-therapy (first 100 words)

"well eh it's eh this eh Cinderella eh eh /hæd/ very two very /hæ/ very /sə/ sisters eh very /hu/ very /kʌn ɪn ə ɪn tu/ eh very eh eh /aʊwə wiwə ði ðə wər/ very /ʌnkunt/ to do /hɑr/ and /mɪt hʌnd/ to /duɑrt/ all /də/ work and /dɪdn/ do give her /hɛ/ any /pɛplɛsə bɛ/ and eh and /ʌn digəʊt wɛt/ up and and little /ðɛ/ were /rə/ rather /ə ʌldwə/ and so eh /də/ eh even /ðɛ ðɛ sɪ drɒdʌm bi bə gɒ də/ (4 unintelligible syllables) /mɛrin mɑis/ because /ɑɪ ria wɛɪv/ eh eh ehm /nʌs/ nasty /mə/ minds"

MB's telling of the Cinderella story—post-therapy (first 100 words)

"eh it /wə wə/ once upon a time /wə/ there were /sɪ/ sisters ... one /wɔ də lɪs ɪtl/ little /sə sɛs/ sister and she / wə/ very badly /titəd/ she /mɛ/ she /wu bɛ bi/ to do all the housework and /ði/ the sisters who /wə/ very /əgrɪp/ people eh /vɛ nə/ nasty people these they eh eh they get they get they get /də dʌ/ right up /əd/ lovely /klɔʊs ʌθi θɛ θɛd/ they the were /fɜɪθ ifə/ thought /utɪful/ and and /də/ little Cinderella had to do all the work and so in a way one day there"

APHASIOLOGY, 2002, *16* (10/11), 1115–1136

The representation of homophones: Evidence from remediation

Britta Biedermann

Albert-Ludwigs-Universität, Freiburg, Germany, and Macquarie University, Sydney, Australia

Gerhard Blanken

Albert-Ludwigs-Universität, Freiburg, and Otto-von-Guericke-Universität, Magdeburg, Germany

Lyndsey Nickels

Macquarie University, Sydney, Australia

Background: This single case study examines the linguistic phenomenon of ambiguous spoken words: *homophones*. In the psycholinguistic research literature the lexicalisation of homophones is the subject of extensive debate. A common assumption is that these words share one word form but have two grammatical representations (lemmas). An opposing view postulates two separate word form entries for homophones—without assuming a lemma level.
Aims: The single case study presented here searches for empirical evidence for the representation of homophones using aphasic speech production. Can aphasic speech production give us some evidence regarding how many processing levels have to be completed prior to articulation?
Methods & Procedures: A treatment study with MW, a man with global aphasia and severe anomia, is presented. Treatment comprised an intensive picture-naming training with exclusively phonological cues. Naming was facilitated using the following cueing hierarchy: (i) giving the initial phoneme, (ii) tapping the syllable number, and (iii) giving the target word for repetition. How this pure phonological training would affect naming performance of homophones, semantically and phonologically related words, and unrelated words was investigated.
Outcomes & Results: The results showed significant short-term, item-specific effects for treated words and generalisation to untreated homophone words alone. The outcome is discussed with reference to the debate regarding homophone production in psycholinguistics and the debate regarding the facilitatory effects of phonological techniques.
Conclusions: The results support the two stage model, with only one word form and two lemma entries for homophones. In addition, the outcome of this phonological treatment supports the common assumption that pure word form training rarely results in long-term improvement or generalisation.

Address correspondence to: Britta Biedermann, Macquarie Centre for Cognitive Science, Macquarie University, Sydney, NSW 2109, Australia. Email: *britta@maccs.mq.edu.au*

We thank MW who offered so much time, interest, and energy participating in this study. We also thank Florian Kulke, Petra Krehnke, Sandra Hollstein, Michael Walter, Tobias Bormann, and two reviewers for interesting discussions and helpful comments on an earlier draft. Lyndsey Nickels was funded by an Australian research Council QEII fellowship during the preparation of this paper, and Gerhard Blanken by DFG WA 509/12-3.

http://www.tandf.co.uk/journals/pp/02687038.html

DOI:10.1080/02687030244000545

When we take a close look at the mechanisms of speech production, the question arises: what happens from the moment of having a thought until these thoughts are put into words, and, more specifically, what basic steps of processing are involved in the generation of lexical items?

One approach to answering these questions is that of the *two stage model* of lexicalisation proposed by Levelt and his co-workers (e.g., Levelt, 1989, 1999; Levelt, Roelofs, & Meyer, 1999). This model contains a concept level[1] that provides semantic information, e.g., CAT has the properties *is an animal, is alive, can purr* etc. Levelt et al. postulate holistic conceptual semantic representations, where one abstract concept rather than a cluster of semantic features represents CAT.[2] After a concept has been chosen, lexicalisation can begin. The lexicalisation process itself consists of two distinct processes. According to the original theory (Levelt, 1989), lemma units, which contain lexically coded semantic-syntactic information, must be activated and selected before the appropriate word form information can be accessed. In the latest version of the two stage model (Levelt et al., 1999), the first step of lexicalisation comprises only a pure syntactic phase (activation of the *lemma level*), which has to be completed before morphophonological features *(word form level)* are accessible.[3] Lemma units are proposed to be modality-neutral representations, thus serving input and output mechanisms in both spoken and written language. Lemmas are activated in parallel by conceptual information (resulting in a cohort of active lemmas) and the lemma with the highest activation is finally selected. This lemma functions as a *pointer,* activating just *one* appropriate modality-specific word form entry. According to Levelt et al. (1999) more than one word form may be activated (as in the case of, e.g., blends), but only in contexts where two lexical targets are highly interchangeable (e.g., synonyms).

DO WE NEED LEMMAS?

A general question that has arisen since the "appearance" of the lemma level (Kempen & Huijbers, 1983) is this: why can't we just assume direct access from the concept to the word form level? Is there really enough empirical evidence to require an intermediate stage where only syntactic information is available?

Early neurolinguistic evidence supporting the lemma hypothesis came from a case study describing an Italian anomic aphasic who was nearly perfect at providing correct grammatical gender information in cases of blocked word form access (Badecker, Miozzo, & Zanuttini, 1995; see also Henaff Gonon, Bruckert, & Michel, 1989 for similar observations). The same Italian patient was also shown to have relatively preserved knowledge about verb auxiliaries in spite of his anomic problems (Miozzo & Caramazza, 1997, but see their interpretation). Similarly, normal Italian speakers were found to be able to report the grammatical gender of the target word in experimentally elicited tip-of-the-tongue situations even when no form information (about metrical or segmental features) was available (see Vigliocco, Antonini, & Garrett, 1997). Of course, the lemma hypothesis can easily account for the dissociations between syntactic and phonological lexical access just described.

---

[1] Whether the concept level includes lexical or non-lexical concepts depends on the version of the model (for discussions see Nickels, 2001).

[2] An expanded discussion of different semantic theories cannot be given here, but for an opposing viewpoint see Bierwisch and Schreuder's (1992) decompositional semantic theory.

[3] For a summary of the differences between the "old" and the "new" lemma see Nickels, 2001.

Is the lemma hypothesis the only theory that accounts for these data? Opponents of the lemma hypothesis express doubts that there is sufficient evidence to require a lexical level of pre-phonological syntactic information, and suggest direct access from a semantic to a lexical form level. They agree that syntactic information is specified and accessed independently from phonological and semantic knowledge. However, in their model—the independent network (IN) model—syntactic information is selected after lexical form selection has been completed (see, e.g., Caramazza, 1997; Caramazza & Miozzo, 1997, 1998).

Kulke and Blanken (2001) analysed the distribution of the syntactic feature of gender in picture naming of nouns for a group of German aphasics. They found that the semantic errors preserved the gender of the target word significantly more often than would be expected by chance. These results, together with electrophysiological (Van Turennout, Hagoort, & Brown, 1997) and chronometrical (Pechmann & Zerbst, 2002) evidence on the time course of speech production in normals, suggest that word form access may indeed be preceded by processes of semantic and syntactic specification as postulated by the lemma hypothesis.

One of the major issues in the ongoing debate about the lemma hypothesis concerns the representation and access of homophones and we will now turn to this in more detail.

HOW CAN HOMOPHONES HELP TO SOLVE THE "LEMMA PROBLEM"?

Homophones are words that sound the same but possess two or more different meanings, e.g., CRICKET (the animal) and CRICKET (the game). Homophones can be *heterographic*, e.g., FLOWER and FLOUR, or *homographic*, e.g., BALL (the game) and BALL (the dance). In speech perception homophones are semantically ambiguous, whereas in speech production no ambiguity occurs: when a homophone is heard or read it can only be disambiguated by the listener with the help of context, whereas when generating a homophone the relationship between concept and word form is clear-cut to the speaker.

Representation of homophones in the lexicon

Do homophones share one phonological entry or is their phonology stored twice? Homophones like MORE (a high-frequency adjective) and MOOR (a low-frequency noun) differ in their syntactic properties and therefore require different representations for their grammatical features. In contrast, the phonological forms are identical, so there might be no need to assume two separate word form entries. If we assume that our speech-processing system is built on the most efficient and economical mechanisms, a reasonable hypothesis could be to assume only one word form representation for homophones.

Analysing speech errors of nonaphasic speakers, Dell (1990) found that low-frequency words are more error-prone than high-frequency words (regardless of whether they are content or function words) whereas high- and low-frequency homophones show no such difference in error rates. Dell explains this homophone effect by assuming that the two homophone lemmas share one word form representation. The lemma entries differ in frequency, but feedback mechanisms between the lemma level and the phonological representation allow the low-frequency homophone twin to benefit from the higher activation of the high-frequency homophone. Apparently, the low-frequency homophone *inherits* the frequency of its high-frequency partner and is therefore less error-prone (see Figure 1).

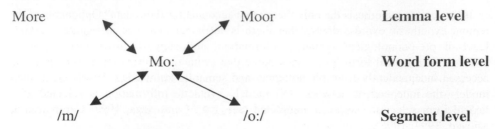

Figure 1.   Homophone representation: Dell (1990) (but see also Dell et al., 1997, where all explicit word-form level is no longer assumed; the adjacent level to the lemma level seems to be the segment level now).

Jescheniak and Levelt (1994) (see also Roelofs, Meyer, & Levelt, 1998 for discussion) also postulate two different lemma entries for homophones, which project onto one word form entry. They use empirical evidence from an English–Dutch translation task, focusing on high- and low-frequency homophones. An English word like BUNCH was visually presented. Dutch students were then asked to translate these English nouns together with their article into Dutch[4] (e.g. BUNCH or FOREST into [de/het] BOS). Jescheniak and Levelt (1994) found that low-frequency homophones had almost identical translation times compared to high-frequency homophones, whereas high- and low-frequency non-homophones, (matched to the homophones) showed a clear frequency effect in translation time. According to their theory, frequency is localised at the word form level. Jescheniak and Levelt assume that the low-frequency homophones profit from a lower threshold level at the word form level, caused by the high-frequency twin. Therefore they infer that homophone lemmas point to one (shared) word form entry (in a strictly feed-forward fashion).

Recently, Caramazza, Costa, Miozzo, and Bi (2001) tried to replicate these results in a Spanish–English translation task with bilingual speakers. They failed to find a homophone effect like that of Levelt and colleagues (see Caramazza et al., 2001). Instead, they found different translation times for high- and low-frequency homophones: the low-frequency twin needs significantly more time to be translated. This clear-cut frequency effect, even for homophone words, supports the hypothesis of two separate homophone representations (but see Jescheniak, Levelt & Meyer, in press).[5] This hypothesis is also strengthened by neurolinguistic evidence, where two aphasic individuals showed a double dissociation between written and oral production for homophonic verbs and nouns (see Caramazza & Hillis, 1991). Patient HW could read, for

---

[4] Dutch differentiates between three grammatical genders. According to the two stage model translating the noun together with the article involves lemma access, because at that level syntactic information including grammatical gender is represented.

[5] In two experiments Jescheniak et al. replicated the results of the Jescheniak and Levelt (1994) English–Dutch translation task in both an English–Dutch and an English–German translation design. They found for both experiments a clear condition effect, where high-frequency non-homophones showed a significantly faster translation time than the low-frequency non-homophones. Homophones, regardless of whether high or low in frequency, showed almost the same translation time and no significant difference could be found compared to the high-frequency non-homophones, except for the English–German translation task. For the English–Dutch translation task no significant difference between word groups was found, whereas in the English–German translation task a significant difference was detected, in favour of the high-frequency non-homophones. Translation time and error rate for all word groups decreased with repetition, whereas the homophone effect was maintained.

example, the homophone noun *watch* but not the homophone verb *watch*, whereas patient SJD could write the homophone noun, but not the verb. Hence, Caramazza (1997; Caramazza & Miozzo, 1998) holds the conviction that the data on homophone processing do not unambiguously support the two stage model and argues that the data support the IN model that assumes no lemma level but just *one* lexical level, and two different word form entries for homophones.

We can summarise the recent debate regarding how homophones are represented in the two diagrams shown in Figure 2.

(a)

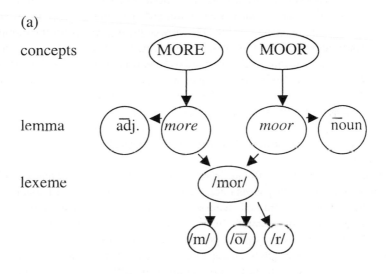

(b)

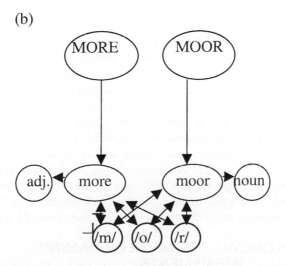

Figure 2. Homophone representation in (a) the discrete two stage model and (b) the "one" stage model of Caramazza (adapted from Roelofs et al., 1998).

EVIDENCE FROM THE TREATMENT OF APHASIA

The starting point of the present study was observations made of the verbal learning behaviour of TH, a man with global aphasia, reported in Blanken (1989). TH was a 62-year-old German printer and engraver who suffered extensive left hemisphere damage following a stroke (haemorrhage) 5 years before the onset of the study, which left him with a severe but relatively fluent aphasia. At the time of examination his auditory comprehension (word–picture matching) and his repetition abilities had recovered quite well at the single word level. However, oral picture naming was very poor, as was his spontaneous output which mostly consisted of real word recurring utterances. His error pattern in naming was mainly dominated by omissions with only a few semantic and phonological errors.

Blanken (1989) reports two verbal learning experiments (both noun-naming tasks). In both experiments only word-form-related treatment techniques were used, including phonological cueing and repetition. While TH showed clear benefits for the trained items, there was no learning transfer from trained to non-trained items either for unrelated words (Experiment 1) or for meaning related words (Experiment 2). However, 10 pairs of homophones of which one "twin" of each pair was used as a training item were included in the second experiment (10 sessions/days of training). On the pre-test (100 targets presented 5 days before training onset) his results were poor with both "twin" sets of homophones (1/10 and 3/10). On post-test 1 (one day after treatment) he reached 8/10 correct responses in both conditions. On post-test 2 (6 days after treatment) he still named 9/10 and 7/10 correctly.

Blanken argued that TH suffered from raised thresholds for phonological output representations and that such patients are predicted to learn in a word-specific manner with no generalisation to untrained materials (see also Miceli, Amitrano, Capasso, & Caramazza, 1996). As an account of the unexpected results with the untrained homophone "twins" he suggested a possible unitary representation for both word meanings at the form level, thus connecting evidence from treatment results with a hypothesis on the psycholinguistic representation of words.

However, in a number of aspects we regard the results from homophone production by TH as preliminary. First, the focus of the study was not on homophone production but on possible generalisation from trained to untrained words in an unrelated and a meaning-related condition. Second, at the time of the study there was no theoretical framework that predicted the special status of homophones. Thus, the results on homophones were a theoretically unguided or post-hoc observation. Third, no condition of phonological relatedness was included for comparison with the semantic and homophone condition. Hence, it was possible that the homophone effect was an effect of generalisation to phonologically related items. Fourth, and as a major methodological drawback, no norms were used to balance the frequency or dominance of usage within the pairs of homophone "twins". Finally, no statistical analysis was carried out in order to demonstrate significant differences between the critical conditions. Thus, having both the "new" theoretical background about homophone representation as well as the listed short-comings in mind, it seemed worthwhile to take Blanken's observations of 1989 as a starting point for a second treatment study that focuses on the production of homophones.

"PHONOLOGICAL" THERAPY FOR NAMING IMPAIRMENTS

What happens when we use therapy techniques that focus on the word form, like repetition, reading aloud, phonological cueing, syllable tapping?

As described earlier for TH (Blanken, 1989), phonological tasks can result in item-specific improvement. Howard, Patterson, Franklin, Orchard-Lisle, and Morton (1985a,b) found that phonological cues had an item-specific, short-lasting facilitation effect, up to 15 minutes with no generalisation, and the effect could be strengthened and maintained up to 1 week, if the cueing techniques were used repeatedly over 1 or 2 weeks. These results can be called the "classical" assumption about the effect of phonological techniques in therapy, and may have led to the prevalence in the use of semantic techniques (perceived to be more likely to produce generalisation). Nevertheless, Hickin, Best, Herbert, Howard, and Osborne (2002) emphasise that phonological and orthographic cues can be highly effective in improving word retrieval. They conclude, "...that phonological and orthographic treatments for word finding difficulties [...] represent an under-utilised and under-researched tool in the clinician's armoury" (Hickin et al., 2002, abstract).

Indeed it has become clear that there can be other possible outcomes in phonological therapy. Studies on the remediation of anomia using phonological techniques have reported contrasting results. They have found *no generalisation*, where improvement is restricted to treated words (e.g., Howard et al., 1985a,b); *partial generalisation*, where improvement transfers to untreated words that belong to the same semantic domain (e.g., Miceli et al., 1996; Raymer, Thompson, Jacobs, & Le Grand, 1993); and also *complete generalisation*, where an improvement of untreated words could be observed, independent of whether or not they belong to the same semantic field as the treated words (e.g., Robson, Marshall, Pring, & Chiat, 1998).

The inconsistent results of these studies are very difficult to reconcile and to compare because different methodologies and therapy designs were used (and, of course, different individuals with aphasia!). So we are left with the question: What is the relationship between the form of therapy offered and its results?[6]

CONNECTING THEORY WITH THERAPY?

This single case study of therapy for anomia aims to answer the two questions that follow. It will address the questions by attempting to replicate and extend the results of Blanken (1989). It reports the results of a phonological naming training with a German anomic man, MW.

(1) Can further neurolinguistic evidence regarding the representation of homophones be obtained?

In order to answer this question, the treatment focuses on one of a pair on homophones (e.g., BALL—a homophone in German as well as English). Will treatment of the homophone BALL (dancing) improve the naming performance of the untreated BALL (game)? If it does (as was found by Blanken, 1989), we can assume *one* word form entry but *two* different lemma entries. In contrast, no naming improvement for the untreated homophone would support the assumption of two separate word form entries.

---

[6] Moreover, excluding semantic influences from phonological therapy—to ensure a purely phonological technique—is an impossible task. Indeed, some authors have suggested that in so-called "semantic" therapy (e.g., auditory/written word–picture matching) it may be the combination of semantic and phonological information that is important for efficacy (e.g., Nickels & Best, 1996a,b).

(2) Is there any evidence that intensive naming training with phonological techniques can result in a significant naming improvement and, if so, what pattern of generalisation is obtained, and how long are effects maintained?

In order to allow more detailed examination of the extent of generalisation from phonological tasks, three further conditions were included in the design (semantically related; phonologically related; unrelated). Will treatment effects be restricted to treated items or will there be generalisation to semantically related distractors (e.g., as was found by Miceli et al., 1996, Raymer et al., 1993, and Robson et al., 1998) or more widely to phonologically related and unrelated items?

METHOD

Materials

The stimuli were 64 concrete nouns taken from Snodgrass and Vanderwart (1980); Neubert, Rüffer, and Zeh-Hau (1995); Druks and Masterson (1999); and from private material. Name agreement norms for the pictures were obtained by standardisation with 21 students (age range 19–29, median: 25, 11 female, 10 male). Stimuli were divided into 32 treated items and 32 untreated control items (see Appendix). The design included four different conditions (homophones, semantically related, phonologically related, and unrelated). Each condition contained 16 items. The items were subdivided into pairs (treated, n = 8; untreated, n = 8) (see Table 1). The pairs were matched for frequency[7] and syllable number (see Appendix). Frequency ranges were established as follows: high-frequency: 211–1267; mid-frequency: 65–210; low-frequency: 0–64. Only two-syllable words were used for the semantically related, phonologically related, and unrelated conditions, but this criterion could not be fulfilled for the homophone condition because of the small number of possible items.

TABLE 1
Experimental design

8 homophone pairs (treated-untreated)		
treated		*untreated*
e.g., treatment of *Ball* (dancing)	⟶	generalisation for *Ball* (game)?
8 semantically related pairs (treated-untreated)		
treated		*untreated*
e.g., treatment of *Fenster* (window)	⟶	generalisation for *Tür* (door)?
8 phonologically related pairs (treated-untreated)		
treated		*untreated*
e.g., treatment of *Vase* (vase)	⟶	generalisation for *Nase* (nose)?
8 unrelated pairs (treated-untreated)		
treated		*untreated*
e.g., treatment of *Geige* (violin)	⟶	generalisation for *Apfel* (apple)?

Experimental design with four different conditions, which are divided into treated and control items. For each condition an example pair is given (see Appendix for the whole corpus).

---

[7] The frequency data were taken from the CELEX Mannheim Korpus of the Institute for German Language, which is based on 6 million entries ($5\frac{1}{2}$ million words were taken from written and $\frac{1}{2}$ million wee taken from oral sources) (Baayen, Piepenbrock, & van Rijn, 1993).

Case history

MW, a 59-year-old man, suffered a stroke in February 1987. The CT scan revealed a fresh ischaemic lesion in the area of the left middle cerebral artery, further lesions in the fronto-parietal and temporal lobes and parts of the frontal perisylvian area. Lesions resulted in a dense right hemiplegia and a severe global aphasia. No visual deficits and no hearing loss could be detected.

Before his stroke, MW worked as an electrician and as an estate agent. He is a right-handed monolingual German speaker. After the stroke he received several periods of intensive therapy in medical rehabilitation centres. At the time of this study he received 1 hour of therapy a fortnight. During this therapy MW concentrated mainly on conversational skills and learned how to use his new computer. There were no picture-naming tasks carried out within these sessions (which overlapped with our treatment only twice). We can therefore exclude any effects on our treatment. This study began in April 2000, 13 years after the onset of aphasia.

Language presentation: Investigation of input and output

Spontaneous speech.   MW's spontaneous speech overwhelmingly consisted of his recurrent utterances "Ja weißt du was?" ("You know what?") and some affirmation and negation particles like "ja" ("yes"), "nein" ("no"), "doch" ("of course"). Spontaneous expressions like "ach so" ("I see"), "gut" ("great") or "ach" ("well") and forms of greeting, names of the week, days, or months as well as names for numbers were observed, but occurred rarely.

Aachen Aphasia Test (AAT).   The results of the AAT (Huber, Poeck, Weniger, & Willmes, 1983) showed the language profile presented in Table 2. MW could be classified as a global aphasic. He was severely impaired in all subtests except for repetition and comprehension where he reached a moderate level of impairment.

Impaired short-term memory.   MW's verbal short-term memory was severely impaired. His performance in digit repetition span was extremely poor (two numbers in a row: 8/30 correct; three numbers: 3/20 correct; four numbers 0/20 correct). Phonological deficits as the cause for poor verbal short-term memory can be ruled out because of superior performances in repetition of four-syllable compound words, e.g., FINGERNAGEL (fingernail) (56/60 correct) and pseudo-compounds like NAGELFIN-

TABLE 2
AAT results for MW

Subtests of the AAT	Percentile ranks	Assessment of spontaneous speech (1–5 points)	Points (1–5)
Token Test	21	Communicative behaviour	1
Repetition	33	Articulation and prosody	3
Written Language	26	Automatised language	1
Naming	22	Semantic structure	0
Language Comprehension	31	Phonological structure	0
		Syntactic structure	0

GER (nailfinger) (46/60 correct)). Although this performance is impaired, MW's ability to repeat was a strength compared to his performance on other language tasks.

Auditory comprehension.   An *auditory lexical decision task* in which real words and non-(pseudo)words must be differentiated, was performed with a high degree of accuracy (see Table 3). Auditory access to the lexical form level itself seems therefore to be relatively intact.

The multiple-choice materials of Blanken (1996) identified that MW had difficulties differentiating between semantically very close concepts but fair performance with more distant foils (see Table 3). In order to further tap his semantic comprehension abilities, the auditory synonym judgement task from PALPA (Kay, Lesser, & Coltheart, 1992) was translated and adapted to German. In this task MW had to decide whether the pairs of words were synonyms or non-synonyms. Overall MW correctly classified 40/60 pairs (see Table 3). His impairment was most marked for low-imageability words. These results were supported by the subtest *word–semantic association*, where a written target is presented together with four written words, two of them semantically related (close and distant) to the target and two of them unrelated. Again, MWs performance for the high-imageability words was slightly better than for the low-imageability words (see Table 3).

TABLE 3
MW's auditory and visual input processing

	First trial	Second trial (1 week later)
Auditory lexical decision		
Real words correct	35/40*	39/40
Pseudo words correct	40/40	39/40
Auditory and visual word–picture matching (Blanken, 1996)		
Part A (4 choices, 3 unrelated distractors)		
Auditory correct	19/20	
Visual correct	17/20	
Part B (4 choices, 5 same-category distractors & 1 unrelated distractor)		
Auditory correct	31/40	
Visual correct	35/40	
Part C (6 choices, 5 same-category distractors)		
Auditory correct	14/20	
Visual correct	17/20	
Auditory judgement of synonyms (Palpa; Kay et al., 1992):		
High-imageability correct	23/30	
Low-imageability correct	17/30	
Overall correct	40/60	
Controls (n = 18)		
Median correct	58	
Word-semantic associations (PALPA; Kay et al., 1992)		
High-imageability	7/15 correct	4/15 (semantic distractor)
Low-imageability	5/15 correct	5/15 (semantic distractor)

* 37/40 including self-corrections.

A picture association task, similar to the *pyramids and palm trees test* (Howard & Patterson, 1992) was successfully completed by MW. All of the 30 triplets (e.g., CHEESE–PIG/COW*)* were matched correctly.

Oral and written word production.   In the Comparative Analysis of Linguistic Functions (CALF) (see Table 4) (Freiburger Funktionenvergleichsprüfung [FFVP]; Blanken, Döppler, Dittmann, & Wallesch, 1988) MW showed high scores in repetition of nouns, matched non-words, and function words. Reading the same items aloud was markedly poorer for nouns, whereas the non-words and function words could not be read aloud at all. MW was unable to perform written word production, and so was not tested. Oral naming was severely impaired, but seemed to be better than spontaneous word production (see results of the AAT, Table 2). Furthermore, MW seemed to be helped by phonemic cues—around 50% of previously failed items were successfully named following a phonemic cue.

MW's naming pattern has been extensively studied in Blanken and Kulke (in press) and Blanken, Dittmann, and Wallesch (in press). For example, for the Snodgrass and Vanderwart picture series he reached 24% correct responses. His error pattern consisted of 54% omissions, 16% semantic errors, 2% perseverations, and 4% other errors including form-related responses, unrelated responses, and a few fragmentary or neologistic responses. In addition, there were some phonetic inaccuracies due to a mild dysarthria that did not, however, affect the intelligibility of his speech. As MW's naming was largely unaffected by phonological errors, we can focus on the lexical component of his naming performance.

Functional localisation of the deficit.   MW showed clear semantic comprehension deficits. Repetition of single words was accurate, hence a phonological encoding impairment can be excluded. The effectiveness of phonemic cues confirms that there was no lexical storage impairment. Hence MW's impairment is localised in access to phonological forms given impoverished activation from semantics.

TABLE 4
MW's results in the Comparative Analysis of Linguistic Functions (CALF)[a]

	MW	*Control mean (range)*
Oral naming (nouns)	15/30	30 (29–30)
Written naming (nouns)	0/30	29 (26–30)
Oral completion (nouns)	23/30	27 (21–29)
Written completion (nouns)	0/30	–
Repetition (nouns)	29/30	30
(pseudowords)	27/30	30 (29–30)
(function words)	30/30	30
Spelling to dictation (nouns)	0/30	30 (24–30)
(pseudowords)	0/30	29 (24–30)
(function words)	0/30	29.5 (27–30)
Reading aloud (nouns)	18/30	–
(pseudowords)	0/30	–
(function words)	0/30	–

[a] Freiburger Funktionenvergleichsprüfung (FFVP) (Blanken et al., 1988).

Therapy method

Over 10 days, the treatment set of 32 items was treated for 1 hour each day. Items of each condition were treated for around 10 minutes a day. The following cueing hierarchy was used, based on exclusively phonological information: (1) initial cue (C + Schwa or V); (2) tapping the syllable number of the word; and (3) repetition.

MW's naming performance was tape-recorded for all 32 treated items in a daily pre- and posttest. In the pre- and posttest no cues were given. In "no response" cases the word was given for repetition to avoid frustration.

MW's naming performance for all 64 items was measured at three different times: (1) baseline testing; (2) posttest 1 (one day after the 10 days of therapy); (3) posttest 2 (one week after the therapy sessions). During these testing sessions no phonological information was given to MW.

RESULTS

Comparing the improvement in the daily pretests with the daily posttest results over the 10 days of therapy (see Figure 3), an improvement within every session can be observed. Hence, a clear immediate *facilitation effect* from phonological training can be inferred. Naming performance for the treated items showed steadily increasing naming improvement for both daily pre- and posttests. Comparing pretest 1 with pretest 10 using McNemar's Test, there are significant differences in error rates (20/32 versus 10/32; $\chi^2 = 10$; $p < .05$, df = 1). The same significant result was found for the daily posttests.

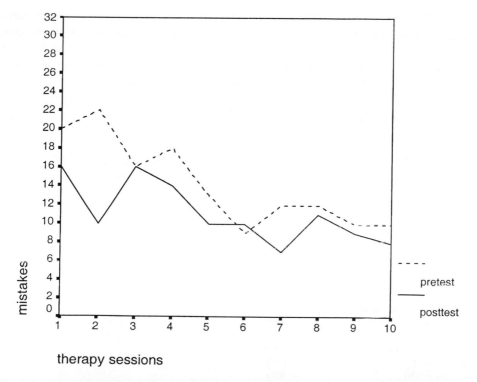

Figure 3. Naming performance for the treated items over 10 days, showing significant improvement in the pre- and posttest (pretest: $\chi^2 = 10$; $p < .05$; posttest: $\chi^2 = 8$; $p < .05$).

Error rate from posttest 1 (16/32) was continuously reduced to 9/32 in posttest 10 ($\chi^2 = 8$; $p < .05$, df = 1). The remaining 32 untreated control items were not given in the daily pre- and posttests.

Results in absolute numbers and percentages of the correct named items in each condition are shown for treated items (Table 5), untreated items (Table 6), and the overall items (Table 7) at pre- and post-treatment. Comparing baseline to post-treatment posttest 1 for the treated items, a significant treatment effect was found (McNemar one-tailed p = .0017). This treatment effect is no longer significant 1 week later (baseline—post-treatment posttest 2: McNemar one-tailed p = .0730). These findings indicate a short-term, *item-specific improvement* effect.

Turning to the issue of generalisation by analysing the control conditions, a comparison between the baseline and the post-treatment posttest 1 of the untreated items showed no significant difference (McNemar one-tailed p = .5000), neither the phonologically, the semantically related, nor the unrelated condition showed any effect

TABLE 5
Correct naming responses

Treated items	Baseline	Post-treatment posttest 1	Post-treatment posttest 2
Homophones	3/8 (37.5%)	6/8 (75%)	4/8 (50%)
Semantically related	3/8 (37.5%)	7/8 (87.5%)	4/8 (50%)
Phonologically related	5/8 (62.5%)	8/8 (100%)	7/8 (87.5%)
Unrelated	3/8 (37.5%)	4/8 (50%)	5/8 (62.5%)

Absolute numbers and percentages for the treated items (n = 32) within each condition (n = 8).

TABLE 6
Correct naming respones for the untreated items (n = 32) for each condition (n = 8)

Untreated items	Baseline	Post-treatment posttest 1	Post-treatment posttest 2
Homophones	4/8 (50%)	8/8 (100%)	6/8 (75%)
Semantically related	4/8 (50%)	2/8 (25%)	5/8 (62.5%)
Phonologically related	6/8 (75%)	3/8 (37.5%)	4/8 (50%)
Unrelated	4/8 (50%)	4/8 (50%)	4/8 (50%)

TABLE 7
Correct naming responses over all items and conditions (n = 64)

Overall items	Baseline	Post-treatment posttest 1	Post-treatment posttest 2
Homophones	7/16 (43.75%)	14/16 (87.5%)	10/16 (62.5%)
Semantically related	7/16 (43.75%)	9/16 (56.25%)	9/16 (56.25%)
Phonologically related	11/16 (68.5%)	11/16 (68.5%)	11/16 (68.5%)
Unrelated	7/16 (43.75%)	8/16 (50%)	9/16 (56.25%)

of generalisation (see Tables 5, 6, and 7). The same results were confirmed when comparing baseline to post-treatment posttest 2 (one-tailed $p = .5000$).

Figure 4 illustrates the results for the semantically related, phonologically related, and unrelated conditions. It was only in the untreated homophone condition that a generalisation effect could be detected. While there was no significant difference between the untreated homophones and the control conditions at baseline (semantically related, phonologically related, and unrelated; Fisher's Exact Test: exact two-tailed $p =$

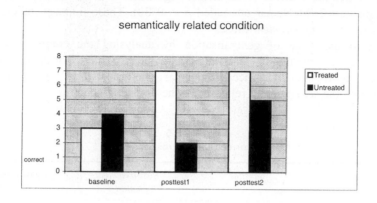

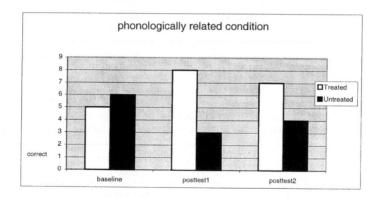

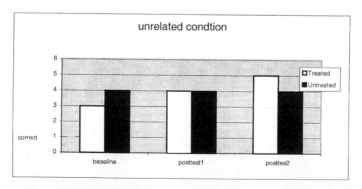

Figure 4. Pre- and post-treatment naming performance for the semantically related, phonologically related, and unrelated conditions.

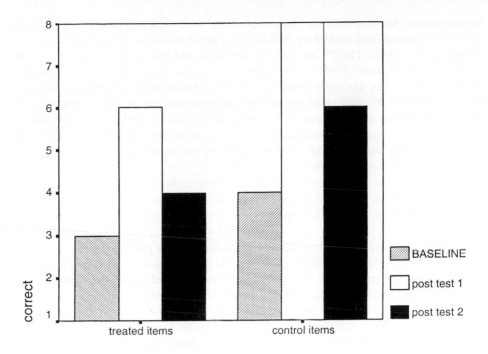

Homophones

Figure 5. Naming performance for the treated homophones: baseline, posttest 1 (1 day after therapy session), posttest 2 (1 week after therapy session).

.4203), untreated homophones showed significantly better naming than the controls at post-treatment posttest 1 (exact two-tailed $p = .0029$) However, this "homophone effect" was not to be maintained—by post-treatment posttest 2 (one week later), there was no longer a significant difference between homophones and controls (exact two-tailed $p = .4203$) (see Figure 5).

Hence, the untreated homophones benefited from the phonological naming training, indicating a generalisation effect of treatment but restricted to homophones.

Unexpectedly, the treated homophones themselves appeared not to benefit from treatment in the same way as the other three conditions (see Table 5). This seems to be a paradoxical effect. However, this contradictory result can be explained by the fact that in some cases the pictures used in the homophone condition depict one homophone meaning better than the other one (see Discussion).

Nevertheless these results show that an intensive naming training with only phonological cues has an indirect effect on the naming of untreated homophones— treating one meaning of a homophone improves the naming performance of the other one.

DISCUSSION

The results of this German single case study showed significant generalisation from treated to untreated homophones, but no generalisation to untreated semantically or phonologically related stimuli. Therefore it can be argued that this pattern supports the assumption of a single phonological representation for both members of a homophone pair. Relating the results to the different theoretical assumptions made about homophone representation, these results are compatible both with Dell's (1986, 1990) interactive activation account, and the strictly feed-forward approach of Levelt and colleagues (e.g., Levelt et al., 1999). The IN model of Caramazza and colleagues (Caramazza, 1997; Caramazza & Miozzo, 1998) is not supported by this study. According to the latter model, homophones are represented as two word forms with different lexical access routines initiated by their different semantic representations. As no overlap in lexical processing of homophone words is assumed, the selective treatment transfer that MW showed for homophones is unexpected within this model. In addition, recall that MW's naming was only minimally affected by phonological errors, ruling out a post-lexical locus of the generalisation effect.

Furthermore, the use of phonological treatment techniques resulted in short-term, item-specific effects in this single case study. No generalisation was found to untreated items, except in the case of homophones. No long-term effects were obtained. These results support the "classical" assumption of Howard et al. (1985 a,b), replicating their effects following phonological facilitation. Because syntactic processing was not required by the tasks, the assumption can be made that the word-form level was addressed by that treatment, not the lemma level. All techniques that were used within the "therapy", like providing the initial cue, the syllable number, or the whole word form, contain information that relates to phonological retrieval and encoding processes. What theoretical assumption can help to explain and interpret these data?

First of all it should be noted that the results presented here must be interpreted with caution, because of the limited number of items treated and the methodological problem in depicting both homophone meanings adequately. As shown earlier (see Figure 5), MW's naming performance for the untreated homophones was better than for the treated homophone condition in posttest 1. It could be argued that possible influencing factors like imageability, frequency, familiarity, and idiosyncratic effects are responsible for this paradoxical finding, but the more obvious reason here is likely to be *name agreement*. The treated homophone pictures overall had lower name agreement than the control homophone pictures, e.g., BANK (financial institution) evoked naming responses like "post office" or "counter" in normal speakers, whereas BANK (bench) had 100% name agreement and hence a 1:1 mapping of semantics and lexical form. Because of the limited choice of homophone items, the investigators attempted to solve the problem of lower name agreement by putting the "problematic" items in the treated homophone condition. It was hoped that the opportunity to influence MW's naming within the therapy session would counteract the low name agreement. As the results demonstrate, this may not have been the case—the variety of possible naming responses could not be suppressed. In terms of the two stage model this would mean that pictures with poor name agreement continued to activate a number of concepts, and correspondingly a number of lemmas. This diffuse activation can hardly help to address one word form node properly. Hence, "No responses" or "semantically related word responses" would be expected from an aphasic speaker.

Nevertheless there was an obvious and significant homophone generalisation effect. How might we explain these results? The theories of both Dell (1986) and Levelt et al. (1999) can account for the homophone treatment generalisation effect. According to the two stage model of Levelt and colleagues, the effect can be explained in terms of a lowered threshold level at the level of the phonological form: repeated activation of the word-form node during treatment lowers the threshold. As homophones share a single word-form node, this lower threshold benefits both the treated homophone and its untreated twin, resulting in greater success in word retrieval for picture naming. In terms of the Dell model one can argue that feedback mechanisms between the word-form level and the lemma cause the homophone effect. Although only one of the homophone meanings is treated, the untreated homophone inherits the activation of its treated homophone twin because of feedback mechanisms from the shared word-form node.[8]

But can we assume that there are *always two* lemma entries for homophone words? In languages like Dutch, Italian, French, or German, different grammatical genders are used, so one can assume that those homophone nouns that differ in grammatical gender—like DIE WAHL (the election) versus DER WAL (the whale)—should have separate lemmas at this strictly syntactic level. Different grammatical representations also seem to be plausible in those homophone words that differ in their plural morphology, like for BANK–BANKEN (financial institution: bank–banks) versus BANK–BÄNKE (bench–benches). Both nouns use the same determiner DIE, but use different plural forms. These homophones fit perfectly into the theory of the two stage model, but what happens when there are homophone words that do not even differ in their grammatical representations? Take for example the German homophone DER BALL (singular)–DIE BÄLLE (plural): both meanings (game/dance) have the same determiner DER (singular, masculine) or DIE (plural, masculine) and the same plural morphology. Might that not indicate that there need be only one lemma entry? For the English language, where there is no grammatical gender, cases analogous to the German example BALL appear much more often. In these cases the lemma level appears to be superfluous. The IN model of Caramazza and colleagues, in which a lemma level is excluded, would provide a good explanation for these homophone words, but still there would be the controversy about *how many* word form entries we have to assume. Keeping the problem of homophones with "identical syntactic properties" in mind, the homophone argument cannot be used in general as evidence for the lemma level.

Turning to the question of how phonological techniques as remediation for word-finding difficulties might work, the outcome here shows support for the traditional view: phonological techniques cause short-term effects but no long-term or generalisation effects (except for the homophone control condition). Relating these findings to previous therapy studies mentioned earlier, this clear-cut finding is not a general rule. Phonological therapy has been shown to produce partial or even complete generalisation to unrelated words, although these findings are more rare. In this study the effect of a phonological treatment can be interpreted in terms of a direct activation of single word-form entries, which lower their pathologically raised threshold level only after being used—indicated by the item-specific effect. This lowered threshold level effect is not maintained over 1 week. The treated word forms seem to be blocked again, presumably through the threshold having risen once again.

These results suggest that the question has still to be left open as to which factors cause reliable generalisation or long-term effects. The discrepancies and inconsistencies

---

[8] That word-form access is critical for MW (and that therefore he should benefit from homophony) is also supported by the study of Blanken et al., in press. Here, MW was required to name targets with or without strong semantic competitors. Omissions clustered around the latter targets and semantic errors around the former with the sum of both error types remaining the same, however. Models of word selection that include a word-form level can account for the data distribution because the word form level is involved in both omissions and semantic errors (see e.g., Morton & Patterson, 1980, for the "response blocking" hypothesis of semantic errors). Models that exclude form information from lexical selection (see introduction) do not predict the observed pattern (e.g., that with decreasing semantic errors omissions increase). The authors argue for a model in which word-form access is crucially involved in lexical (mis-)selection.

shown across therapy studies (see Nickels & Best, 1996a,b) suggest that there is still a long way to go before we can detect all possible interfering variables.

While being aware of the limitations of these data, this single case study provides a further explanation of the homophone treatment effect found initially by Blanken (1989), and as such it is a further support for a theory that incorporates a single phonological form for homophones. We are currently extending and replicating these data in English, using the same "therapy" techniques. It is hoped further replications will shed still more light on the representation of homophones and the effects of phonological therapy.

REFERENCES

Baayen, R.H., Piepenbrock, R., & van Rijn, H. (1993). *The CELEX lexical database [CD-Rom]*. Linguistic Data Consortium, University of Pennsylvania/Philadelphia, PA.

Badecker, W., Miozzo, M., & Zanuttini, R. (1995). The two-stage model of lexical retrieval: Evidence from a case of anomia with selective preservation of grammatical gender. *Cognition, 57*, 193–216.

Bierwisch, M., & Schreuder, R. (1992). From lexical concepts to lexical items. *Cognition, 42*, 23–60.

Blanken, G. (1989). Wortfindungsstörungen und verbales Lernen bei Aphasie – Eine Einzelfallstudie. *Neurolinguistik, 2*, 107–126.

Blanken, G. (1996). *Materialien zur neurolinguistischen Aphasiediagnostik. Auditives und visuelles Sprachverständnis: Wortbedeutungen.* Hofheim: NAT-Verlag.

Blanken, G., Dittmann, J., & Wallesch, C.-W. (in press). Parallel or serial activation of word forms in speech production? Neurolinguistic evidence from an aphasic patient. *Neuroscience Letters*.

Blanken, G., Döppler, R., Dittmann, J., & Wallesch, C.-W. (1988). *Die Freiburger Funktionenvergleichsprüfung [Comparative Analysis of Linguistic Functions]*. Freiburg University (experimental version).

Blanken, G., & Kulke, F. (in press). Die Verarbeitung von Genusinformation bei schwerer Aphasie. Eine neurolinguistische Studie. In C. Habel & T. Pechmann (Eds.), *Sprachproduktion*. Opladen: Westdeutscher Verlag.

Caramazza, A. (1997). How many levels of processing are there in lexical access? *Cognitive Neuropsychology, 14*, 177–208.

Caramazza, A., Costa, A., Miozzo, M., & Bi, Y. (2001). The specific-word frequency effect: Implications for the representation of homophones in speech production. *Journal of Experimental Psychology: Learning, Memory and Cognition, 27*(6), 1430–1450.

Caramazza, A., & Hillis, A.E. (1991). Lexical organisation of nouns and verbs in the brain. *Nature, 349*, 788–790.

Caramazza, A., & Miozzo, M. (1997). The relation between syntactic and phonological knowledge in lexical access: Evidence from the 'tip-of-the-tongue' phenomenon. *Cognition, 64*, 309–364.

Caramazza, A., & Miozzo, M. (1998). More is not always better: A response to Roelofs, Meyer, and Levelt. *Cognition, 69*, 231–241.

Dell, G.S. (1986). A spreading activation theory of retrieval in sentence production. *Psychological Review, 93*, 283–321.

Dell, G.S. (1990). Effects of frequency and vocabulary type on phonological speech errors. *Language and Cognitive Processes, 5*, 313–349.

Dell, G.S., Schwartz, M.F., Martin, N., Saffran, E., & Gagnon, D.A. (1997). Lexical access in aphasic and nonaphasic speakers. *Psychological Review, 104*, 801–838.

Druks, J., & Masterson, J. (1999). *An object and action naming battery*. Hove, UK: Psychology Press.

Henaff Gonon, M.A., Bruckert, R., & Michel, F. (1989). Lexicalization in an anomic patient. *Neuropsychologia, 27*, 391–407.

Hickin, J., Best, W., Herbert, R., Howard, D., & Osborne, F. (2002). Phonological therapy for word-finding difficulties: A re-evaluation. *Aphasiology, 16*, 000–000.

Howard, D., & Patterson, K.E. (1992). *Pyramids and Palm Trees*. Bury St. Edmunds, UK: Thames Valley Test Company.

Howard, D., Patterson, K.E., Franklin, S., Orchard-Lisle, V., & Morton, J. (1985a). The facilitation of picture naming in aphasia. *Cognitive Neuropsychology, 2*, 49–80.

Howard, D., Patterson, K.E., Franklin, S., Orchard-Lisle, V., & Morton, J. (1985b). The treatment of word retrieval deficits in aphasia: A comparison of two therapy methods. *Brain, 108*, 817–829.

Huber, W., Poeck, K.-J., Weniger, D., & Willmes, K. (1983). *Der Aachener Aphasie Test (AAT)*. *Handanweisung*. Göttingen: Hogrefe.

Jescheniak, J.D., & Levelt, W.J.M. (1994). Word frequency effects in speech production: Retrieval of syntactic information and of phonological form. *Journal of Experimental Psychology: Learning, Memory, and Cognition, 20*(4), 824–843.

Jescheniak, J.D., Levelt, W.J.M., & Meyer, A.S. (in press). Specific-word frequency is not all that counts in speech production. Evidence from the production of homophones in Dutch and German. *Journal of Experimental Psychology: Learning, Memory and Cognition*.

Kay, J., Lesser, R., & Coltheart, M. (1992). *Psycholinguistic Assessments of Language Processing in Aphasia*. Hove, UK: Lawrence Erlbaum Associates Ltd.

Kempen, G., & Huijbers, R. (1983). The lexicalisation process in sentence production and naming: Indirect elections of words. *Cognition, 14*, 185–209.

Kulke, F., & Blanken, G. (2001). Phonological and syntactic influences on semantic misnamings in aphasia. *Aphasiology, 15*, 3–15.

Levelt, W.J.M. (1989). *Speaking. From intention to articulation*. Cambridge, MA: MIT Press.

Levelt, W.J.M. (1999). Models of word production. *Trends in Cognitive Sciences, 3*(6), 223–232.

Levelt, W.J.M., Roelofs, A., & Meyer, A.S. (1999). A theory of lexical access in speech production. *Behavioral and Brain Sciences, 22*, 1–75.

Miceli, G., Amitrano, A., Capasso, R., & Caramazza, A. (1996). The treatment of anomia resulting from output lexical damage: Analysis of two cases. *Brain and Language, 52*, 150–174.

Miozzo, M., & Caramazza, A. (1997). On knowing the auxiliary of a verb that cannot be named: Evidence for the independence of grammatical and phonological aspects of lexical knowledge. *Journal of Cognitive Neuroscience, 9*, 160–166.

Morton, J., & Patterson, K. (1980). A new attempt at an interpretation, or, an attempt at a new interpretation. In M. Coltheart, K. Patterson, & J.C. Marshall (Eds.), *Deep dyslexia*. London: Routledge & Kegan Paul.

Neubert, C., Rüffer, N., & Zeh-Hau, M. (1995). *Neurolinguistische Aphasietherapie. Materialien*. Hofheim: NAT-Verlag.

Nickels, L. (2001). Producing spoken words. In B. Rapp (Ed.), *A handbook of cognitive neuropsychology*. New York: Psychology Press.

Nickels, L., & Best, W. (1996a). Therapy for naming disorders (part I): Principles, puzzles and progress. *Aphasiology, 10*, 21–47.

Nickels, L., & Best, W. (1996b). Therapy for naming disorders (part II): Specifics, surprises and suggestions. *Aphasiology, 10*, 109–136.

Pechmann, T., & Zerbst, D. (2002). The activation of word class information during speech production. *Journal of Experimental Psychology: Learning, Memory, and Cognition, 28*, 233–243.

Raymer, A.M., Thompson, C.K., Jacobs, B., & Le Grand, H.R. (1993). Phonological treatment of naming deficits in aphasia: Model-based generalisation analysis. *Aphasiology, 7*, 27–53.

Robson, J., Marshall, J., Pring, T., & Chiat, S. (1998). Phonological naming therapy in jargon aphasia: Positive but paradoxical effects. *Journal of the International Neuropsychological Society, 4*, 675–686.

Roelofs, A., Meyer, A.S., & Levelt, W.J.M. (1998). A case of the lemma/lexeme distinction in models of speaking: Comment on Caramazza and Miozzo (1997). *Cognition, 69*, 219–230.

Ruoff, A. (1981). *Häufigkeitswörterbuch gesprochener Sprache*. Tübingen, Germany: Niemeyer.

Snodgrass, J.G., & Vanderwart, M. (1980). A standardized set of 260 pictures: Norms for name agreement, image agreement, familiarity and visual complexity. *Journal of Experimental Psychology: Human Learning and Memory, 6*, 174–214.

Van Turennout, M., Hagoort, P., & Brown, C.M. (1997). Electrophysiological evidence on the time course of semantic and phonological processes in speech production. *Journal of Experimental Psychology: Learning, Memory, and Cognition, 23*, 787–806.

Vigliocco, G., Antonini, T., & Garrett, M.F. (1997) Grammatical gender is on the tip of Italian tongues. *Psychological Science, 8*, 314–317.

APPENDIX

Frequency details (according to CELEX) or dominance (standardised with 21 students, 23–29 years old, 12 female and 9 male), details of syllable number and initial syllable structure. NB: There was no CELEX frequency for *Schloß*. Therefore the frequency was taken from Ruoff (1981).

Item	Treated/ control	CELEX frequency and dominance	Syllable number	Initial syllable structure
Homophones				
(Blumen)Strauß (bunch of flowers)	treated	non-dominant (5/21); 100	1	CC
(Vogel)Strauß (ostrich)	control	dominant (16/21); 97	1	CC
(Tanz)Ball (ball/dance)	treated	non-dominant (1/21); 365	1	CV
(Spiel)Ball (ball/game)	control	dominant (20/21); 365	1	CV
(Box)Ring (ring/fight)	treated	non-dominant (1/21); 275	1	CV
(Finger)Ring (ring/jewel)	control	dominant (20/21); 275	1	CV
(Schlüssel)Bart (key bit)	treated	non-dominant (0/21) 71	1	CV
(Gesichts)Bart (beard)	control	dominant (21/21); 71	1	CV
(Menschen)Mutter (mother)	treated	dominant (20/21); 599	2	CV
(Schrauben)Mutter (bold)	control	non-dominant (1/21); 599	2	CV
(Königs)Schloß (castle)	treated	dominant (16/21); 56	1	CC
(Tür)Schloß (lock)	control	non-dominant (5/21) 3	1	CC
(Geld)Bank (bank/money)	treated	dominant (14/21); 829	1	CV
(Sitz)Bank (bench)	control	non-dominant (7/21); 541	1	CV
(Gockel)Hahn (rooster)	treated	dominant (20/21); 41	1	CV
(Wasser)Hahn (tap)	control	non-dominant (1/21); 41	1	CV
Semantically related				
Zeitung (newspaper)	treated	1061	2	CV
Buch (book)	control	1093	1	CV
Fenster (window)	treated	534	2	CV
Tür (door)	control	739	1	CV

Item	Treated/ control	CELEX frequency and dominance	Syllable number	Initial syllable structure
Auto (car)	treated	688	2	VV
Flugzeug (aeroplane)	control	446	2	CC
Radio (radio)	treated	367	3	CV
Telefon (phone)	control	1142	3	CV
Paprika (sweet pepper)	treated	8	3	CV
Tomate (tomato)	control	30	3	CV
Bürste (brush)	treated	12	2	CV
Kamm (comb)	control	48	1	CV
Gabel (fork)	treated	26	2	CV
Messer (knife)	control	50	2	CV
Krug (jug)	treated	27	1	CC
Tasse (cup)	control	61	2	CV
Phonologically related				
Kirche (church)	treated	1267	2	CV
Kirsche (cherry)	control	15	2	CV
Kiste (box)	treated	132	2	CV
Kissen (cushion)	control	41	2	CV
Nase (nose)	treated	211	2	CV
Vase (vase)	control	34	2	CV
Sonne (sun)	treated	212	2	CV
Tanne (pine)	control	9	2	CV
Wiege (cradle)	treated	32	2	CV
Ziege (goat)	control	49	2	CV

Item	Treated/ control	CELEX frequency and dominance	Syllable number	Initial syllable structure
Rutsche (slide)	treated	6	2	CV
Kutsche (carriage)	control	13	2	CV
Tablette (pill)	treated	16	3	CV
Pinzette (tweezers)	control	2	3	CV
Kessel (kettle)	treated	4	2	CV
Sessel (arm chair)	control	99	2	CV
Unrelated Zigarette (cigarette)	treated	305	4	CV
Baum (tree)	control	381	1	CV
Flasche (bottle)	treated	216	2	CC
Geld (money)	control	1204	1	CV
Hose (trousers)	treated	138	2	CV
Bett (bed)	control	709	1	CV
Vogel (bird)	treated	235	2	CV
Koffer (suitcase)	control	123	2	CV
Gürtel (belt)	treated	42	2	CV
Topf (pot)	control	61	1	CV
Zange (pliers)	treated	18	2	CV
Angel (fishing tackle)	control	32	2	VC
Löffel (spoon)	treated	37	2	CV
Mütze (hat)	control	63	2	CV
Geige (violin)	treated	16	2	CV
Apfel (apple)	control	47	2	VC

Subject index